THE
BOXING
DIARIES

THE
BOXING
DIARIES

THE
BOXING
DIARIES

Marion Dunn

Saraband

Published by Saraband,
Digital World Centre,
1 Lowry Plaza,
The Quays, Salford, M50 3UB

ISBN: 9781912235551
ebook: 978191223568

Printed and bound in Great Britain by Clays Ltd, Elcograf S.p.A.

10 9 8 7 6 5 4 3 2 1

Please note that for privacy reasons most of the names in the text and some of
the locations have been changed.

This book is dedicated to Anthony, Michelle and Stephanie

YEAR ONE

1

FIRST STEPS

It is 7.45 p.m. on a Monday night in October 2013, and I swing the car round into the car park off the small side road. It is not actually snowing yet, but nearly. Over the previous few months, I have festered, putting on unacceptable amounts of weight. This has led to a search for cheap gyms in my local town. According to various websites, there is a gym here at the youth club just down the road from work which is open to the public three evenings a week. I am not flush with cash so the advertised cost of £2 per session is the decider. Although I am no youth, I push the doorbell and wait.

A largish, friendly man opens the door and introduces himself as Stuart. He leads me into the recreation room, which contains a tatty, blue table tennis table plonked in the middle, plus a few plastic tables and chairs set out for drinking tea and coffee. Next door is a kitchen with a serving hatch. Two podgy kids with thick glasses are pinging and ponging their lives away. I look through two dusty internal windows into the gym itself. I am expecting deep carpets, svelte people in Lycra, coffee and other glistening machines, but instead there is a slightly drab and silent gym. The surroundings are Edwardian – no, Victorian, but for the presence of electric light. The walls are lined with bricks, painted in powdery red up to half the wall height, then above a stark, military grey. An ancient football has become lodged in the dusty ironwork that holds up the ceiling. There is a yellowing linoleum floor marked out in white paint as badminton and basketball courts.

Suddenly there is a blast of noise, which sounds much like very garbled speech reverberating. I see the back of a man's head bobbing up and down through the internal windows, then ten children, ranging in age from about eleven to sixteen, leaping and jumping up in time with the shouts. There are four boxing bags hanging from sturdy, black iron stanchions in the opposite wall. The children become locked in their own worlds, pummelling away on the bags for all they are worth. There is a brief lull in proceedings when the shouting stops. Then more shouting, jumping and pummelling.

Stuart tells me that he is the senior youth worker there and introduces me to the cheap delights of the adult boxing club: 'The adult session follows the youth session. It is free for the first night, £2 per session, and then £10 to join – insurance, you see.' I have somehow materialised in a boxing gym. *Well, give it a go*, I think. At the age of fifty, I've got no shame and have nothing to lose except my pride. As I optimistically part with my £10, I wonder what I am insuring myself against. Possibly the most dangerous aspect is deciding to turn up in the first place. This Christian youth club is subsidised by the charity Children in Need, and I wonder if God would approve of all that pummelling, and if I already am or will be 'in need'. My previous encounters with boxing were nil as a participant, and only limited as a spectator, although I do remember choosing a boxing book out of the school library when aged about seven and being quite fascinated by it. Perhaps it was the sheer quirkiness and the slightly transgressive element that appealed to me, as in the late 1960s this was not a sport promoted for girls.

Brendan arrives; I later find out that he lays carpets on oil rigs for a living. He looks like he knows what he is doing, and I watch intently as he puts on the boxing wraps, long strips of fabric that he winds around his hands.

Eventually the pale, sweaty kids heave out of the gym and lurch for their various electronic devices, then parents. They all look exhausted. That will be me in a minute, only much worse. Rather nervously I enter the gym. It smells of toil and sweat and chalk. I explain to the boxing coach, Gerard, that I would like to get fitter.

'How fit d'yer think yer are, love?' he says, in a thick Scouse accent and with a wry smile.

I say rather lamely that I have a chequered history of various outdoor pursuits, including potholing, and that I am not as unfit as I might first appear.

'If yer can stick the first month, youse'll be well on the way, love. I'll ask yer again in six weeks,' he says without a flicker of malice.

I suspect that he is one who has seen it all before, legions of youths and adults and their aspirations, hopes and dreams come and go. François arrives. He is a dapper French chef, with a sharp haircut, who kindly gives me a bottle of water which he says I will need. I later discover that his name is not François at all, but Gaspard. Gerard calls him François and no one seems to mind.

No one can pronounce my actual name, so I immediately and permanently become my boxing alter ego, Marianne.

Peter arrives. He is late and is sworn at by Gerard as soon as he enters the gym. He is black and has a public school accent. He is known as the Politest Man in the World, and he is. Nobody knows much about Peter except that he is extremely well mannered, owns a nice Border collie and washes up in a pub.

At Gerard's barked-out command, we all start to skip. It is exhausting. I have not done this since the playground over forty years ago, and none of the right muscles or even bones are in place. My feet ache, my shins ache, my knees ache, in fact all of me aches, but I keep going, the rope swishing and slapping onto the floor, feeling heavier by the second. By chance, I have picked out an orange plastic skipping rope of exactly the right weight and length. It will become both friend and foe over the coming months.

I am severely out of breath, but I carry on as Gerard swears his own kind of encouragement. 'You lazy f—kers,' he shouts. 'You've all got lazyitis!' He turns to me apologetically, 'Not you love. Sorry for the language.' But there is no need for apology. Next we run around the gym, alternately dropping left and right hands to the floor, lurching from one direction to the other as Gerard shouts: 'Change! Change! Change!'

Against all modern Health and Safety legislation, Gerard's Staffordshire bull terrier DJ runs around the gym with us. I like DJ, but I wonder about what happens if he gets overexcited and starts nipping at our heels. Next we do some stretching, arms whirling and legs thrown to each side. The dog barks and jumps to waist height as if on springs. All my joints loosen. I am dripping with sweat and very glad for that small bottle of water that Gaspard has provided. DJ stops orbiting the room and finally calms down. This is a relief to us all.

I go into the boxing store to get my first ever pair of worn, red boxing gloves. The store is a small, dark room next to the gym. It has its own smell of ancient leather, dried sweat and something unidentifiable. There is an old weighing machine painted in telephone-box red in the corner of the room, similar to the 'Speak Your Weight' machines that used to be popular in penny arcades. Rows and rows of boxing gloves and headgear are ranged in size order on wooden shelves. A decaying wooden desk in the corner has drawers which are stuffed with boxing wraps. Like multicoloured carnival ribbons, they spill out onto the floor. Spare boxing bags are stacked like coffins near to the door and twenty skipping ropes of differing weights and lengths dangle from hooks on the wall.

Brendan shows me how to put on the boxing wraps. Apparently, the wraps are not really designed to provide cushioning for the hands. Instead, they pull together all the small bones of the hands, so that any impact does not allow them to splay outwards. This reduces the chance of a broken hand now and arthritis later. It is the gloves that provide the cushioning. The wraps also absorb sweat from the hands, and prevent the passing on of any blood-borne infections. I have read that the famous boxer Muhammad Ali had to have cortisone injections into each knuckle prior to a boxing match. Ouch. I learn that if you bash your hands too much, bad things follow.

The others go to their stations at the boxing bags and I to the appointed spot with Gerard. I stand in front of a mirror propped up vertically on one side of the bare gym wall. Gerard looks wiry and is about five foot seven. When I see and hear him punch the boxing bag, every sinew strains, as his whole body's power gets eliminated in a single bullet-crack punch. It has to be heard to be believed. He says that he won sixty fights out of sixty-eight when an amateur boxer, and even knowing nothing about boxing I can well believe it. I learn that amateur boxers can only fight competitively and be insured up to the age of forty, leading to a surplus of coaches in their late thirties and beyond. Gerard is somewhere in his late forties, I guess.

Gerard tells me to walk forwards three steps towards the boxing mirror. As I am a right-hander, I start forward with my left foot, take three steps and turn my feet through 45 degrees to the right and lift the back heel of my right foot. This is called the 'boxing stance', the position that you must adopt in order to throw any successful boxing punch. It feels very unnatural. How am I even going to stand like this, never mind punch anything? I teeter on the balls of my feet, like a clumsy ballerina. As I turn to try and throw a left jab for the first time, I lift my shoulders awkwardly and wrongly lean forwards into an imaginary punch zone. My body feels as tense and static as a piece of wood.

Gerard tells me to aim for a cross made of yellow tape in the middle of the mirror. This, I presume, is a proxy for my opponent's face. I slam my hand into the mirror, hoping that it is plastic. I am as weak as a kitten. The power needs to come from the body, from a twist in the hips, from the floor and feet, not the arms.

I drop my hands and my face is unguarded. I am told that if I drop my hands in the boxing ring, even for a microsecond, I will be punched in the face. I am tense and thoughtful, then thinking so hard that I forget my stance; then I forget how to punch; then I forget to breathe and run out of oxygen. Finally, I forget which hand is which.

Gerard moves on and leaves me in the care of Janine, his glamorous girlfriend who also works as a boxing coach. Janine is very patient, even though I fail to deliver the shots time after time.

Humiliating circuit training and bench exercises follow. We are allowed a glorious two-minute rest, and then we line up on the first of the white lines which criss-cross the gym floor like the rungs of a ladder. We have to run like mad, touch the two short opposing walls of the gym, perform a particular exercise on each of the twelve white lines that traverse the floor, and then slowly reverse back down the same twelve lines until we are at our starting point again. Some exercises accrue more cumulative pain than others if performed in quick succession, especially bunny-hops, press-ups and squats. Arms and legs shake and buckle as Gerard bawls encouragement. Speech is not possible and only pain registers in the brain.

The final stings in the tail are the bench exercises. These are a particular form of boxing torture which never get easier as the ante is continually upped. One round of these just consists of two minutes of press-ups, sit-ups and dips. It doesn't sound like much, but time stretches in the boxing gym. When waiting for a kettle to boil, two or three minutes seems like nothing. On the benches it seems like an eternity. While the others sweat and groan, I manage only a few. Rather menacingly, Gerard faces us from an opposing bench as we dip up and down to exhaustion. He dips too, and says, 'Stay with me,' as in vain we try to keep up with him. It is not his vanity that makes him do this – he is genuinely trying to encourage us, but for now he is king of the dips.

The next set of bench exercises consists of jumping or walking over the benches in a figure-of-eight pattern, turning alternately to the left and right. Peter tells us that he is mildly dyspraxic, and for some of these walk-over bench exercises Gerard therefore takes Peter's hand or shoulder to lead his confused turns to the left and right. Gerard has the patience of a saint and they make such an unlikely dancing pair that their ungainly three-legged shenanigans make us all laugh out loud. However, Peter has the last laugh as he keeps going long after we have tired. After the bench sessions, Peter has enough energy left to thwack the heaviest boxing bag in the gym into oblivion. We are aghast at his physical indestructibility.

Then it is all over. Peter has to be dragged off the heavy bag, before we finally put the boxing bags away. I race to the edge of the gym and all of us gulp down pint after pint of water. Peter says what a novice he still is, how he will never get any better and how age and decrepitude is against him. Brendan confesses that he has been out on the lash again, that his beer belly is returning and that his ex-wife has been giving him grief over his divorce. In addition, he is desperate to see his kids. It is a pretty heart-rending tale. Janine recounts in a completely matter-of-fact way that she has just been in hospital again, having had more cancer treatment. Thus, she has not been able to keep up with her training. We all sympathise, marvelling at her stoicism.

I am pleased and surprised to have made it through the first hour-long session. The other boxers tell me that new recruits usually drop out after about twenty minutes, but somehow I have managed to stay the course, feeling at the end like I have undergone instant liposuction without any anaesthetic.

'Did you enjoy it?' Somebody asks. This is a difficult question to answer, as an hour of being trashed can hardly pass as enjoyment, but without hesitation I say yes, as I find the sense of camaraderie and achievement much stronger than I expected. I also see the appeal of a perfectly balanced boxing equation, where you clearly get out exactly what you put in. As a self-confessed nerd, I find that I am entranced by the myriad of boxing technicalities that have been demonstrated on that first night. These are to be studied, practised and hopefully mastered. More than that, I see the glimmer of a beautiful addiction about to start.

⊙

It is a cliché, but true: the following morning, I find that I am aching in places that I didn't know could ache. But I am back on Wednesday, bringing a bottle of a glucose-laden sports drink for Gaspard, to say thanks for the bottled water that he gave me on that first night. I am armed only with water for the second session, where there is more emphasis on technical boxing, and for the first time I try and punch the boxing bags.

This is not as straightforward as it might first appear. Each bag is different. There are four ranged out along one side of the gym. Each hangs from a thick, black stanchion that can be hinged back against the wall when not in use. The extreme left-hand bag is the hook bag. This is the lightest of them all and is moulded into the crude shape of a human body – a bit like the army uniforms filled with hay used for bayonet practice. On first inspection this is possibly a little too human. It is made of quarters of blue and white leather, and the head and shoulder sections are designed to be a testing ground for uppercuts and hooks. Although the hook and uppercut are advanced shots, I give them a go. Gerard explains that in the case of the uppercut, the entire twisting power of the body should get behind a single upwardly mobile punch which should be delivered to the opponent's chin. The punching arm should not move. It is as constrained as a piston, hunched upwards by a corkscrewing motion of the body. It is a very difficult shot to do, especially at speed, as you have to wind up the body like a spring before letting the punch go, without advance warning to your opponent. A common mistake with the uppercut is that the arms wave around too far from the body. Here the punch loses power, as only the arms deliver the shot without the ballast of the body behind.

The second bag is known as the heavy bag. This is a long, heavily weighted bag of blue leather with red ends. It is indeed a heavy bag, and when I punch it for the first time it barely moves. I am told by the other boxers about the history of the heavy bags: in the past they were routinely stuffed with rags, rubber pellets and sawdust or army blankets. Apparently the 1920s American championship boxer Jack Dempsey specified various recipes for making your own heavy bag, using a duffel bags and wood shavings. (His instructions also assume that you have a barn at your disposal in which to hang it, as everyone did in rural America one hundred years ago.) Another suggested alternative is to suspend a tractor tyre from an appropriate fixing. The heavy bag in our gym is very unforgiving and bears terrible grudges. It has the annoying knack of yawing back at you without you noticing, so that your effective punch range subtly alters.

The third bag is initially my favourite. This is a light, anony-mous, black bag filled with something foam-like. A novice like me feels that they are making great progress when hitting this bag. It responds with a satisfying thwack, even in response to a light punch, and jumps away in an instant. It does not creep up on you with a slow rebound like the heavy bag. However, like low-hanging fruit, I discover that it is the shirker's prize.

The final bag is another blue and red number, a bit like bag number two. The significance of this bag is not in its demeanour, but its position. This is the last bag in the sequence of four. Being another heavy bag, it is of strength-sapping proportions. Crucially, the station that follows is a session on the boxing pads with Gerard, but every ounce of energy and shred of concentration has just been drained away by the might of bag four.

Our standard training schedule is to box for anything between four and eight two-and-a-half or three-minute rounds on the bags, with a thirty-second rest in between. For greater effect (aka pain), there is sometimes a minute or two minutes' exercise added in between each bag round before a rest is allowed, but for the time being we luxuriate in our thirty-second rest, with no added extras.

The simplest boxing punches are the jab and the right hand. It is only possible to throw any punch from the correct starting position or boxing stance. Most right-handed people, like myself, adopt the 'orthodox' stance, with their left shoulder facing the middle of their opponent's chest, left foot forward, with the right foot triangulated to form two parts of a three-part tripod. The feet are initially flat on the floor and parallel to it, angled at 45 degrees from the line of the left shoulder to your opponent's chest.

Then the experts start to disagree. There is much argument about how the front foot should be placed. Fast boxers can point the left foot directly towards their opponent, but then the open body alignment presents a dangerously large target. It is more common to align the left foot at 45 degrees or even 90 degrees to the opponent line. This automatically turns the body into a more defensive stance, allows the left shoulder to protect the face and lessens the target area. The right foot should remain in its 45-degree position but be stepped a little to the right, so that one foot is never directly behind the other, as this leads to instability.

There is much debate as to whether your weight should be equally distributed between the feet, or if the weight should be tilted slightly forwards or slightly backwards. If slightly forwards, there is a temptation to lean into your opponent's punch zone and for this reason alone, I find I favour the weight slightly tilted onto my back foot. However, a common approach is to have the weight evenly distributed between the front foot and the back foot. The knees should be slightly bent and relaxed. The right heel should always be lifted, and sometimes the left too. The hands should be up beside the chin, protecting the face, although there is much debate about the exact position of each hand. The elbows should be tucked in, protecting the body. This is the basic boxing stance. If this is wrong, everything is wrong.

There are so many mistakes it is possible to make with the boxing stance that I cannot list them all, but these are a few common ones (and I make all of them, most of the time): legs too close; legs too far apart; right heel not raised; left heel not raised; both heels not raised; weight not on back foot; legs too much in line; leaning forwards too much; left foot facing too much in forwards direction; knees not bent; arms too tense; shoulders too tense; body too square on; hands not against cheeks; hands dropped (the worst sin!); chin too raised; just plain wrong. At the outset I find the boxing stance particularly hard to master.

Most left-handed people adopt the 'southpaw' or opposite stance, with respect to left and right. Highly skilled boxers can change from a southpaw to orthodox stance to confuse their opponents, the gifted doing this instinctively, but I discover that although legal this is sometimes seen as bad form.

From my perspective as an orthodox boxer, the workaday punch is the jab, thrown with the left hand. This should be relentless, continually weakening your opponent. I say 'thrown' because all the power of the body should be behind it by means of a rightwards twist of the hips, and a sharp flick and twist upwards of the right heel. This launches the left hand out like a slingshot. The jab should be like the long tongue of a tropical frog catching an insect in milliseconds before being retracted in double-quick time. It should pierce the jawline of your opponent before he has even noticed, and your hand must be back in position immediately ready to deliver the exact same thing, all over again.

There are variations on the jab. Jack Dempsey called his own special jab a 'jolt'. His version always involved a long, lightning step forward with the left foot pointing forwards, and the right foot resolutely stationary. If effected correctly, this adds a short burst of phenomenal power, and makes the jab into a proper power punch. The step forward is aided by a falling motion, which imparts the force of gravity to the shot. It works well, but relies totally on speed, as the front foot has to be retracted very quickly indeed after the shot has been deployed. If you are too slow, the forward front-foot position and direction makes you into a ready target. I have seen other boxers twist the left heel outwards and clockwise when throwing a jab, essentially pivoting on the ball of the left foot.

For the first time, I find myself watching various TV boxing matches from the perspective of an insider. There are many variations, but it seems like all great boxers have an accurate and powerful jab. There appears to be no substitute for it.

⊙

Meanwhile back in the real world, even a barely acceptable jab is hard to achieve. On top of all the impossible constraints of the stance, you have to be relaxed when delivering a jab, otherwise you do not get the full 'throwing' effect.

As a right-handed person, I initially find the jab impossible to deliver. My elbows flail uselessly outwards, a boxing crime known as 'chicken-winging'. I do not twist my hips enough, or even at all. I do not twist my hand to the correct position – the flat of my punching knuckles should lie flat on the bag – instead my hand merely slides off. I stand too close to the bag, so I bend my arm and the jab loses power; I stand too far away from the bag and I lean forward into my opponent's punch zone to deliver the jab. I am too square on, and I cannot throw it at all. Worst of all I drop my hands, and I am in no position to throw anything in the first place.

Even when I do throw the jab, I start to wind back my left shoulder in preparation. This is a grave error, even if it lasts only for a split second, and is known as 'telegraphing'. If I am telegraphing, my opponent – thankfully only the boxing bag at this stage – can predict which punch I am going to throw and respond in double-quick time. At times I am telegraphing so badly that it constitutes a kind of boxing semaphore. I then discover a further sin of which I am also guilty. This is aptly named 'painting and decorating'. I concentrate so much on pushing the punch out, that I leave my hand out in the punch zone, failing to retract it, 'admiring my own handiwork' so to speak, hence the DIY tag.

I read in Jack Dempsey's book, *Championship Fighting: Explosive Punching and Aggressive Defence,* that he has another nasty jab variant. Normally the jab is delivered with the hand in a slightly open position, but for extra bite Jack Dempsey suggests closing or 'freezing' the hand at the point of delivering the punch.

The right hand punch is known simply as the 'right hand'. The right hand is the power punch, and hopefully having softened up your opponent with the jab, you spot a chink in his armour, and then deliver your knockout right hand. Many have been caught unawares by a sneaky right hand punch. As a sideways body shot or in the solar plexus it can wind or temporarily disable an opponent. A nasty visceral side shot known as the liver shot can fell a giant if underpinned by a strong right hand.

The key to delivering a good right hand is being in the correct stance in the first place and in having really good hip action, as you swivel your right heel up and rightwards, and turn the right knee inwards and to the left, pivoting on the ball of the right foot. The right hand usually follows on from the jab, as the backwards momentum of the returning jab propels the right hand forward via the hips and shoulders. For a right-hander like myself, the right hand punch feels like quite a natural punch and to start with I overuse it instead of perfecting the jab.

The most common and simplest of punch combinations is called the '1-2', a jab followed by a right hand. I practise this first on the bags, and then on the pads which Gerard holds up. The pads are like specially padded gloves with a flat or slightly curved palm, worn by the coach or training partner. They are held up at head height or at various positions on the body as a punching target. There is a definite art to holding up the pads for another boxer. Your pad hands have to provide enough resistance to make your partner feeling as if they are punching something, but not too much, as your arm has to be relaxed enough to allow the pads to take most of the shock.

Being of comparable height is helpful in pad-work, and if your technique is good it is possible to hold up the pads comfortably for a very strong boxer. If your boxing partner is very strong, trained and fight-ready, it is advisable that the pad-holder wears headgear and a gum guard, just in case of an unintentional swipe. As well as mastering the boxing stance itself, judging distances is the next big problem: if you are too near to or too far from your target, you cannot punch anything for toffee. In an orthodox stance, the right hand has further to travel than the left, so the right hand generally sets the range. Turning the hands inwards when punching increases the length of the arm, and increases the reach, by half an inch or so. It also increases the pressure points from the knuckles on the target, and in the boxing ring can add some bite to the punches.

The next level of complexity is punching a moving target. This usually involves your boxing partner moving the pads first slowly, then circling slowly or stepping quickly around the boxing ring. I find that the minute Gerard moves in any direction with the pads I am instantly bamboozled and lose the correct boxing stance. If boxing for real I would be reduced to instant mincemeat.

I have read that to be a good boxer you need both heart and spite, and I quite preternaturally find my inner spite. However, I learn quickly that it is a sign of inexperience to hit the pads as hard as you can, and attitude is no substitute for technique.

Gerard makes me punch the pads in a simple 1-2 repeating pattern for a total of a minute. As the last ten seconds approach, he smiles an evil smile and says: 'Marianne – you are getting weaker.'

With my last gasp of breath, I say, 'No, I am not,' but we both know that this is untrue. Pad-work is completely and surprisingly very exhausting, but in a good way. Chest heaving and sweat pouring, I make my way self-consciously to the edge of the gym. Here, I can look incredibly wasted with a small degree of privacy.

I secretly think that I must look awful, as any make-up I have applied has completely melted off my face (sad insight: at my age, I mostly regard make-up as essential to selfesteem) but plainly I am the only one that cares. This is the first joy that I discover in the boxing gym, that no one really cares about anything – who you are, how old you are, how you look, where you are from or even how fit you are – except that you give it your all. After the pad-work I am so exhausted that I cannot tell my left hand from my right, a common training problem in boxing – when all your energy has gone, there is no oxygen left in the brain to process the simplest of thoughts.

I also realise that Gerard has eyes in the back of his head. Occasionally he slips out of the gym for a glass of water or cup of tea, or to see that DJ is alright if he has been left in the car outside. Even if he has been out of the room for only a minute he knows by osmosis whether you have been slacking or not.

I have never entirely solved the mystery of why boxing is so tiring. Erudite books state that you burn about 800 calories per hour while sparring, about double the burn rate of running. Jack Dempsey put this down to the unpredictability element, as body and brain are constantly re-evaluating a new configuration of micro-events in the boxing ring, and in so doing are using up all their available resources.

I trust Jack Dempsey. Everything that I have read in his boxing book makes sense, and this seems like a plausible explanation. His book contains informative hand drawings of boxers in plain white shirts, black army shorts and boots undergoing various drills and throwing sharp shots, along with terse descriptions in simple English. Jack Dempsey's narrative contains only a little homespun philosophy. This breeds confidence and does not play to vanity or ego. Jack Dempsey speaks the truth.

2

TOUGHENED UP

After the first six weeks of boxing training, I finally stop aching and start getting into the swing of things. My technique is still very poor but there is no doubt that, even at this very early stage, I am building up strength and stamina. I spend some useful time with Janine, who is a competent boxing coach. Janine is patient, and even I have to admit that my boxing is improving incrementally, although it is still awful.

I learn a sort-of technique for punching on the bags, moving around the bag in a rudimentary, shuffling kind of way. As I improve, I find that I can push myself further and further. However, Gerard is all-seeing and all-knowing, and the immediate cure for any so-called 'lazyitis' is usually ten or twenty press-ups. Peter also cops for this, as he is always late into the gym but cannot possibly arrive earlier because of his pub work.

Somehow, I get through the Monday, Wednesday and then the Friday sessions of the first few weeks, then months. The Monday and Wednesday sessions last for an hour, but Friday comprises a full hour-and-a-half accompanied by the youth boxers. There is more of a fun feel to the Friday session, but it is longer and more tiring.

Spring finally comes into view and the nights are lighter. We now have sprinting sessions out in the youth club yard, interspersed with other forms of boxing training. We do 'walk, jog, run' sessions in the yard – a form of interval training, where the continual change of pace ups the effort.

I invest in a proper pair of cushioned shoes to take out the grief of skipping on the hard gym or yard floor. Having never been able to skip much before I am now becoming proficient, even trying a few party tricks with the skipping rope, much to everyone's amusement. In ancient boxing books the experts say that being able to skip and master the speedball makes you feel like a boxer, and then once you feel like a boxer you morph into the real thing.

⊙

My colleagues at the local school where I work as a laboratory technician think that I am mad, and secretly in pursuit of men with sculpted bodies. Worse still, my partner, Haydon, openly hates me pursuing boxing of any kind, as he imagines that I am participating in the heavy-slugging professional game and getting severely beaten about the head at every turn. My brother-in-law warns me that I am in the middle of a mid-life crisis if only I could but see it.

Nothing could be further from the truth. I am finding the boxing training genuinely interesting and entertaining, though what exactly I am training for I do not know or dare not think. In part, I think I find the sport appealing because it is monumentally not boring.

In my teens, constrained and bored by suburban life in the small northern town of Culcheth, and burdened down by my parents' overblown academic expectations, I sought escape, freedom and kindred spirits. I fell in with a group of potholers based in Bolton, where I went to school. Every weekend I cadged a lift north to the Yorkshire Dales, Britain's premier caving and potholing area, staying in a semi-ruined farmhouse for a peppercorn rent on the moors near the town of Settle and exploring caverns measureless to man.

At the farmhouse, there was no glass in some of the windows, and a sheep's skull hung ominously on a rope in the front room window. The only source of heat was a single wood-burning stove known as 'Old Faithful'. Someone had had a tussle with Old Faithful and had inadvertently got their potholing gear burned. The remains were nailed to the front-room wall as a warning. There was an outside chemical toilet in a barn, patrolled at night by a huge rat.

On summer days, when there was nothing much to do, we could drag the musty furniture out into the nearby field or set fire to various things. A dear friend was rugby-tackled by another when he threw a full-size gas canister onto a bonfire 'just to see what it would do'. In the winter, we could be snowed in by six foot high drifts for days on end, surviving on baked beans, until the snow-plough came through.

On more active days, my companions and I obsessively explored the caves and potholes beneath the Yorkshire Dales. Caves are more or less horizontal and relatively easy to navigate, but the term 'potholing' is reserved for caves with vertical drops, known as 'pitches', which require competency in rope-work. Trips varied in length from a couple of hours to ten or even twelve hours to descend Dales' deepest caves, which were about 550 feet deep.

Although I already had undertaken a couple of very simple caving trips while a member of an outdoor activities club at school, my first real introduction to potholing was to descend a pothole called Cherry Tree Hole on Darnbrook Fell near Settle, with the Bolton group of potholers. It must have been about 1980 as I was seventeen. The entrance to the pothole involved shimmying down a 25-foot-deep rift in the limestone rock.

In the UK, caves and potholes are graded in difficulty from one to five, five being the most difficult. Cherry Tree Hole was graded four with elements of five, and soon I was to find out why. In the initial sections of the cave there were very few places to stand up. We followed a torturous and constricted route through the rock, stooping and crawling, roughly following the course of the underground stream we could hear rumbling below, out of sight.

At a T-junction we ventured upstream, where the cave passage gradually lowered until it was less than eighteen inches high and mostly filled with water. Close to the end of the navigable parts of the cave, there was one improbable section, about twenty feet long, with only one or two inches of airspace above the water. This section was so low and wet that it could only be negotiated on your back with nose pressed to the cave passage roof. Only one person could go through at a time, as the presence of another could cause the stream to back up and fill the cave with water.

Summoning up nerves of steel from somewhere, I entered this section with trepidation. Once in, there was no going back. I felt the freezing cold water hit my ears as it lapped right up to the corners of my eyes. As I had no wetsuit hood, the cold water induced instant dizziness.

Beyond this section we found ourselves in a very remote part of the cave known as Blackstone Chamber. Here, the cave was strikingly beautiful and pristine, festooned with startling white stalactites and stalagmites, that had presumably been seen by only a very few. Despite the extreme cold and dizziness, I was still glad that I had witnessed the stark and perfect beauty of Blackstone Chamber. Early experiences such as these fostered an interest in cave exploration, but also a lifelong interest in geology.

Not all of my potholing experiences were as extreme, but the attitude of northern potholers at the time was to downplay and normalise extreme physical hardship and the bucketfuls of bravery which were usually required to survive a standard caving trip.

Understatement was the order of the day. Wet caving trips were described as 'sporting' or as 'a bit aqueous'; trips actually described as 'wet' usually required dry-suits, boats, diving gear or hundreds of feet of swimming in ice-cold water. Yawning underground chasms, which no sane person would cross, were described as 'perhaps needing a rope' or as a 'bit of a bad step'. Squeezes through body-sized, constricted spaces were described as 'a bit tight'; those described as 'very tight' were best avoided, and the local Cave Rescue Team had a subset of very thin men known as 'The Thin Mans' Team' to take charge if anyone got stuck in these, and cracked ribs usually resulted. Crawling beneath tons of loose, rickety boulders known as 'boulder chokes' was merely described as 'interesting' or 'entertaining'.

On one memorable occasion, Haydon and his companion, Bob, described entering a cave with a loose, teetering boulder choke where the boulders actually moved as they crawled through them. 'How was your trip?' I asked, afterwards. 'Oh, fine,' Haydon replied. Then, after pausing for a moment, 'Although at one point Bob was weeping.'

Truthfully, I always thought of myself as one of the more fearful potholers, a grafter rather than a 'natural', and my companions much tougher and more competent than I.

With the benefit of hindsight, I can see now that the extreme had become normalised for all of us, and without realising it I had become quite toughened up. Perhaps initially we had been drawn to potholing because of its quirkiness, the satisfaction of overcoming physical hardship and of facing down real objective dangers. In the end the real driver became the joy and wonder of exploring a largely unknown, beautiful and mysterious underground world.

Anyway, my phlegmatic caving companions, who grew prize-winning dahlias, drank tea and read the *Guardian* in their spare time, would never have thought of themselves as athletes. They did not have a shred of ego, yet they were some of the toughest and most self-effacing people that I have ever known. It was a no-brainer making the move to the Yorkshire Dales with Haydon in 1988, as the area already meant so much to us both. I was fortunate in that many potholing friends from the Manchester area had already relocated for similar reasons and were living close by. This is how, in the Yorkshire Dales, I truly found freedom, interest and companionship, and got toughened up into the bargain.

However, in my late thirties, I began to find that even one decent caving trip feels like too much effort when balanced with other necessities of life. Reluctantly, I decided to give it up, with rock-climbing coming more to the fore, its risks more control-lable, its logistics less complex, but with a similar appeal.

In my forties, I fulfilled a lifelong ambition to complete a part-time master's degree in geology, in a subject area of my own choosing at Sheffield University. This takes six years, as I am working full-time for the duration. It is a self-funded labour of love, aided and abetted by two genuinely enthusiastic and supportive academics to whom I will be ever indebted. I collect limestone samples from various locations in the Yorkshire Dales and analyse their tiny fossils under the microscope, relating this to ancient climate change. At the end of it, I am poor, exhausted and fat, but my brain works magnificently. Along the way, I have also had a fascinating glimpse into Earth's history 330 million years ago. However, further study is stalled, as my supervisors at Sheffield University retire, and I can find no one else within the UK university system who really shares my academic interests. Moreover, the constraints of full-time work and a lack of money kick in.

Having always been reasonably fit, I found that I was viewing middle-aged spread as if staring down the barrel of a gun. At fifty, I know full well that any attempts to regain fitness will involve several years' hard work, and in truth I dread the boredom of the gym.

One of the strong motivators is that I would like to gain enough fitness to go caving again. I read an inspirational article by the journalist and caver David Rose. David was a keen cave explorer in his twenties, being involved in many pioneering expeditions in the 1980s to explore and survey very deep and arduous caves in the Picos de Europa area of northern Spain, including Pozu del Xitu at *c.* 1160 metres deep. Thirty years later, he puts himself through a formidable fitness programme, redescending Pozu del Xitu and heroically reaching his previous exploration 'low point'. I doubt I can match David's efforts, but I scrolled through various fitness options on-line. In the end, I decided that the gym was the most efficient option, as it involves simple no-nonsense graft, the activities are not weather-dependent, nor do they require a partner.

Thus, my lurch towards the gym and inadvertently to boxing was fated. Perhaps after years of potholing I am tougher than I think, and after three months of boxing training my decision is also vindicated, as I am most definitely not bored. My progress is at a snail's pace, yet there it is, plain to see. I am light years away from facing anyone, even a sack of potatoes, in the boxing ring on grounds of age and lack of experience, but I do definitely have a new spring in my step.

3

BETTER THAN YOU THINK

I find that I am really enjoying my visits to the boxing gym, which now feel routine. Everything just seems better. The longish commute from the Dales to my workplace seems less of a nuisance and I generally have more energy on the drive home, as I watch the pale halo of the sun disappear behind the Lancashire hills.

At the youth club gym we graduate from rest sessions between the bag rounds to a cache of other exercises that fill up any gaps. I am introduced to the new torture of tuck jumps, pike jumps and snake curls, the last exercise where the body is contorted into an uncomfortable S-shape while trying to do a press-up. The body reaches a 'wall' after a certain level of oxygen demand, but I discover that the wall is a moveable feast. We try to improve explosive leg power by jumping up and down on things. One boxer, Steve, impresses us mightily by jumping from a standstill onto a four-foot high stage at one end of the boxing gym. None of us can do anything like this, and due to the very real risk of injury (for the moment) dare not try.

In fact, every time I visit the gym, the training exercises seem to become incrementally more bizarre and extreme. At first I think this is just my imagination, but the other boxers notice it too. We try press-ups with our feet braced very high up against the gym wall, and even handstand press-ups which are plumb vertical. I have only seen these done on TV in prison cells where space is very limited. I cannot do them but I try, somebody helpfully dangling me upside down by my feet to take some of the weight.

Another evening Gerard gets into a mood, decides that we are all slackers and that he will put us through our paces. I think that this is some kind of secret evaluation. These sessions are genuinely hard, but significantly none of us actually gives up. Gerard pushes us almost to our limits but is never that psycho that we hear about at other boxing gyms who pushes you so hard that you faint or throw up.

On one occasion he shouts to me while we are doing dips on the bench: 'You f—king little tart, get yer a—e on the floor' – a reference no doubt to not doing the dips thoroughly enough. I am put out, not because of the language but because of the accusation, which I feel is false as I have been genuinely trying my hardest. At the end of the session I decide, as a wind-up, to put on my best hangdog expression and say how upset/offended I am. Gerard is genuinely regretful, and profusely apologises, 'I'm so sorry, love, but I was talkin' to Brendan behind yer.'

As the sessions pick up in momentum and numbers, previous gym inhabitants reappear. Two brothers, Mark and James, clearly experienced boxers but slightly out of condition, don their head-gear and gum guards and spar in the corner of the gym. They are initially rusty but their elegant sway is apparent. We novices look on, impressed. They are both originally from Barnsley and by a quirk now live in the same street in the local town.

Becky, a former youth boxer, starts attending the adult sessions. The youth boxers have a scheduled session earlier than ours, so we rarely get to see them in action. Becky has been boxing for six years, since the age of eleven, and she is easily the best technical boxer in the entire club. Quiet, fearless and fast, she is also said to pack the biggest punch. There is a rumour that she has been spotted by a North West regional amateur boxing team. Her tall frame is quite slight, leading those who don't know her into dangerous underestimations. Her technique is superb as she has speed, skill and good movement around the ring. She is the queen of long, looping, hammer blow hooks which rain down relentlessly on any unsuspecting opponent.

I hear the crack, crack, crack of jabs, straight rights and hooks of all persuasions on the pads which Gerard holds up for Becky. I notice that she is leaning into her would-be opponent's punch zone, but guess what? It doesn't matter. No one could get through that barrage of superfast punches. I give my best, stern advice to any male boxers who are looking as if they might want to make their mark: 'Don't get in the ring with Becky.'

I have conflicting views about children being allowed to box. Clearly there are some risks, but most clubs that adhere to Amateur Boxing Association rules allow sparring between children aged ten and above. This seems far too young and at this age I worry about the vicarious ambitions of adults being projected onto the children in question. Furthermore, in the adult game, boxers are able to understand the risks and apply self-discipline. In training, a stronger opponent will usually deliberately pull punches against a weaker opponent to make the experience more valuable and evenly matched for both.

In reputable boxing clubs, it is seen as very bad form to attempt to pulverise your opponent during a routine training session: the main aim is to outwit them. So-called 'hard-sparring' is usually only reserved for the run up to a competitive fight, when both boxers are fight-ready and then only under very strict supervision.

Real risks in training seem to come from mistaken judgement or a stumble or slip, which leads to the occasional unplanned shot. Sometimes boxers just get a bit carried away by the drama of it all – hence the need for someone else looking on. However, the biggest injury threat in boxing is football: footballing boxers are always off sick, with something nasty like a split kneecap.

I continue to watch various TV boxing matches, and this is a bit of guilty pleasure, as I am genuinely at odds with the very violent aspects of the professional game, where the boxers sometimes sustain severe injuries, even death. But neither can I deny that the professional game has a sort of old-school valour, which I feel is missing from many modern sports.

I watch because of the sheer technical brilliance and endurance of the athletes, as I try to grasp the huge range of different boxing styles: the heavy-sluggers, the volume-punchers, the defensive boxers and the punch-traders. The TV cameras always focus on the boxers' heads and hands, but because of my own atrocious footwork I always want to see their feet.

Anyway, I am all fired up after watching old video clips of Muhammad Ali in the famous boxing match known as 'The Rumble in the Jungle'. This seminal event was held in 1974, in Kinshasa, Zaire (now the Democratic Republic of Congo). Ali was the underdog who beat George Foreman ('Big George') by knockout in the eighth round. Ali deployed a clever rope-a-dope strategy, where he lay back on the ropes in a defensive position for most of the rounds, letting Foreman tire and punch himself out. Fresh as a daisy towards the ends of the rounds, Ali then sprang off the ropes, surprising Foreman with a major offensive attack.

With renewed and misplaced optimism, I ask Gerard to try and teach me the left hook. The left hook is so complicated that I will not attempt to describe it yet. Suffice to say that I fail at it miserably, as my arms are all wide and spidery instead of having the 'windscreen wiper' precision required.

⊙

After one memorable session, Peter and I are left behind in the gym, after the others have gone home. We indulge in a black, self-deprecating, no-hope conversation about all our old and new boxing mistakes, our failure to correct them and how age, time and everything else is against us. We do not realise that Gerard is lurking out of sight in the boxing store next door and can hear every word.

He storms into the gym with ballistic force and it is the only time that I ever see him genuinely angry. 'Youse both are NOT CRAP!' he shouts. 'I will not have that talk in this gym! Youse are both improving! And, by the way, I'LL DECIDE if youse are f—king crap, or not, and YOUSE ARE NOT F—KING CRAP!'

We are both dumbstruck and heartened by this stinging endorsement and agree that it is the nicest thing that anyone has ever said to us. Gerard mumbles something else and locks up the boxing store. 'See youse on Wednesday,' he shouts, as he leaves the gym.

Peter and I mumble something in reply, then immediately collapse to our knees in a fit of hysterical giggles.

4

IN THE RING

It is the Easter holidays and the youth club is temporarily closed, so I decide to take matters into my own hands. I decide to attend a professional boxing gym and try to master the hook.

I used to live near the small coal mining town of Leigh in southern Lancashire and went to school in Bolton. I still feel a sort of kinship with Bolton and, for no other reason than I already know the geography, I search the internet for boxing gyms there. The First Rate Boxing Gym in Bolton looks a bit more respectable than the rest. I also know that this is one of the training gyms used by a well-respected professional boxer from my local area. So, one Saturday I take my chance and turn up for a training session at 11 a.m., parting with fifteen quid.

Boxing gyms are always in the 'nicest' parts of town, and this is no exception. It is in the war-torn and left behind backstreets of Bolton, full of decaying mills and boarded up two-up two-downs in red Accrington brick. I read in the paper there has been a serious armed bank robbery only a block away one week previously. I don't know if this is an urban myth or not, but someone has told me that you never get your car broken into in a boxing gym car park, so I have no qualms about leaving my car. I will not pretend that I would like to live in this area of Bolton, but aspects of it, such as the Victorian buildings, I find genuinely beautiful.

The modern way is to romanticise poverty and victimhood. The Sunday papers are full of what I call 'poverty porn': the unfortunate situations of the urban English or American poor are presented as some kind of art, and the poor are venerated as heroic and real. The truth is that no one wants to be poor or live in a rundown area. Without any slack in the system, poverty forces even the strongest to lead chaotic lives. Only photographers such as Don McCullin manage to tell it like it is without fear or favour (P.S. I love you, Don).

The boxing gym is indeed in part of an old mill building that is still being used for something. On the ground floor there is a small textile firm probably only hanging on by a thread. I go up a single flight of very dark, grimy stone steps onto the first floor. I open the fire door and immediately there is the throb of house music dampened by thick black rubber mats, which cover most of the floor. There is the smell of sweat, anguish and possibly triumph. I feel inexplicably at home.

The original cast iron pillars which form the fabric of the mill building pierce the gym space, and at the far end is the boxing ring in all its glory. There is a small ladies' changing room on the left near the entrance door. This is very basic with a mirror and cheap, packing-crate benches, with an equivalent room for men on the right.

I have signed up for a women's boxing session, and in the changing room I speak to a woman with badly dyed blonde hair and a slightly mad glint in her eye. She tells me that she has been in the boxing ring fighting competitively as an amateur but has been recently injured and has lost fitness.

I change into my gear and have a little last-minute shadow boxing session in front of the changing room mirror before the main session starts. Even though it is supposed to be a women's only boxing session, we are initially directed to a largish group of men and women, where we warm up under the watchful eye of the coach, skipping and shadow boxing interspersed with other familiar exercises. We have to sprint in a dogleg pattern across the gym floor to avoid the Victorian ironwork.

The room seems to be divided into two halves. Most of the women are directed into the right hand half of the room and, mysteriously, the woman with the mad glint in her eye, the men and I are directed into the other half, where things begin to look a bit more serious.

I have had to fill in an online form about my boxing skills (or lack of them), so surely the coach must know that I am still a novice? The boxers in my group appear to be more experienced, carded or ex-carded types, which means they either carry or have recently carried medical cards to allow them to box competitively in the ring. After a few further exercises I am paired up with the woman with the mad glint in her eye, and I get my first taste, or rather trial by fire, of defensive boxing.

She throws a sharp jab. I am not expecting this so rather embarrassingly I am still wearing my glasses. I block the shot with my left hand, with my hand in a vertical orientation and the palm facing inwards as I have seen the other boxers do at my local gym. She throws a right hand – I parry or push it out of the way with my right. This goes on for a bit. We stop for a breather.

I warn her that I am wearing a rather expensive pair of glasses that I don't want to lose. We start up again. The glasses seem to have enraged her somehow. The jabs and right hands come thicker, faster and harder, and my glasses are knocked to the floor. I am having real trouble blocking the shots now. I sense that she has it in for me, and I am cross because it should be obvious that I am novice and will gain nothing from the session if she treats it like a boxing match. Neither will she. I guess that she is somehow frustrated by her injury. The coach rushes over and without hesitation slings her out of the gym, and that is that. I am glad to say that this is the one and only time I have experienced this type of undisciplined behaviour in any boxing gym.

I attend two further sessions at the same gym over the next few weeks and both are worthwhile. In the first session one of the professional coaches who has a cauliflower ear spends time with me going right back to basics with my boxing stance. This is incredibly worthwhile. I practise moving around the boxing ring for the first time. I am told to 'swing my hips like Elvis' which I try in vain to do.

In the second session I am paired up with a much saner female boxer, Michelle. We both practise some genuinely useful defensive moves at a more civilised pace, before enduring a fairly punishing fitness session. At the end of this session, I am placed in the boxing ring with a much more experienced male boxer for five three-minute rounds. My sole purpose is to try and break down his defences and to see if I can score any points against him at all.

I consider myself to be quite fit now, but rather cruelly I am not allowed to rest between the rounds. Instead, I am given a series of exercises including fast step-ups on a bench to keep me 'occupied'. Apparently, this keeps the necessary blood pumping round the muscles between the rounds.

My opponent is not throwing any punches at all at me, but even without this obvious distraction it is completely exhausting work. Because he is an experienced strategist, somehow he is making me do all the work. I seem to be whirling round and round the edge of the ring, feebly throwing punches into the air. He can read me like an open book and merely ducks, slips or rolls out of the way of my clunky jabs. He barely seems to move as I try my hardest. It is abundantly clear that he is completely at ease and well able to defend himself from any of my rather pathetic attempts. In fact, his is a textbook demonstration of proper boxing defence. In a way this gives me hope as I see that good defensive boxing is at least possible by *someone*.

Something must change, I think, as the bell rings and rings and the fourth round starts. For the first time ever, I actually start to engage my boxing brain. I must try something new or face complete humiliation in the eyes of the few onlookers. I feint a right hand shot. This causes him to momentarily drop his guard, and I plant a good left hook. I drop towards the floor by flexing my knees. He doesn't know what's going on, and this temporarily confuses him. I move forward in a display of pretend confidence. He moves back onto the ropes, and I deliver a couple of good body shots, then I am spent. The bell rings. At least I have managed something. The fifth round passes in a blur of exhaustion without event, but I do manage to deliver punches right to the last.

I thank my opponent and we fist-bump gloves in the time-honoured way. He takes off his headgear and smiles. He has barely broken into a sweat, but I am all in. I ask him for his honest comments. 'Well, you are clearly a novice and lack technique, but there is some determination and punching power there. You were even punching quite well in the fifth round.'

Though not a proper boxing match or even a sparring contest, this experience did have a sense of reality about it, and from now on, I think, I will never be afraid to step into the ring under the gaze of onlookers, as long as I am adequately prepared. Perhaps this means never.

After getting changed, I have the immediate and quite primal desire to eat. It is an overpowering sense of hunger that I have rarely experienced. Fortunately, I have a couple of cereal bars in the car. Feeling faint, I wolf these down. Perhaps these will stifle the hunger pangs before I can reach my favourite café in Rivington village, a couple of miles away.

After driving only one mile along the Bolton Ring Road, I turn off into a small park. God Help Me! I have to eat again. Right Now! I fumble in a rucksack in the boot of my car and thankfully I find a few soggy glucose tablets right at the very bottom. Simultaneously, I glug down a whole flask of sugar-rich coffee. Then I feel as high as a kite as my system is simultaneously swamped with endorphins, sugar and caffeine. It is the most glorious feeling imaginable. It makes me wonder what real boxers must feel like after a real match.

Eventually I make it to the Rivington café. It is an old, slightly damp, churchy building stuffed with wet dogs and their earnest owners out for weekend walks on the Bolton fells. Years ago, I recall that my partner shamed me in this café by asking for Eccles cakes. 'They're Chorley cakes round 'ere, love,' came the swift reply.

I ask for beans on toast with scrambled eggs, and pray, pray, pray for it to be quick. I am thirsty again and ask for a pint of tea loaded with sugar, then another one, then another one. It might be the road to diabetes hell, but I need it right now.

I sink into a dreamy torpor. I am tired, but also alert and

incredibly elated. The food revives me enough to make it back home by teatime. I wonder if I will ever replenish my reserves of energy.

The following day, I lie languidly on the sofa and eat three enormous meals, one after the other, one of which is just a giant pan of spaghetti. 'You're never going eat all that?!' Haydon says, aghast. I know that it is slightly disgusting, but I just stuff it straight in, gratefully all the same. I am still ravenous.

'After all,' I lie, 'I'm allowed – I'm a boxer.'

☉

I am just about recovered from this epic by the following Friday. After the Easter holidays, Gerard is absent – and unusually only Peter and I turn up. Peter starts his own particular routine and I am just about to put myself through my own well-worn paces, when the gym door creaks open and Declan appears. From what I remember he is a young boxer of some style, who appears infrequently. He is a traveller from Bishop Auckland and a part-time salesman, who occasionally visits and stays in the local area with his sister. He tells me without a hint of boastfulness that he has been boxing since the age of eight.

We are not supposed to spar without a coach present, but in the rush to do something productive we genuinely forget this. We set up a makeshift ring in the corner of the gym using gym benches, and Declan asks Peter if he will join him in the ring. He says no. Anxious to do something, I say that I will try and breakdown Declan's defences like I did in the pro-gym, a week earlier, and I say that he is welcome the throw the odd punch at me, just to keep me interested.

He agrees that this will be a great idea and of use to us both. We warm up by skipping and square up in the ring. Declan tells me that he is not been in the ring for a while and I am surprised. He also warns me that he is very unfit, which I doubt. I am fully recovered from the exhaustion of the previous week in the Bolton gym and feel fit and ready for anything. We use the alarm on my phone to time the rounds which are three minutes, with a minute's rest in between.

First of all I try a jab. It is clearly far too slow. Declan can see exactly what is coming, and without expending any energy he drops to the floor, and I swipe hopelessly into the air. I am 'telegraphing' again needlessly, bringing back my left shoulder before I unwind my too-slow jab. He seems to have an incredible economy of movement which means that he is standing in the middle of the ring as I trundle around the outside, expending all my energy. This will not do. I try the tactic of moving forward, in a false show of confidence. This spooks him a bit, and I feint a right hand and push him back onto the 'ropes'. I deliver some good body shots, while simultaneously apologising, then finish off with a sort-of left hook.

The bell rings and already I feel that I am starting to tire, even after the first round. I know the immediate signs, but also I know that I still have plenty of energy left, and the capacity to recover quickly. I rush for my bottle of water. Declan advises, 'A boxer should never apologise for delivering a good punch.' I agree and hope that I will have the chance not to apologise in the next round.

In round two I decide that a full on assault is the best strategy as I try to get my opponent on the back foot. I try some newly learned pivots so that I am out of line of his occasional punches. I push him back onto the ropes again with a nicely aimed double jab, but this will be the last jab that hits its target as Declan slips and rolls and then hunkers down.

Both his gloves suddenly cover his face, a style of boxing formally known as 'peek-a-boo' and his head becomes an unassailable fortress. There is really no way through. The bell rings again and not a second too soon. I greedily gulp down more water while Declan grabs a ham sandwich. He offers me some, but I politely refuse, saying that I am a lifelong vegetarian and think that the long-distance transport of livestock is incredibly cruel. Declan muses for a minute, then says that he doesn't think that animals have souls, and therefore cannot suffer. 'Says who?' I reply and he quickly responds: 'God.' I decide that we cannot have a full-blown philosophical discussion about God, and what he approves and disapproves of, against the clock, as the bell signalling the third round dings and dings.

I decide that since my right hand is my strongest punch. I must get it through somehow. I move forward and back, forward and back, in unpredictable shadow boxing manoeuvres to try and confuse. I pretend to stoop down to deliver an uppercut – a punch that I am in fact incapable of delivering anyway – but at the last minute get into a perfect side-on stance and deliver a great right hand body shot. This is the kind of shot that resounds throughout the gym on the bag or pad. I know that I have hit my target, and I bite my lip so that I don't apologise. This ups the ante a bit, and Declan begins to grapple rather than step back, a sign that he is also starting to tire. The bell rings and we are both grateful for the end of round three.

As I drink an impossible amount of water, I notice that Declan still has the energy to practise on the bags between the rounds. 'Help me out, Peter!' I gasp. 'Can't you go in the ring with Declan just for one round to give me a breather?'

Peter hesitates: 'It is not really my thing, you know.' I know it is not, but even at this early stage I could desperately do with the break.

During round four, Declan develops this infuriating habit of simply hunkering down on the ground with his gloved hands glued to his face. Once he adopts this pose there is very little I can do, except bend my creaking knees even lower and try and deliver some not-very-good uppercuts. I wonder if his approach is legal within the rules of boxing, with which I am not really yet familiar. Eventually he tires of this, and we are both up and about again, with me helplessly orbiting the ring. He has the ability to bend backwards at the waist superfast, and all of my punches simply fall into the air. There is a special name for this type of manoeuvre which I readily forget as any stored strength evaporates.

My strategy of coming forward briefly works again as he moves back, then further back, his punching space diminishing till he can punch no more, and I see the opportunity for two left hooks which I manage to deliver one after the other.

I definitely begin to tire after round four, but on and on we go, in much the same fashion, except that my punches get weaker and wilder, until finally at the end of round eight I have to throw in the towel. I breathe pathetically in slow heaves at the side of the ring, like a marooned goldfish gasping for water.

We both fist-bump gloves in the usual way and manage to raise weak smiles. Declan is a good and disciplined opponent. He could knock me unconscious with a single hook, but instead chooses to hone his own defences and to help me with mine, and I am grateful. He is by far and away my best and most good-natured sparring partner, although the thought of ever taking him on for real is genuinely formidable and outrageous.

I ask him for his comments and advice. Dryly he says, 'Learn to compose yourself in the ring.' He is right – when I am composed, I can obviously box much better. However, when I say how weak I felt in the eighth round he says that I was still actually packing some quite hard punches. This is similar to comments that I have had before, and I take heart in the knowledge that I do now have some real physical strength. It is a lesson in how to dig deep mentally, keep calm and above all to keep going when you might mistakenly feel that you are spent.

5

WHITE COLLAR MADNESS

The following Monday there is an influx of boxing refugees from other clubs. Gerard is away again. Unfortunately, his absences will increase, as he fulfils a lifelong ambition to set up his own boxing club elsewhere to his own exacting requirements. Dai steps in as our voluntary coach. Dai has occasionally filled in for Gerard, and we already know him a bit. Dai tells us that he is an ex-army championship boxer, brought up quite toughly in warmer climes. He tells us that as a child he used to box fifteen rounds with his brother in the heat of the midday sun. This laid the foundations for an illustrious boxing career in the army, first as an infantryman in the light infantry and then in the 3rd Battalion, light infantry. We first see Dai in his late forties, a ska music enthusiast with a suedehead haircut. He is an accomplished footballer and referee who plays in a local team and has a penchant for West Ham. Dai has a dry wit which we will come to know and love, but for the time being he is an unknown quantity. Our first impression is that he is totally fearless and utterly reliable.

We arrive early and see that Dai has set up the proper

boxing ring in the corner of the gym. Normally the ring is just set out crudely using the gym benches, but tonight Dai has gone the whole hog, setting up the ring pillars, which slot into pre-drilled holes in the gym floor and form the four corners of the ring, and thick hemp ropes which are tensioned up between the pillars using ancient metal ratchets. The ring has the look and smell of an old ship about to be cast out to sea. I long to have another go in the ring, but know in my heart of hearts that I do not really have the skills, and dare not admit to my eight illegal rounds with Declan during the previous weeks. Peter too has been sworn to secrecy.

We watch Dai spar with a new boxer, Brent, for a couple of rounds. Both look the real deal and Dai is extraordinarily fast. Though a third of his age, Brent is no match for him. Dai expertly weaves back and forth delivering perfect quick-fire jabs and Brent starts to crumble. I am in Dai's corner, delivering encouragement which he does not really need (but it all adds to the atmosphere), and Peter is in Brent's corner, with Brendan acting as referee.

We decide that it is all over in the fifth round, and Dai is the clear winner. This is rough justice. Dai has known Brent in a past life and blames his indolence in training. Brent has all the innate skill and some of the technique, but none of the work ethic, and so his fitness is lacking. The origins of Dai's fitness are clear. That same night he shows us an old video on his smartphone of one of his army boxing matches a quarter of a century earlier. Dai is obviously proud as hundreds of military colleagues cheer him on. His speed in the ring is blistering, and we have seen that some of that old magic is still there.

As a trick, Dai asks me to stand in the ring. He says that he will come out of the corner and deliver a light punch. All I have to do is get out of way. Nothing more.

The odds are stacked against me. Like a silent owl, Dai looms out of the corner, throws his punch and is back in the corner before I can even blink. It is a true demonstration of speed and skill, especially for a man approaching fifty, and we are all a bit awestruck.

We joke with Dai that he should go back in the ring as a veteran, but it is not actually a joke as we all feel he could do really well. There are some incredibly old timers on the pro-circuit including one pro-boxer who is actually aged forty-nine. I secretly try and imagine what mind-boggling torture they have had to undergo.

Wednesday sees Gerard's continued absence, and Dai therefore continues as overlord to us all and especially to several new recruits: Bernard, Sean, Will and Donny.

Bernard is a charming and modest ex-boxer, aged only twenty-one. He confesses to us that over the last sixth months he has foolishly got into MMA cage fighting, which he describes as a 'complete nutter's game' where the worst elements of the local council estate have tried to beat him unconscious, again and again. He explains that he has cheated certain death on a number of occasions, every time he entered The Cage, and is now fully grateful to be alive. Bernard says ruefully that it was only his sheer physical strength that has saved him from these lunatic gladiator opponents with their no-holds-barred approach. He certainly looks strong, and he says that his ability to hold his opponent in a headlock was his one saving grace. Once again, he is glad to be in the safe and familiar bosom of traditional boxing.

Sean is a big bear of man, quiet and unassuming, and we all think rather naive, even for his eighteen years and eighteen stone. He has signed up for a white-collar boxing match in a Burnley nightclub a few weeks hence, with an audience of 700. These so-called white-collar boxing matches are outside normal boxing jurisdiction: some are completely respectable, with an appropriate infrastructure; others are no more than bare-knuckle fights in basements with no ringside medical cover or insurance. We regard some of these events with a healthy suspicion. Some unscrupulous boxing trainers market themselves to no-hope have-a-go desperados, put them through an intensive programme of boxing training over about eight weeks, and shove them out into the ring as cannon fodder or for financial gain. There is insufficient time to develop proper boxing skills or fitness, and most result in slightly manicured brawls.

We all like Sean and admire his bottle, but he is in no way fit enough to go into the ring. We urge caution, but Sean smiles and gently dismisses us. Dai has the difficult task of assessing and improving his fitness while simultaneously dissuading him from taking part. Dai must also build his confidence should he decide to go ahead with his summary execution. After just one training session, all can see that Sean is the least fit in the gym. He huffs and puffs at the skipping and the bag-pummelling as Dai shouts in vain: 'You lazy motherf—ker.' Sean is not lazy – but he is serially underprepared, and Dai knows this.

The following week Dai sets up the proper ring again. Only Peter, Sean, Declan and I are in attendance. Since the only two possible sparring partners are Declan and Sean, Dai pairs them up but will keep his beady eye on both. It is not really a fair pairing. On the face of it, at almost twice his weight, I predict that Sean must surely have the advantage. How wrong I am. Sean shuffles and lumbers his weight around the ring. He cannot move. He is virtually static. He immediately falls prey to

Declan's lightness of foot and target-perfect punching. We can see that Declan is deliberately taking his foot off the pedal so as not to embarrass Sean. Sean quickly tires and we see that Dai, normally optimistic, does not really know how to proceed.

The plan of action is to give Sean his pre-ring pep talk, fill him with false confidence, but also with a respectable and shameless exit strategy should he need it. We suspect that Sean may need some money from his boxing dalliance, but we cannot bear to see his demise. After a post-training session conference when he is absent, we shamefully become deserters who decide not to attend.

We hear a week later that he has been beaten to a pulp in the first round of the match and that the referee has had to stop the fight. We are very relieved to hear that he has survived, but we never see Sean again.

We hear on the grapevine that Gerard has recently got engaged to Janine. We are very fond of them both, but have not seen them for some time. In the middle of one of Dai's training sessions they suddenly appear out of the blue, having arrived in Gerard's brand new, shiny BMW. They say that they are going for a romantic weekend to an expensive hotel in the Lake District and, dewy-eyed, Janine very proudly shows us her diamond engagement ring. DJ the dog looks very fetching in his new diamante collar as he barks approval. We want to chat, but are only allowed out of the gym for a barely permissible thirty seconds to say 'Hello' before Dai drags us back into the gym for more punishment.

Two college boxers join us, Will and Donny. As the weeks roll by, they join Peter and myself as regular fixtures at the gym. Declan appears only intermittently, as his travelling work permits.

Dai cannot be around as he is in demand elsewhere as a football referee and so as summer approaches, no coaches routinely appear at our boxing sessions. I step into the breach, running one or two sessions – not because I am any kind of expert, but simply because I do not want us to lose any of the fitness and discipline that we have built up during the season.

We are fortunate to have an ex-army PT coach, Fred, who also usually attends. As well as being a competent boxer, Fred is a qualified first aider. He is happy to look on when I am running the classes as I'm particularly concerned about anyone getting injured on my watch. Fred has extraordinary levels of energy, and to our amazement, he casually mentions that he has climbed Mont Blanc, in the five-day time gap between our usual Wednesday and Monday sessions. His vigour and enthusiasm in the boxing gym remain undiminished by alpinism. The others say that they enjoy my training sessions but (unbelievably) complain that they are too hard. The numbers in the boxing gym funnel down to a regular core of grafters.

YEAR TWO

6

HEROES

After these few months of uncertainty, in late summer 2014, without faff or complaint, Dai takes the reins for our routine Monday and Wednesday training sessions, on an unpaid, no-expenses-paid basis. For this, we are eternally grateful. He also takes the youth boxers under his wing, running their training sessions before ours.

Dai and clones of Dai populate Britain enhancing the life of millions through sport, turning up week after week, year in, year out, always there, always committed, always encouraging, always uncomplaining, attending despite storms, droughts, floods, traffic jams, family illness and work. The phrase unsung hero doesn't really cover it.

On the internet I see a range of boxers and others, all with their own equally dedicated versions of Dai: street boxers trained by Alan Duarte in the favelas of Rio de Janeiro at the Abraço Campeão (Embracing Champions) boxing project. I see Muslim girls training in the Pak Shaheen Boxing Club in Karachi – their male coach, Younis Qambrani, frequently taking the flak for breaking cultural norms.

A special place in my heart is reserved for the magnificent Lorraine Jones. Her son, Dwayne Simpson, was an innocent bystander tragically murdered in a street incident in Brixton, London. Lorraine continues to run and expand Dwaynamics, the community boxing gym he had set up, and encourages those who might otherwise have strayed into street gangs onto a straighter path. I make a small donation towards the purchase of a boxing ring for Dwaynamics. I get a warm and fulsome email from Lorraine who addresses me straightaway as Dear Sister. (Not even my own sister addresses me thus.) I am genuinely humbled even to be vaguely associated with this legion of superheroes, and boxing moves in mysterious ways.

◉

Although we are small in number, we train regularly and hard. Dai brings out the 'Board of Death'. This is a white board which has no doubt been in the boxing store since antediluvian times, and at least since the birth of Methuselah. It is simply a numbered list of exercises that must be performed in order in a five-minute round (without rest), and then repeated four times, so that the total number of rounds performed is five in twenty-five minutes. A one or two-minute rest is allowed between the rounds.

I feel that I must record the oxygen-sapping contents of one round of The Board: twenty press-ups; twenty dips; twenty sit-ups; twenty press-ups again, or even snake curls if you are up to it – ten, if you are really struggling; twenty tuck jumps; twenty pike jumps; twenty star jumps; twenty burpees; twenty double-squat thrusts; twenty single-squat thrusts; twenty squats and two minutes of shadow boxing. Then, collapse on the floor. Before the start of the rounds, ten laps of the yard outside are traditionally required, but we are usually relieved of this because of rain, darkness and general feebleness.

Dai tells us that there is one lad in the youth boxers group who will never be able to do a particular exercise involving the core muscles. Dai tells us that he has a modern condition known as 'gamer's stomach'. This means that he has no core muscles at all as a result of spending years hunched over an iPad or laptop.

It is reported in the media that National Statistics reveal a worrying trend: successive generations are weaker than their antecedents: younger generations are taller due to good nutrition but weaker due to lack of exercise, as no one apart from labourers has to go outside any more. The prophecies laid out in H. G. Wells' book *The Time Machine* have finally come true. The Eloi and Morlocks are alive and kicking. (Perhaps, I am a sort-of Morlock.)

Allegedly, carded boxers should be able to perform five rounds of the board once they are officially fighting fit. No one at the club in living memory has managed five or even four rounds of the board, even though vintage photographs of the club show that it has definitely produced British Championship boxers, who presumably fell into this category. We usually save The Board for the end of a session, when we are already in an imminent state of collapse, and it is sure to finish off the hardiest. Only sparring sessions surpass it in terms of energy burn.

At the absolute peak of my fitness, I manage two-and-a-half rounds of The Board, but am utterly wasted afterwards, and more usually two is my absolute limit. Peter, while telling us all how desperate it is, easily manages three rounds of The Board, and actually has the energy to talk while doing the exercises.

The others manage between one and two rounds. At the end of it all, the floor of the gym is awash with sweat which trickles around in slow pools. No one speaks at first, and then only in rasps and gasps. Even Dai finds it hard to speak, despite his football refereeing training and hours of running along Morecambe Promenade. We both love and hate The Board. Like a bitter medicine, we know that it does us good and therefore feel bound to ask for it.

The two brothers, Mark and James, appear intermittently at these sessions and beat the hell out of each other in the most good-natured way. They toil away in the corner of the gym, their improvement marked by thunder-crack shots getting louder by the week. In the gym, we discuss TV boxing matches and music gigs. One August evening in 2014, I am mesmerised by Scott Fitzgerald in the Commonwealth Games Welterweight boxing final in Glasgow. He has a neat, determined style, and his business-like approach almost conceals his perfect jab which, like a steam-driven ramrod, wears down his opponent, Mandeep Jangra, again and again. Mark and James both love music and state proudly that they attended a Kate Bush concert, one of a unique series to be scheduled in modern times, thirty-five years after her last appearance. Around the same time, I relive my youth, worshipping at the altar of The Smiths and attend a Morrissey gig at the O2 arena in London in November 2014. (I say 'relive', but the lyrics seem far more relevant now than they ever did when I was a moody teenager.) Morrissey is a treasured, but increasingly controversial cultural icon, who inspires an almost religious devotion amongst many. Hence, the gig at the O2 is destined to be a crazy affair and it is. I am told that extra security guards have been employed on the night to hold back us middle-aged fogies, and they do. Unabashed, I sing my loudest. My boxing training (and elbows) are for once genuinely useful when I am crushed by love in the deepest heart of the mosh pit.

Back in the gym, Peter is getting stronger too, and although forever claiming that he is a novice we hear his punches slap onto the pads that Dai holds up for him. Dai shouts desperately: 'Peter – hit me like you mean it!' Peter tries and fails to bury his lifelong politeness, but is nonetheless now an effortless big hitter.

Will attends frequently. He is a law student from the local college. He says that he has never done any boxing before, but no one believes him. Easy going and with a natural boxing style, he is softnatured. He rescues cats and kittens in his spare time, which he and his girlfriend keep in their flat very much against regulations. He is burdened down by academic study, yet always manages regular attendance. Will is also a crack table tennis player, and if we both arrive early to our training sessions, we usually slug it out in a table tennis match, each claiming to be not-at-all competitive and me ruing a misspent youth.

Donny, ever cheerful, is an economics college student of Far Eastern extraction. He has a boundless boxing energy, and his hips are worthy of mention as they have the most rotation we have ever seen. This gives the quite slight and smiling Donny a cracking punch of gargantuan proportions. Donny is always late due to academic commitments and is therefore greeted by Dai in the same way every week as soon as his front foot crosses the threshold: 'Donny – you lazy f—, motherf—ker, you're late' followed sometimes by: 'Twenty press-ups.' Ever smiling, Donny takes his punishment well without complaint. One night, after many months, we remonstrate with Dai for his continued harsh treatment of the very genial Donny. That evening, as soon as Donny arrives late on cue, Dai shouts: 'Donny, Good Evening –' (a pause for comic effect) '– in your own time!' We howl with laughter as we see the one and only occasion that Donny's smile is wiped from his face as his jaw drops in amazement.

⊙

After fourteen months of training, I reach a sort of plateau fitness-wise, and technical progress stalls. I struggle to find the necessary motivation to push myself into a different zone, where I know things will get much more demanding. I am helped in this regard by a series of excellent boxing videos in the 'Sneakpunch' series made by one of my boxing heroes, Cornelius Carr. I do a few boxing moves during my tea break at work to amuse my colleagues. As the weeks roll by, they tell me that I am moving better and faster and that I look stronger, but I am all too aware that I'm still technically very deficient. Word gets around the students that I am a boxer of sorts. The boys take a real interest, while the girls think that I cannot possibly be any kind of boxer, presumably on grounds of age and sex. Perhaps, they are more far-sighted than I and can see beyond my naive optimism.

I am starting to get a few minor injuries from the intensity of all the training. This is disheartening, and after the initial rush of excitement and relatively fast improvement, I find that I am making the same technical mistakes again and again. Determinedly in for the long haul, I feel that I have to make more of the right sort of effort to improve, and having reached a boxing impasse, I need help and have resigned myself to forking out some cash for extra boxing tuition. I start researching other gyms, where different types of training might be available which could be added into my routine.

According to the internet, Mr Kelly trains professional boxers at his gym near Blackburn. Kelly's Gym is tacked onto the side of a posh hotel, as I guess the professional boxers do not like slumming it. I clock Kelly's gym as a future option, as it is also open to the public and has the obvious advantage of having a full-size boxing ring. In addition, Mr Kelly has a couple of professional boxing coaches on the premises whose services can be hired by mere mortals like myself.

I also join a local community gym in the Dales nearer to home. This is run by heroic volunteers with support from the local authority – remember those?! It is usually quiet at the times when I appear. The facilities here have been well very thought out and are well cared for. All the familiar tools are here: the usual gym machines in a single, carpeted room; a proper, heavy bag hanging in a spacious, high-ceilinged room with sprung floor, where there is actually room to swing a skipping rope. Best of all, there is a wall of mirrors in which to admire all your boxing mistakes. The modern way is to cram punters into small rooms, but in these old spaces there is room to expand and breathe.

The typical Dales' view from the long, grey, Victorian gym windows is tremendous, and is motivating in itself. In the foreground, grey-walled fields are framed by the angular, green fell tops which form the backdrop. The whole is backlit by yellow sunlight or white rain. At dusk grey and orange light piles into the room, changing the colour of the duck-egg blue walls. I can concentrate in this gym. It has a calm, vintage ambience which is somehow conducive to boxing.

I spend time in this Hall of Mirrors shadow boxing and trying to work on my rather poor boxing stance. At least I start to

believe that I can improve. Even Dai notices some mild improvement. After what seems like whole lifetimes, I finally begin to
practise the classic defensive moves of ducking, weaving, slipping and rolling, and some simple combinations of punches. My
speed and strength ratchets up another small notch.

In November 2014, I change jobs and start working as a
laboratory technician at Lancaster University, running a large
teaching laboratory in the Environmental Science faculty. The
university has a reputation for an excellent boxing club, and
I decide to join them for a training session. They have about
twenty carded boxers, all match fit and preparing to fight in a
major competition the following week.

I turn up for their college training session one Thursday
night. They wrongly assume that I am spectator, presumably
on account of my age, and they are surprised when I proffer
my £4 to participate. I sail through the two-hour session
fitness-wise, but find the technical boxing very challenging
and interesting.

I am paired up with a serious-minded lad of about twenty-
two, with dark hair and a beetling brow, who takes me through
the basic defensive manoeuvres of blocking and parrying or
pushing shots out of the way. He also shows me an elegant
little shimmy to the side which allows the avoidance of a
painful body shot, known as the liver shot. I gradually get
the hang of this and other small tricks of the trade. The coach
commends me for getting through the session, which is quite
heart-warming, but I am far from complacent.

That Sunday afternoon I turn up for a sparring session with
the same group of boxers. I stand on the sidelines, hoping to
be paired up with another similar novice, but there are none.
The other boxers are clearly way beyond my league in terms of

technique and the sparring is fight-ready hard-sparring, which I would never survive.

⊙

I am still feeling the mild after-effects of that Thursday session when I turn up for the usual session at the youth club the following Monday. Christmas is approaching, and I spend an enjoyable Saturday helping with the youth club Christmas fair. I ice cakes, wrestle with a snow machine, move tables and sell raffle tickets.

There is a wooden stage at one end of our boxing gym, raised about four feet off the deck. We normally use this for the various improbable high-angle press-ups. During the Christmas fair, the stage is at last used for its proper purpose: a small girl sings songs from the musical *Frozen*, belting out tunes as a crowd claps enthusiastically. Her triumph is all the greater as she has stepped into the breach at the last minute, as her friend who was going to take the lead role is off sick.

What surprises me the most are the huge crowds that our small event draws. I meet the generations that have benefited from the youth club. Granddads, grandmas, dads, mums, lads and girls all swarm in. Many older men recall their young boxing days here, training in the same gym that I have come to know and love, and there is talk of the past British champions, that I only know about in theory, produced on this very spot.

I discover that the youth club is underfunded because it has a relatively 'posh' postcode, which is at odds with some of the kids that I see attending weekly, including those in care who arrive sullenly with patient and upbeat minders. The local mayor visits briefly and I mumble something embarrassing to her about the transformative power of boxing. A group of footballers from Merseyside provides the main entertainment of the day running popular football training sessions for both boys and girls. They buy me cups of tea all day, as I sell raffle tickets. I hear that we make about £800 in all, which is very, very pleasing.

⊙

Dai suggests a boxers' night out in town as Christmas approaches. It is a running joke that Dai mumbles a bit, as Gerard did before him. Though we are generally attuned now to the reverberating warbles that are Dai's gym commands, many newcomers are not, and it is sometimes very hard to make him out. Time and again we fail to hear the name of the pub we are invited to attend, and however many times it's mentioned during the course of the week, we still cannot make it out. Despite everything, we are all still slightly frightened of Dai, and no one will ask him outright.

At the eleventh hour we finally learn of the appointed venue. Fred is a picture framer by trade and he says that he will frame some ska and two-tone pop-art posters from 1980s, which we hope Dai will like. We club together to get him a bottle of single malt whisky, which we feel is a safe bet.

When we arrive in the pub, Dai is cheerful and already pretty well oiled. I sit next to him but cannot make out a single word he says. This is not much different from usual, except that he is obviously slurring his words so there is absolutely no chance of a two-way conversation. I just smile and nod in the right places. The other boxers do the same. A couple behind us is trying to have a romantic meal. They are sitting closer to Dai than we are, if on a separate table, and clearly some of Dai's choice language does not pass them by as he gives a graphic and adventurous account of soldiering abroad. I cannot hear exactly what is being said, which is probably just as well, but I gauge its effect by catching Mark's eye who sits opposite me with a permanently raised eyebrow.

My partner is scheduled to pick me up later and I see him arrive early, clearly having some difficulty of his own at the pub door. We are unworldly country bumpkins, unversed in the ways of the town. He has inadvertently worn tracksuit bottoms with deep pockets which instantly makes him a drug dealer in the eyes of the door staff. I learn later that, being a man of a certain age, he has had to ask to go to the toilet. Against his wishes the burly door staff follow Haydon into the gents, believing him to be up to no good.

Unaware of this unfolding drama we seize the moment and present Dai with his carefully chosen Christmas gifts. Dai is well-chuffed as we pass over the framed posters and the whisky, which we suspect may not last much beyond the next week. He expects nothing from us, except for us to turn up week after week, to be shouted and sworn at, to be moulded to his own exacting requirements and to be enveloped in his own particular brand of tough love. Yet our gifts are clearly a bounty beyond words. Unable to say anything more of value, in our stilted northern way, we slap Dai on the back, wish him a Happy Christmas and go home.

7

A CHANGE OF SCENE

I hate Christmas and I jump for joy when all the sham and glitz is over. The New Year brings not inactivity exactly, but a nameless ennui followed by a frenzy of sorts. I am not normally bothered by my weight, but I strive to hack off the extra few pounds that I have gained over the holidays. My back has been giving me some gip and I have had to visit the doctor, dreading the outcome. As I enter his den, he is engrossed in his computer screen and says without looking up, 'Now, take a seat. What do you think is the matter?'

In my dreams, I am assertive and say: 'Well, from an internet search, I judge that there are about thirty possibilities from the utterly benign to the imminently fatal, and I can only narrow them down to eight. You are the f—king doctor, so you tell me if it's spinal cancer or a pulled muscle.' I find that everything in modern life has been reduced to a politically correct puzzle or riddle, where everyone has to pretend to be equal in all regards. No one says what they mean, and the doctor has to pretend that I know better than him, even though he has had at least seven years more medical training than me. After all, that is why I am there in the first place.

In reality I sigh, and submit. It is not a counsel of despair, but it will take a visit to the physiotherapist and a good few exercises to undo various past abuses. Of course, friends and family heap blame upon blame and say that it is my fault, as they tut-tut at the ridiculousness of someone my age attempting to learn to box. But I know that boxing is only partly to blame, with a lifetime of other abuses taking their toll. When I do finally get to see a physiotherapist whom I trust, he mainly blames other things such as driving and repetitive lifting at work, and says that actually the boxing is doing me a power of good, and I should continue with it at all costs.

It is a sobering observation, but in general I find that men dissuade and women encourage. For instance, men who are not boxers tend to ask the same, dull, silly and slightly sexist questions. They ask about women boxing, whether there are other women boxers in my club, how it makes me feel if there are none, how it makes me feel if there are any, how concerned I am about potentially destroying my looks(!), how I feel about boxing men, how I feel about getting injured, etc. In fact, I am not in the least concerned with any of these things, and neither is anyone else in the boxing gym, man or woman. No man who is not a boxer ever asks me an interesting question about any of the technical aspects of boxing, or considers that I might be remotely interested in them (even though *I really am*).

By contrast women tend to ask if the environment in the boxing gym is overly macho, whether it is encouraging or not, how I am coping with the boxing fitness regime and whether I am getting any injuries. I honestly reply that the environment is distinctly inclusive and non-macho, and that I am really enjoying the fitness regime, but have to admit that I am starting to pick up the odd injury or two, necessitating my visit to the physiotherapist.

I always aim to be organised when visiting the physio, to arrive early with a reasonable set of sports kit to change into. This never happens. I am always disorganised and late. With horror, I notice that on one particular visit I have a small hole in my tracksuit bottoms just above the knee. They look as if the cat has slept on them, which he has. I decide that my visits to this physiotherapist are cursed, as whenever I plan a visit, motorway junctions and one-way systems are mysteriously out of action, leading to immediate panic and despair. Only a simultaneous car crash combined with the actual loss of a leg and its fantastical replacement with a wooden leg could make things worse.

It is ironic that the only person who is truly sympathetic to my position is an ex-military physiotherapist at my workplace, who is by chance undertaking a degree at the university. We do not cross paths until, due to mutual incompetence and us both working late, neither she nor I can find the exit to the maze-like building we inhabit. There are never-ending building projects on the university site, which make the route out of the building more and more like an obstacle course, and the route changes daily. She notices that I am limping slightly and gives some sanguine advice. In a no-nonsense way she reduces my back problem to simple mechanics. I am a blameless broken machine that can be fixed without guilt or shame, as long as I do what I am told.

⊙

It is mid-January 2015 and the usual suspects appear at the youth club. Will and Donny appear fresh and full of energy due to the respite of the university holidays. Donny is early for once. Dai looks sweaty and pale, as he confesses to a couple of ridiculous drinking sessions. He growls, 'You bunch of lazy motherf—kers,' as we grab our instrument-of-torture skipping ropes. Dai is wearing a striking fluorescent orange hat, which must surely be the boxing equivalent of a Christmas jumper. The hat serves as a warning beacon for punishments to come.

As a magnanimous gesture, we are initially allowed thirty seconds of rest between the two-minute skipping sessions. We have already been skipping for ten whole minutes when Peter saunters in. 'Peter! You're f—king late! You f—king f—ker!' shouts Dai with a crocodile smile. But we know his bark is worse than his bite. There really is no answer, except to grab a skipping rope as fast as you can and skip for all you are worth. Instead Peter diddles around at the side of the gym and, with an apologetic shrug of the shoulders, slowly starts putting on his boxing wraps. This sends Dai momentarily into orbit: 'Peter! Skip! You f—ker! Just f—king skip!' Peter duly does. We cannot decide if Dai is really in a proper mood or just putting it on.

Anyway, even with Dai's sacred and profane encouragement, we are all exhausted from bag punching due to the usual Christmas excesses. As Dai holds up the pads for me, I make the same mistakes over and over again, dropping my hands and throwing weak, flattened punches. It is disheartening. He throws a sharp jab, which concentrates the mind just enough for me not to drop my hands, but only once. Then I am punching the pads for a whole minute – a barrage of 1-2, 1-2, left hook, 1-2, 1-2, left hook, right hook, 1-2, left hook, right hook, uppercut, uppercut until I finally tire. Even with Dai urging me on, my fourteen-ounce gloves feel as if they have been filled with molten lead.

⊙

The next few weeks drone on in a similar vein and eventually there are microscopic levels of improvement.

Gennady Golovkin has become another favourite in terms of boxing style. He is also known as 'Triple G' or 'The Kazakh Thunder' and is an almost unbeatable middleweight Kazakh professional boxer, who looks as if he has been out for a gentle stroll after twelve professional rounds with anyone. In a gripping late night televised boxing match in February I watch him destroy Martin Murray, a tall and very powerful-looking middleweight hopeful from St Helens. Murray is probably near the top end of his weight range and game. Golovkin does one thing that Murray cannot cope with: he constantly moves forward, so that Murray constantly has to move backwards to create his own punching space. Psychologically this is damaging, as Golovkin is always seemingly on the offensive. In addition, Golovkin has the perfect jab and he knows it. It is devastatingly accurate and fast and he knows exactly when and where to deploy it. Golovkin barely seems to move, except to throw the jab. There are no wild or rangy punches from Golovkin. Each one is delivered like a perfect package on time to its destination with no fuss, delivered with a barely detectable smile.

In a fit of boredom, I decide one Sunday to go to another boxing gym just to get a change of scene. It is in the East Lancashire town of Nelson. Here, northern English manufacturing died and was never revived. No inward investment ever found its way into Nelson. Only the Manchester music mogul Tony Wilson tried to effect his own type of rescue for East Lancashire, rebranding it as Pennine Lancashire, but sadly Tony and his immediate ambitions have now passed away.

I drive through the leafy environs of Barrowford, stuffed with posh hairdressers, nail bars and superfluous shops where the only-just-upwardly-mobile buy useless, vintage ornaments made out of papier-mâché. Only 200 yards away, over the M65, the town of Nelson lies in ruin. The streets have grand names that ape London's most famous, regal streets and speak of long-gone prosperity and success. Little corner shops are beacons of light and prosperity, as they stick two fingers up at the Bargain Booze, payday loan, pawn and betting shops which dominate the main streets. The latter are abominations that lay waste to human happiness. I do not pity the people of Nelson, but I do feel angry on their behalf.

The boxing gym is part of a larger 1960s-style sports centre in the northern part of the town, just as it edges out on to the hills. The sports centre is a modernist, concrete building with none of the drill-hall romance of the older boxing venues. Here I pay £4 for the use of a serviceable boxing gym on the first floor. The room is shabby and lined with a fading and frayed blue carpet, but has edifying views out onto the Lancashire moors.

There are a couple of wall mirrors, eight assorted boxing bags hanging off the ceiling and a large iron frame. There is a simple, unflashy floor-level boxing ring in the corner of the room. Two Asian lads are sparring in the ring. They are fast and slick, but their speed belies a total lack of technique, even though they look superficially impressive. They are not wearing headgear or gum guards, even though the punching is hard. When I politely challenge them they tell me that it is better 'to take a few punches' which, of course, it is not. Their boxing stances are all wrong, and their front feet are facing each other in a straight line, which means they are both much too square on, poorly balanced and are 'chicken-winging' some of their

71

punches. Their offensive skills look good, but they move round and round the ring superfast, wasting precious energy.

However, their defensive skills are poor as they box with their hands in the default down position. This is usually a sign of misplaced confidence in amateurs. If you adopt this position you are effectively saying to your opponent that you can put your hands up and punch them in less time than it would take for them to travel over and punch you. Only exceptional professional boxers like Muhammad Ali, Lee Selby and Naseem Hamed could box successfully from their own strangely invulnerable hands-down positions. They also had the speed and chutzpah to simultaneously taunt and unnerve opponents with smiles, waves and other showboating flourishes.

I grab a very fancy speed rope from the rack on the wall and skip for fifteen minutes. The rope whirrs round with the sound of a purring cat. This is one of those breadandbutter activities that are part of the boxing soul: boxing and skipping; boxing and the whirr of the speedball. Joe Frazier remarked that just being able to hit the speedball in rhythm makes you feel like a proper boxer, and it does.

I spend a full two hours on a variety of bags, heavy and light, including an extremely heavy bag which I can hardly move. I seem to be punching the bags quite hard, but it is difficult to hear the glove-slapping volume of each uppercut or hook over the obligatory house music. The Asian boxers are friendly and give me a few much-needed tips on my jab. By the end of this session I am relaxed and moving well.

Two days later, I have a chance meeting in another local gym with Trent, the only professional boxer that I ever come across who is local to the Dales. I have heard about him and his progress over the preceding year, but only via third parties.

Trent is gracious, and watches me on the bags, making helpful suggestions. However, he is nursing a surgically rebuilt broken hand and explains that he has undergone six-months of one-handed boxing training. This surely smacks of either religious devotion or desperation. I ask about his boxing history and training regime. Having obviously excelled on the amateur circuit, he tells me that he turned professional at the age of twenty, and is now twenty-five. He says that he is currently overweight, and will have to lose two stone before fighting in the ring again in two months' time, while still performing his sixteen training sessions a week. He already looks as trim as a lat, and my mind stalls at the prospect.

8

LIVERPOOL REVISITED

Seeking further inspiration, I pay £20 to watch the Elite National Championship in May. This prestigious event is the national amateur boxing finals, which is held at the Echo Arena in Liverpool. It takes place one Sunday afternoon in late April and showcases Britain's best amateur boxers, male and female. I have never been to a live boxing match and I do not really know what to expect. My conscience is partly salved, as hopefully this is neither the heavy-slugging professional game nor white collar lunacy, and I will see some excellent boxing without anyone having to be stretchered off. I arrive and park in the concrete jungle car park populated by security men on the Liverpool Waterfront.

I have not been back to Liverpool for years and family memories come flooding back. Over many years I had visited my paternal grandparents at their home in Anfield. The last time I found myself in Liverpool was in early 1990, on the day when my widowed grandmother, Grandma, ended her residence of over sixty years in her two-up two-down terraced house, at 67 July Road, Tuebrook, and moved to a nursing home in

Southport. Shortly afterwards, in March 1990, my father, Harry, her eldest son, died of leukaemia at a relatively young age. He was therefore not around to evaluate or help with her situation. I was very fond of Grandma and it was always a joy to see her, but visits to Southport were always tinged with sadness as she missed her son as much as I missed my father.

Waves of unconditional love knocked you flat as soon as you entered the same room as Grandma, and her face lit up whenever I appeared. Although I lived in the Dales some distance away, I visited her frequently in the home, taking her out for a drive onto the breezy front if she was up to it.

Grandma's middle son, Daniel, an extremely caring man of good sense, lived relatively close to the nursing home, in Formby. Daniel and Nerys, his second wife, made sure that Grandma was well attended to and genuinely happy in her final years. In her former working life, Nerys had managed a very large care home and her default mode was kindness mixed with warmth and a high degree of competence. She was (and is) stylish, witty, fond of music and could sing well, which had made her an instant hit with the Dunn family.

Daniel had worked as a tourism and marketing manager in the Southport area. He was always very well turned out, his positivity reflected in his attire. In the winter he wore a stylish black overcoat, with matching tie and handkerchief often in bold, fashionable colours. In the summer he was dapper in a smart, lightweight suit with the same matching accoutrements. Sadly, Daniel, too died of cancer at a relatively young age, and is sorely missed by all. His life was marked by seeing everything in a positive light, a fortunate trait which does not seem to have been entirely heritable. When asked by a colleague how best to market Southport as a sea-bathing town – when the tide was frequently so very far out – he replied emphatically: 'Miles and miles of golden sands', an apt description of how he viewed his own life.

As I drive into the city, I recall members of the Dunn family, past and present, and how, like me, they were held hostage by their own various quirks and unconventional obsessions. Most seemed to have had strong personalities, with compelling and diverse interests outside of work, which sometimes dominated their lives, and occasionally got out of control. This certainly feels familiar.

The modern Dunn family story starts with Marcella Dunn, my granddad's mother. Her family were refugees originating from the Austrian Tyrol, migrating to Liverpool in the nineteenth century. Marcella was born in Liverpool in 1861. She was a woman of strong character who separated from her husband and brought up three sons on her own: Ike, John and my granddad, Henry Conrad Dunn (b. 1897). Henry Conrad was also the name given to my father. Very unusually for a woman of that era, she went out to work to support her three sons.

My father and his brother Daniel remembered Marcella well, but also knew her from various family anecdotes and quotes, passed down through the generations. Apparently she was fond of saying things like: 'When I want your advice, my good woman, I shall ask for it.' She had a penchant for Botany wool stockings which were very hard to come by particularly after the First World War. There were no compromises in Marcella's world, as only real Botany wool stockings would do, making her life very difficult. Although she had no formal education, she was well read and took up a position as a political campaigner for women's rights, regularly attending protest marches in London.

In later life, Marcella lived with her long-suffering sister, my Great-Great-Aunt Mary Ann (b. 1858), near Sefton Park in Liverpool. In the 1930s, when both were in their late seventies, they would routinely walk across the city on Sundays to visit Grandma at July Road. Marcella would be very indignant that she was tired, even though the two old ladies had walked the seven mile round trip.

Aunt Mary Ann was a sweet lady, whose views were frequently at odds with Marcella's. Mary Ann's life was governed by folklore and hearsay, whereas Marcella generally favoured science. Mary Ann would never eat cabbage because she had been told that it contained oxygen. Neither would she eat apples from a tree next door, where neighbours had buried their beloved pet dog years earlier.

Marcella longed for progress, and wanted electricity installed in the house, but as a girl Mary Ann had been told that Electricity Would Set Fire to the World, so instead the two old ladies crept round the dim house lighting gas lamps – a huge fire risk, which seriously worried the rest of the family. After Mary Ann died, Grandma cared magnificently for Marcella, whom one imagines must have been difficult. Throughout her life Marcella had worked as a medium, and now she promised Grandma emphatically that she would come back and haunt her as a means of repaying all her kindness. Grandma was thankful that Marcella never did manage to keep her promise.

I have a treasured photo of Marcella as an older woman, where she does indeed look formidable, wearing a stiff-necked, dazzling-white blouse with a ruffled neck and a long, black skirt. She stares into the camera with a steely glare, but also with a twinkle in her eye. In the picture she is framed by potted palms in a photographer's room. I have another photo of her as a much younger woman, perhaps in her twenties, wearing a Victorian dress and floppy hat. Her expression looks single-minded and uncompromising, and I see elements of myself resolutely staring back from the ether. Dai has often told me that I have a certain focused look in the boxing ring, which others find intimidating. For this I heartily thank Marcella.

At some point in the 1920s, Marcella and her family moved to 58 August Road, Tuebrook, within walking distance of the famous Liverpool FC football ground. As a young man, granddad took up a motor mechanic's apprenticeship, becoming one of England's first motor mechanics, then a cutting edge, hi-tech profession.

Grandma (then Margaret Noonan, known as Maggie) and her family lived in the next street, at 63 July Road. The rest is history, with Grandma and Granddad meeting and marrying young and moving to 67 July Road around 1925. They had three sons: my father Henry Conrad Dunn, born on 16 May 1925, followed by Daniel and then Patrick. Thereafter, the geographical hub for all family exploits was Grandma's house, and I visited often, up until 1990, when she finally left the house.

My first memories, as a young child, of Anfield in the late 1960s are of areas clearly past their best. The area known as Tuebrook, or simply 'The Brook', was centred on a small section of Rocky Lane which contained a row of small family run shops and businesses, now all gone. Grandma lived off Lower Breck Road in an area between Newsham Park and Anfield, on one of a distinctive set of streets named after the months of the year.

Grandma's house was a traditional red brick Victorian terrace fronted by a bay window, and a tiny low-walled area of garden, filled by dark green shrubs. A path of old quarry tiles, laid in a diamond shape, led up stone steps to the dark red front door. The steps were worn and grooved due to the passage of many feet. There was a short, dark hallway lit by a dim lamp and any daylight which filtered in through a red, fan-shaped piece of glass at the top of the front door. An ancient Bakelite telephone sat high on a glass table. In Grandma's house, if anyone rang whom we didn't want to talk to, we were allowed to answer the telephone with the words: 'Hello. This is Chorley Brickworks' to put them off. It usually worked, but the difficulty lay in mimicking a sufficiently strong Chorley accent.

The door into the front room was immediately on the left of the short hallway, followed on the left by a very steep single flight of stairs to the upper floor. The living room was straight ahead on the ground floor and beyond that the kitchen, back yard and the back entry.

The front room was an Edwardian relic, looking exactly the same, I imagine, as it had for fifty years or more, and had been given over to music. When I knew it, the room was always cold and mostly unoccupied, with a slight antiseptic smell. Along the back wall was a dark wood Van Gruisen upright piano and a standard lamp. On a table against the side wall was a primitive electric gramophone flanked by two huge orange, Chinese cracked-lacquer vases and potted palms.

The living room in Grandma's house was at the end of the hallway. On entering, a blast of warmth was felt. All comers were welcome, and a perpetually lit coal fire roared in the grate of the black, cast iron Victorian range. A brass fender stopped any hot coals from rolling onto the rag rug which covered the hearth. To the right of the grate was a bread oven with a creaking, black door, where my father recalled making bread as a boy. Above the fireplace Grandma had a fine collection of horse brasses, a nod to her Irish antecedents.

Various comfy chairs with cushions were set about the room, and straight ahead was a large window, overlooking the back yard. To the left of the window, there was a large wooden table with sturdy legs, covered with a beige oilcloth. The pictures on the walls had a religious bent, consisting largely of cherubs and the Virgin Mary.

There was a large, metal hook embedded in the ceiling, next to the window. In the distant past, this had held the cage of Polly, the African grey parrot. Polly had been brought back from abroad by the sailors in the family fifty years earlier and had passed into family mythology. She was taught various utterances, and could apparently impersonate the priest rather well. Tragically, she had died of fright during an air raid in the Liverpool Blitz in 1941, even though the house was not hit directly, as it was forbidden to take any animals or pets into the protection of the air raid shelter. Polly was so beloved that no one could ever bear to take down the cage hook, and it was still there in 1990.

A love of animals was also pervasive throughout the Dunn family, and in the 1960s Patrick became interested in exotic animals. There were tanks of terrapins and the odd grass snake at Grandma's house, as well as the usual cats and dogs. Patrick genuinely tried to cater for his animals' needs, but his interest spectacularly backfired.

In his first marital home on Lower Breck Road, around 1970, Patrick purchased a miniature alligator, having been told that it would remain a manageable six inches long. However, he had been sold down the river, and the creature eventually grew to about three feet. Patrick loved that animal, but a crumbling Victorian terrace in inner city Liverpool was not a suitable place for the animal's (or anyone else's) needs to be met.

As a child of seven, I remember seeing the alligator hanging from the curtains in the living room and making a barking noise. It looked very large even at that time, although it must have been only about two feet long. At other times it lay in the bath. My parents were very unhappy about me or my sister being in the same room with it. Not unreasonably, Patrick's wife was afraid of doing the hoovering, and I suspect that Patrick was offered some kind of ultimatum. Eventually, I believe that the creature was rehomed to Edinburgh Zoo. Patrick emigrated to Australia, making a much better life for himself and his family than Liverpool could offer at the time.

There was a strong creative impetus running through the family, which expressed itself in various ways as a love for music, dance, storytelling and love of language. I have always attributed this to the Liverpool-Irish branch of the family on Grandma's side and it occurs to me now that, perhaps, boxing represents my rather clunky way of learning to dance.

Between the wars, the front room at Grandma's house had hosted rousing family sing-songs when those of Irish descent (which was nearly everyone) would belt out the old songs at full blast. An old Edwardian songbook remained forever on top of the piano.

As a child I was fascinated by these songs written in arcane music hall language from a bygone era: 'Down by the Salley Gardens', 'The Anchor's Weigh'd', 'Come into the Garden, Maud', 'Danny Boy' and 'I'll Take You Home Again, Kathleen' are all etched in my mind. Recordings of the northern opera singer Tom Burke, 'The Lancashire Caruso', were reverentially played at 78rpm on this ancient machine, his mellifluous tones forever tarnished with a crackling hiss.

Grandma would recall the family sing-songs with joy and sadness, as she was always reminded of her beloved brother and dancing partner Jim, who had died young. I never knew Jim and only ever saw a single photograph of him. He was tall, thin, slightly stooped with a wide, toothy smile. It is bizarre that even though he died around a hundred years ago, I still have a strong sense of what he was like from Grandma's vivid descriptions, his ghostly trace fading into the oral tradition, a carbon copy of himself growing ever fainter.

In the 1960s, Grandma moved the ancient gramophone into the living room. By this time the music had evolved to include Johnny Cash tracks, and country and traditional Irish dance music. A particular favourite was Luke Kelly's 'Black Velvet Band'. Although normally quite shy, Grandma would throw off her shoes and dance round the tiny kitchen, singing loudly.

Music permeated the lives of Grandma's sons. For much of his adult life, Daniel had been a talented, part-time club singer and entertainer in Liverpool, along with his much younger brother, Patrick. In addition to other full-time careers, both went on to have successful part-time careers as musicians and entertainers as a duo, and as solo artists. The two brothers had shared a bedroom at Grandma's house in July Road as teenagers and then as young men. Apparently, this was full of magicians' props, ventriloquists' dummies, accordions and even greasepaint. (Later on, they developed other obsessions including a love of boats and sailing. On an ill-fated trip to France, Patrick sailed his own boat across the Channel, but was arrested on landing on the French shore as he failed to produce the correct paperwork).

Just as punk and indie liberated youth in the 1970s and 1980s, rockabilly and skiffle had done the same twenty years earlier. With a rash of confidence, bands had sprung up from the ordinary streets. Patrick was part of a successful R&B band, which formed at the tail end of the Merseybeat sound and recorded two successful singles for Decca Records.

Patrick said that occasionally his band had backed The Beatles at Liverpool's famous Cavern Club. I have a photograph of Patrick taken around this time. He is standing moodily in the street, the embodiment of rockabilly rebellion, with slickbacked hair and winkle-picker boots. An admiring posse of girls stands nearby. Winkle-picker boots were a fashion item adopted by the Mod movement in the 1960s, ankle boots with an extremely long pointed toe – the longer and more pointed the toe, the more status the boots had. The band disbanded in 1966 having not enjoyed the commercial success that they deserved.

The Dunn family musical gene has largely passed me by, in the sense that I am certainly no performer and have no desire to be on stage. My real love is indie music, and I am not alone in admitting to a lifelong interest in The Smiths and Joy Division.

One of the things that strikes me is the presence of music in every boxing gym that I visit, and in my usual haunts the only thing that boxers potentially come to blows about are the music choices. I notice that many boxers genuinely seem to have a strong connection with music, and especially rhythm, and many (such as Dai) are drummers in bands. My nephews both turn out to be talented drummers, with semi-professional careers and so, in a sense, the beat goes on.

As well as having musical leanings, Daniel was very well read and witty, gregarious and a natural storyteller. He was the wordsmith of the Dunn family, the self-appointed custodian of family anecdotes that stretched back to the middle of the nine-teenth century. In my mind's eye, I see him and my father, Harry, now retelling these long lost family tales, with tears streaming down their faces as they cried with laughter and we laughed just as hard. I guess I am fated too to retell some of these family anecdotes with my own embellishments and inaccuracies.

My father was a quiet, bookish boy, christened Henry, but always known as Harry or Hal, who went to St Edward's Catholic College, off Queen's Drive. My father pursued his own quiet obsessions, which were different from those of his brothers. He loved science and chemistry from an early age, managing to carry out many sophisticated chemistry experi-ments in Grandma's bathroom without anyone batting an eyelid. Health and Safety didn't exist then and so my father's sense of enquiry was untrammelled.

Eventually, my father won a scholarship to read chemistry at Liverpool University. It was wartime and degree programmes were accelerated. My father was bright and went to university a year early, aged only seventeen. He had finished his first degree aged nineteen, and went on to study for a PhD inves-tigating the chemistry of fats and lipids that were extracted from tropical nut and seed oils. He was methodical in his working methods and suited to laboratory work, traits which I have obviously inherited. In his early career, he would receive huge shipments of exotic nuts and seeds from the Tropics for analysis at the university. On delivery, giant tropical spiders would run out causing fear and panic. My father told me that he spent a good deal of time rehoming the spiders at a local zoo, and acclimatising others to them.

My father finished his PhD at the age of twenty-one and then undertook war work that he rarely spoke about, as he was exempted from military service because of his status as a scientist. I guess that this was emotionally challenging work, as he never wanted to talk about it.

His own life was saved by Liverpool University, by luck rather than by design, as he was still suffering from leukaemia while a student, although he didn't know it. One day he collapsed in the laboratory and his professor, Professor Hilditch, realised that he was very, very unwell, and referred him to a friend of his who was an oncologist. Against the odds, my father managed to survive the crude 1940s radiotherapy treatment, being in remission until the 1960s, then again until 1990.

He married my mother, Rena Gracie in 1958. She was born on 20 July 1927 into a poor, working-class family from Carntyne, in the East End of Glasgow. My mother and her younger sister Marion were brought up by their widowed father, Willie Gracie, after their mother died of a hereditary heart condition, when my mother was twelve. Resilience was an important characteristic on my mother's side of the family, as the family endured poverty and Willie worked a six and a half day week as a railway worker to hold the family together.

Encouraged by her father, who strongly believed in education for women and girls, my mother blazed a determined trail through school at Whitehill College, while her younger sister, Marion eventually went on to study at the Glasgow School of Art and became a professional designer. My mother excelled at maths and chemistry, eventually winning a scholarship to Glasgow University to read chemistry, and became a working industrial chemist in the linoleum and paper industries in Fife, Scotland, in the 1950s. Over a similar period, my father was employed as a works chemist for a rival firm in the same locality, and thus they met, with my mother being unceremoniously given the sack once their engagement was announced due to the sensitivity surrounding trade secrets. In 1960, she and my father then moved south to Culcheth, a small, nondescript town near Warrington, where he joined the United Kingdom Atomic Energy Authority at Risley, as a nuclear research chemist and administrator, and she retrained as a maths and chemistry teacher.

My father had an irrepressible love of languages and took a delight in conversing with anyone in any language. In the family tradition, probably under the influence of his grandmother Marcella, he became fluent in German, and then later in Russian. During the war, he jumped at an additional option to study Russian and Egyptology in addition to chemistry. True to family form, my father's preferred choices were rather unusual. As child it was a joy to go around Bolton Museum with him, as it had a vast Egyptology collection. (It still does and this is really worth a look.) My father could read the hieroglyphics, bringing the papyrus fragments and sarcophagi inscriptions to life. My two nephews are of the same ilk, both being effortlessly fluent in French, Italian, Dutch, German and Russian.

As I survey the Dunn and Gracie family history, I can see clearly that what comes around goes around, and it seems inevitable that I have turned out to be a bit of a science nerd with other rather singular, obsessive interests. There are elements of toughness and resilience on both sides of the family, although I do not particularly think of myself as either.

No one on either side could be ever be accused of complacency, and I wonder if this family trait has prepared, predisposed or propelled me towards an interest in boxing.

Certainly, the desire never to give up is present. I have been told by various boxing coaches that I 'never give up', though in boxing this is a negative as well as a positive trait. Knowing when to hang back rather than come forward in the ring is a real skill which is difficult to master, and being too dogged can result in injury – in life as well as in boxing. Perhaps my 'kamikaze' strategies are just heritable traits.

⊙

Driving into Liverpool to watch my first live boxing match, I turn my attention back to the present and the city I see now. I have not been back to Liverpool for fifteen years, regretting now that I have lost touch with too many members of the extended Dunn family – something that I vow to change. The present city seems to have none of the old world charm that I remember.

I have taken the route from the north via Bootle along the edge of the water, and I am astounded to see row after row of ancient Victorian grain silos, warehouses and derelict docks, some partly demolished, or used for new, unsuitable purposes. These are ghosts of buildings with their eyes put out, but still just about standing, hope against hope. Their dereliction is all the more shocking against the new glamour of Shard-like super-modern edifices of the city centre. These stretch to the sky, all woven glass and metal in the so-called trendy new district of Liverpool One. I wonder why we fail to build anything beautiful anymore and if this is really contingent on money.

As I walk towards the Echo Arena, I cannot help but think back to the TV wrestling matches that Andrea, my younger sister, and I used to enjoy watching at Grandma's house on Saturday afternoons in the late 1960s. The TV wrestling, which was the highlight of the day, started around 3 p.m. on Saturday afternoon. The TV was a tiny, black and white set, perched high on a wall-mounted stand in the living room, so we all had to stand up to see it, adding to the excitement and giving the sense of a live match. The wrestling was a theatrical music hall treat of grandstanding, showboating and pretend slips, trips and falls. The same improbable characters took part every week: Big Daddy a corpulent man, wobbling like a jelly, barely contained in a leotard, who overturned Mick McManus in a cartwheel of pretend hatred every Saturday until teatime.

At around 4 p.m., our too-posh parents would return from their town shopping trip, expressing mild dislike at the wrestling. Someone got thrown against the ropes. Along with Grandma we 'oohed' and 'aahed', egged on by her slightly transgressive enthusiasm. Throughout the proceedings, Granddad would hide, mute, behind the newspaper, usually the *Liverpool Echo*. He would be propped up in an impossibly large antique wooden chair by the fire. My conclusion was that in the 1960s any woman at a wrestling or boxing match would needed a good pair of lungs, a large, square, heavy handbag to wield on the front row, and possibly a beehive of back-combed peroxided hair and heavy black eyeliner.

I hope and expect that some aspects are different now, but I guess that modern regulations have probably squeezed much of the fun and drama out of the proceedings. Now, thankfully, you are much more likely to see women in the wrestling or boxing ring and not just on the sidelines. Visions of vital female boxers such as Nicola Adams from Leeds give me a grain of hope. I am fifty-two but I feel twenty-eight. My late parents would turn in their graves if they could see what I am doing now, but rule-breaker Grandma would surely be cheering me on. I therefore conclude that I must be doing something right.

9

BOXING – ALIVE, ALIVE O!

The Echo Arena is a modern concrete and glass ball, like that in every other city – a nameless, faceless concourse, leading to a nameless, faceless foyer. A little big wheel, substantially smaller than the London Eye, is set outside the entrance, rearing up from the pavement, so that for a fee you can take in the sweep of old and new Liverpool and make your own assessment of its mixed fortunes.

Inside the arena there is a sense of high excitement, and the boxing ring is floodlit yellow and red in theatrical style. I estimate that there are about 1,500 people present. The bouts are staged throughout the afternoon and early evening. The women's bouts are alternated with the men's bouts and the weight categories of the boxers are scheduled to increase as the bouts progress throughout the day.

I arrive during bout three at about noon. I notice that the boxer in the red corner has impossibly long arms, and his long reach is proving too much for his opponent who is being gradually worn down by his relentless jab. Both parties are cheered on by supporters, who spontaneously stand up in the audience when their boxers appear, like squares of waving grass on a mown lawn.

A memorable bout in the early afternoon is the 60kg women's category. This is refereed by a smart, businesslike woman in a starched shirt, bowtie and dark trousers – the only female boxing referee I will ever see. Both women boxers are excellent technically, fast, fearless and unafraid in coming forward. They are very evenly matched, resulting in a thrilling set of four two-minute rounds. A split decision by the judges rules one the marginal victor, but both receive rousing cheers from the audience. Once their headgear is removed they no longer look like the gladiators they are.

I speak to a woman sitting in the audience next to me. We agree what a thrilling match it has been, but I can see that her mind is elsewhere. She is wearing an official-looking lanyard and I ask if she is watching or competing. I learn that she is Binah from Haringey and that she is competing in Bout Twelve. I ask her about her training programme. This consists of two hours of boxing per day with only Sundays off. I ask her how on earth she manages to gain enough rest between training sessions, and she simply shrugs her shoulders. She says that unlike her opponent she has very little ringside support, so I offer to throw off my inhibitions and shout encouragement during her bout.

Half an hour later Binah is limbering up beside the ring. Her opponent, Danielle, also from London, has a lot of vocal support from her loyal audience and looks very chipper. As they enter the ring, Binah crosses herself, and I hope too that God is adjudicating. Unfortunately, in round one she looks like the underdog, as Danielle is extraordinarily slick and fast. Binah has a good jab and, when she has the confidence to move forward, she uses it to great effect. I scream ear-splitting instructions to Binah across the ether. I wonder if she will hear or is in some mind-zone far beyond instruction, where only instinct and muscle memory rules.

I shout: 'Binah! Jab! Jab! Move forward! Use your jab!' She manages to do this for a bit, then, to my horror, I see her hands drop – the cardinal boxing sin. In vain I shout again: 'Binah – hands up!', but I fear it is too late. At the end of round two she looks like she is starting to crumble. In rounds three and four she is continually pushed back onto the ropes, but is still throwing the odd sublime shot. I am sure that it is all over, but the judges have clearly seen her brilliance and to my great delight she is victorious (but only just).

The afternoon progresses and the heavier-weighted boxers appear. I feel less comfortable as the harder punching begins in the welterweight bouts. As a welterweight myself, I feel compelled to stay on, just to see how the welterweights and middleweights fare.

The doctor's presence increases at the ringside, as eyes are checked and bruises are inspected. There are more standing counts, and after three rounds some boxers are starting to look decidedly unsteady. Even at a distance I see the unmistakeable red sheen of blood on one of the super-middleweight's faces, and there are cries from the audience for the ref to stop the bout.

It continues, and I feel that this is the point at which I must take my leave. The late afternoon drinkers start to bay for their bit of blood, no doubt in anticipation of the heavy slugging to come. By any rational measure, this is a crazy pastime; yet it is the best antidote I have ever found to the over-sanitised modern lives that we are now forced to lead. However, my conscience is pricked as I realise that my subscription has paid for the whole shooting match, not only the part that I have chosen to see.

On leaving the venue I momentarily block one of the major exits to the multistorey car park, as I have misunderstood the traffic flow. A parking official who must have spied my idiocy on CCTV appears from nowhere and has time for a chat as I pay with my cash card. We both agree that Tuebrook, where my grandma used to live, now has the feel of the Wild West. Outlaws roam the streets, murdering the innocent. My grandma's old end-of-street pub, The Claremont, which had been derelict was then reopened, but has been closed again after a senseless spate of violence. He says that Norris Green, where his mother lives, is not much better. As I leave, I think of this man stuck in his concrete jungle kiosk for hours on end, with the wild sea, which might as well be another planet, only a few hundred yards away, and I think that surely there could not be a bigger contrast.

On the way home I take a wrong turn and head into Walton. Walton makes parts of slipshod Nelson look like Manchester's upmarket Bowdon and Hale. There are frequent shootings and knifings in Walton. Although I am sure that there are many decent folk living there, I shamefully lock the car doors against unknown perils as I drive through. They lock with a reassuring 'brrr' and clunk.

I have rarely seen so many boarded-up shops and houses, and over such a wide area, for mile after mile. These are the most appalling scenes of Dickensian drear; there are no amenities of any kind and the poorest shops imaginable have their shutters firmly down. There are suspiciously few people on the streets, apart from a few kids buzzing about on cheap mountain bikes and shouting. Men in wife-beater vests, bonehead haircuts and expensive sunglasses stand on street corners outside pubs, fretting and bellowing into their mobile phones. It is easy to imagine a rash of drug-dealing, but I hope not. The pubs are the only visible signs of life and have grand names like The Regent and The Prince Albert in gold lettering plastered across their beautiful and ornate exteriors – reflecting an age when superfluous adornment was still eminently affordable.

A vortex of failures has gathered pace here, unchecked. This neighbourhood represents abandonment. Why is this district, so close to a large and thriving city, allowed to be effectively laid to waste? Why is this happening in my own country and in this century? I contact Walton's MP, but he dissembles, having no real answers. The truth is that this is due to unacceptable failures of society, culture and economy. The government should act as a backstop, but it hasn't. I am glad to leave Walton and its Third World misery behind. I have really enjoyed watching the boxing match, but the state of the city leaves the biggest and most woeful impression of the day.

10

FIRST BLOOD

It is the last training session of the boxing year with Dai as he has football refereeing commitments about to start next month. The year has mysteriously crept forward to April without me noticing. For the whole of the summer we will be left to our devices to flounder or flourish as the mood takes us. Dai works us very hard in this final session, and ten minutes of skipping is followed by a circuit of physical jerks and by eight three-minute rounds on the bags. There is little time for rest or banter as we sweep round the gym for circuit after circuit.

Donny is absent due to the harsher punishment of exams. Will is similarly preparing for academic warfare, and steps bleary-eyed from the university library into the gym.

He is very stressed because he and his girlfriend are overwhelmed by their dedication to the flotsam and jetsam of unwanted animals. They have a very emaciated black and white cat, Sonny, who has had a single seizure and consequently nobody wants him. He is waiting at the vets, facing an uncertain future. At the eleventh hour a good home is found for him, and I hope that Sonny's future will be a little brighter.

Even near the end of the boxing season, hopeful newcomers appear – two new lads dressed in dazzling white gym gear turn out to be affable ex-boxers, both carrying a small amount of extra weight. Their skills immediately surface, as their heavy punches echo around the gym like the clang of bells.

After several months of improvement, I find that once again I am sliding backwards. I am getting some consistent power in the jab from a twist of my opposing foot, but my boxing stance is suddenly all wrong. In that final training session, my crazy movement is as if I have been strapped to an invisible board.

Peter has seen the trouble with my boxing stance and offers to be a foil for the final five minutes of the session. I try and break down his defences, and in so doing I start to move around in a much more fluid and less crab-like style. Anxious not to injure him, I throw only light punches with the wraps still on my hands, as I have removed my gloves. He neatly parries most of these out of the way. However, a few make it through, including a steady right hand body shot, which we both agree is a punch of some substance.

He responds with a jab which I just about manage to block, but I am the one who is worse off, as I feel the bone-crunching effects of not wearing my boxing gloves. I feel like I have just hit a wall, and I promise myself that I will be much more careful in the future. Broken fingers are a fairly common occurrence among the careless in the boxing gym, and now I see why. As usual, machine-like Peter is smiling and as undamaged as The Rock of Ages as I nurse my injured hand, trying not to make a fuss as he looks on concerned. As I shut the door on the youth club gym with my only functioning hand, the start of the summer beckons with the equal hope of recovery and self-improvement.

⊙

A Monday night in mid-May feels like the start of a long and lonely road in the boxing gym, as Dai is defined by his absence. I have put myself through a tough training session the previous Friday at a local gym, including my own version of the Board of Death. Even in a different gym, The Board gnaws ominously at the unsuspecting body, revealing a host of weaknesses.

On Saturday night I go to the local pub with my dear friend June. She has been travelling alone in Nepal, trekking to Everest Base Camp a fortnight earlier. I offer her a lift as she will be drinking and I will not. June is my old potholing partner, whose good company and conversation are always a boon. She is a tough nut, unphased by most things, and is always kind and funny. Her catchphrase is obstinately 'Hey ho', and it is her indomitable hey-ho attitude that has moved her effectively along every inch of life, supporting her husband, a delightful man, through a series of difficulties and illnesses.

One of my favourite anecdotes concerning June is from when we were on a potholing expedition to the Felix Trombe cave system in the French Pyrenees in 2001. June had broken her foot in a minor potholing accident several weeks earlier. She blamed this on complacency, as she had slipped and fallen during a small vertical climb which she had attempted unroped, in a cave called Sunset Hole on Ingleborough, one of Yorkshire's Three Peaks. Ironically June had been involved in the original exploration of this cave and had descended it many times.

She had travelled out to the Pyrenees with another mutual friend, Amelia, who is a doctor. On arrival at the French campsite close to the caves, June emerged from Amelia's car on crutches. Amelia rolled her eyes in disbelief as June proudly displayed a rubber boot that she had had specially made to go over the plaster cast of her foot, so that she could go potholing despite her injury. True to her word, I have an abiding memory of June inching her way determinedly on two crutches along the most slippery limestone bedrock imaginable towards the mouth of a waiting cave and further broken-leg shenanigans.

In April 2015, June had been caught in the Nepal earthquake. She recounted how she escaped the worst of the quake by running out of her eighth-floor guest room in a hotel in Kathmandu, rushing down the stairs and outside into a public park full of toppling statues. She was then holed up for a week in a friendly but rather spartan Ghurkha army camp, courtesy of the British Embassy, before being flown out of the country.

Mercifully, she and her Nepali friends survived, but many tens of thousands did not, as aftershock after aftershock brushed away the country's fragile infrastructure. June had been 'lucky' in the sense that a bout of altitude-induced cerebral oedema had precipitated her early and serendipitous evacuation to Kathmandu.

Over many years of visiting the country, June has made many genuine friendships with Nepali mountaineering guides and their families, supporting them via various voluntary projects. June had grafted away for years under the banner of UNICEF, helping to build hospitals and schools and to install basic sanitation in the more remote parts of the country. After this episode, June tells me that she has made the very difficult decision never to return to Nepal, and she never does. Through tears, she grieves for never being able to see her Nepali friends face-to-face again. She is fearless and worries not a jot about her own personal safety, but is seriously concerned about being a potential drain on the strained infrastructure of the country. Now aged sixty-one, her lifelong commitment to UNICEF continues. She tells me of the urgent need for cash in Nepal and begins a vigorous fundraising campaign.

June tells me that before her last visit to Nepal she had, for a wheeze, entered an 'overactive pensioner' competition which is run annually by the *Daily Mail*. I promise to vote for her, as we predict that she will be a certain winner.

We get back from the pub, and in the confines of June's kitchen I carelessly and rather smugly invite her to throw a punch at me (which I am sure I will be able to block). However the joke is on me, as of course I have no boxing gloves, and I forget that June is not a boxer. I am expecting her to take a few minutes to square up to me in a perfect boxing stance. Instead she immediately lunges forward, encouraged by a few pints of bitter, and punches me hard on the chin. She has a teaspoon in her other hand, which catches me, drawing actual blood. We collapse on the floor with laughter as her husband rushes in from the room next door and demands to know what is going on. A fair question, I think, as I protest lamely, 'Look, June has drawn blood!' I hold my hand up as evidence of the lethal force of the teaspoon.

⊙

I snuffle with a cold during the following Sunday, but still force myself out for a bracing run over the Yorkshire fells at the head of the Kingsdale near Ingleton. It is a daft kill-or-cure strategy, which I should be old enough and wise enough to resist, and sure enough it nearly kills me. Feeling every inch the ancient, decadent Westerner that I am, I huddle under a blanket on the sofa that night determined that I will do something however pathetic and small to help those desperate people in Nepal.

I am physically recovered by the Monday night, and I notice that there are pink ripples of cherry tree blossom across the pavement outside the youth club, and daylight even on the drive home. Peter and the two brothers, Mark and James, appear, together with Jayden, one of the boxers who always dresses in white. Jayden is training hard and we remark on his dividend of having shed a few pounds over the last few weeks. He smiles a big smile, while executing a few pike jumps – not an easy feat. We do our best and skip for the appointed ten minutes, but Dai is not there to shout at us, and my favourite orange skipping rope is temporarily out of action, as one of its handles is missing. It has been my friend, but I have destroyed it. Unaccountably we all like this rope and have vied over it during a hundred training sessions. I opt for a much inferior pink rope that I have bought over the internet, but it is not the same. Likewise, my boxing gloves are on their way out, as the cushioning inside has begun to warp and spill, rather like my body, I am inclined to think.

Peter adopts his machine-like pose at the bags and will not be budged or distracted for a full hour, all the while muttering to himself that he is not moving well around the bags, which he is. He delivers an array of thunderous left and right hooks which actually make the gym floor shake. Before Mark and James start their sparring session, James watches me on the bags, heavy and light. He lifts a boxing death sentence as he tells me that I am no longer guilty of dropping my hands! Hurrah! Hurrah! Hurrah! The reward of twenty months' training is that I have finally corrected this most nagging of faults – for the moment.

However, I am still guilty of many second-degree sins: I am leaning much too far forward, right into my opponent's punch zone: consequently I am losing power in my punches, and not springing enough off my right foot. James takes the time to make further suggestions. Like an avid child wonkily riding a new bike, I am determined to make the necessary adjustments to my boxing stance. Finally poised and successfully anchored on my back foot I deliver some more-than-passable jabs and right hands. I relax. At last, I am really throwing the punches and can feel the power coming up from the floor and feet, via twisting hips, and onto the bag. James makes some encouraging noises, while the sound is no longer of feeble one-hand clapping but a baton round of small, cracking explosions, which I feel in every tendon and sinew. There is no throbbing house music to drown out my triumph as I throw a 1-2, 1-2-1, 1-2-1-2 until exhaustion finally intervenes.

That same Monday night, on the bush telegraph, we hear that Gerard and Janine are not only alive and well but have got married. We break into spontaneous applause and for the moment all is well in our little boxing bubble.

11

ALONE IN THE SUMMER

It is May 2015, and the final Wednesday of the amateur boxing season. Like aging trustees, Peter and I are the only recidivists who appear without the encouragement of a coach. The shining evening sun has derailed the other boxers, and I imagine them sitting outside sunlit pubs with birds tweeting, enjoying the silvered laughter of friends, as we take to our sunless, indoors habitat. There have been very few youth boxers in the preceding session and not all of the boxing bags are set out. We haul our old friends out of the boxing store, one by one, ready for their obligatory punishment: the body-shaped hook bag, the heavy bag and the two lighter bags.

Like an old married couple who have nothing to say, Peter and I do not chat as we each immerse ourselves in our own particular rituals. We skip for fifteen minutes, allowing ourselves luxurious sips of water that would not necessarily be permissible if Dai's beady eye were upon us. My boxing gloves are now totally spent, as indeed I am. There are new gloves in the post, and I promise myself a week of rest and renewal after this session is over.

After five rounds of continuous pummelling, I discover that my jabs are now hard enough to make even the heavy bag jump to attention. I feel vindicated in my strategy of perfecting the jab before anything else. Without the jab, no boxer is anything. Now, I really know this.

I feel ready at last to take Peter's good advice on hooks left and right. Hooking is a shapeshifter's art that starts with stepping forward, bending down and sometimes being on your toes. The body has to be coiled like a waiting spring, partly anchored into the ground, ready to jack-in-the-box up and out with a simultaneous twist of the feet. I try and try but still cannot do it, managing only a bit of useless teetering about.

The jab has taken me a mere twenty months to sort and I see years of my remaining life already flashing by in pursuit of the perfect (or any) hook. As the clock shows that it is already 8.30 p.m., Peter and I take off our gloves for a final impromptu light sparring session. He moves backwards at the speed of light and I am constantly running forwards, abandoning any kind of boxing stance in order to throw any punches (not good). I then decide to stand my ground and wait for him to move forward. I feint a series of shots, and, unexpectedly, I shove a good right hand through. He throws a jab which I manage to parry out of the way, and so on, and so on, until Stuart appears at the gym door calling time, as we both realise our exhaustion not just from this session, but from a whole two seasons of our peculiar tussle with boxing. We wish each other well, as we bundle everything into the boxing store for the summer recess.

12

MIXING IT UP

As the summer waxes and wanes, I ply my peripatetic boxing trade in various establishments. I am really missing the certainty of Dai's training sessions, where you know what you will get and may be surprised by what you achieve. I try out a series of local gyms, but these seem only to have boxing kit included as an afterthought: the boxing bags are extremely lightweight and no good; they will never allow the accrual of any real strength.

A week later, one June afternoon, a nagging toothache which has been gradually worsening over the previous month reduces me to tears, forcing a swift exit from work and an emergency visit to my dentist, Mr Farron. During this ordeal, a small tube of lignocaine gel bought from the local chemist's shop has been my only friend. I wonder how many other poor unfortunates arrive at the dentist's surgery in the same terrible state.

The dentist says that my pain is due to wear and tear, which is almost certainly age related. Since I expect monstrous root canal work every time I visit, I am truly grateful for the welcome news that a bit of fluoride-rich araldite mixed with something powerful and painkilling will quickly fix my problem. To distract me, the dentist tells me about the successful career of his cousin, Scott Fitzgerald, a welterweight boxer from Preston who has won a gold medal in the Commonwealth Games. I know about this already, as Scott Fitzgerald easily has the best jab of any British boxer I can think of, and without any exaggeration I truthfully say how I regard him as a boxing hero. Mr Farron beams as he applies the magical tooth liquor. I am doubly grateful, as this quick fix releases time for a quick visit to Kelly's Gym, near Blackburn, a professional boxing gym that I have been meaning to try out for some time.

When I arrive, one of the professional boxing coaches, Jamie, is training Frank, who turns out to be a novice amateur boxer. After a few minutes of observation, I am convinced that Jamie knows what he is doing.

Frank is not comfortable in his boxing stance. He inadvertently drops in and out of it making himself vulnerable. He is a big bloke whose size and bulk is also making it difficult for him to move round the ring. He makes the same perilous mistakes time and again. He leans forwards with dropped hands, which wastes the potential power from an otherwise good jab. On the plus side, I can see that Frank has innate speed and is a quick and determined learner. He responds to Jamie's encouragements, eventually managing some strong punches, but his feet are all at sea.

I don't have a training session booked, but I explain my interest in boxing and Jamie gives an impromptu assessment of my boxing skills. The main outcome surprises me. Jamie tells me that I am already the proud owner of an almost perfect and quite powerful jab, which would easily pass muster in the professional gym. As ever, a few tweaks can still be made – my only real failure is concentrating too much and not relaxing. Jamie tells me to try not to think the punch through; I should surrender to muscle memory and innate feeling rather than enforced thought. I practise snapping out and withdrawing the jab so fast that the bag does not even move – a worthwhile professional boxer's training trick, which is supposed to develop speed and strength.

Over the summer of 2015, I try to keep my boxing training going, persisting with solo training sessions in a number of different gyms and mixing this up with other activities such as walking, cycling and yoga.

I also make another a visit to the boxing gym at the modern sports centre in Nelson, as they have the best range of boxing bags of anywhere in the district. Once again, I marvel at the sense of a border crossing from Barrowford to Nelson, and pay £4 for a full hour of very heavy bag pummelling. It is only for one hour, as it is the height of summer and the early July sun streams in from the moors, frying all of us gym monkeys alive in the canned heat.

I skip for fifteen minutes with ropes that are either too long or too short. It is one of those days where nothing is quite right, and I can barely drink enough to keep going at all. A slight injury to the shoulder weakens my right hand shots, but I snap out perfect jab after perfect jab. (The taxman is directly responsible for my deficit, as I have been the victim of an evil electronic tax form. This has dominated my life for around three months, and so much so that computer work has wrecked my shoulder.)

I try and fail to perfect a left hook. I am getting the parallel swivel in both legs and hips, but my stance still has to be much more open to start with and I need to be boxing very close-up or on the 'inside'. The stance and starting position are the key factors and I vow to practise in front of the mirror more instead of a lazier hit-and-miss approach. Speed is of the essence too, as you have to get out of your opponent's firing range once you have delivered the hook. I try to imagine a jumping spider or grasshopper as I shuffle slowly backwards.

Three Polish kickboxers are training in the same room. We compare jabs. They seem to throw theirs from the shoulder rather than using the opposing power of the right leg to get the whiplash action into the shot. I wonder if this is inexperience on their part, or if this is the way that they normally throw the jab. Certainly, my jab is as strong if not stronger than theirs, and this gives a certain satisfaction.

One kickboxer is clearly more experienced than the rest. He is tall with rather scary, glassy-blue eyes. I remind myself never to take up kick-boxing as he throws his feet up to shoulder height, sometimes with a jump which brings both feet off the floor simultaneously, thwacking the bag with an incredible force.

I wonder how broken feet are avoided and ask. He says that when you first start kick-boxing you feel that are you are about to break your feet, but in fact never do. Gradually the feeling of impending broken feet somehow diminishes and is eventually forgotten. 'Yes,' I say empathetically, but really I mean 'No', noticing that his feet are quite heavily bound with substantial boxing wraps. This looks dangerous beyond belief to both protagonist and sparring partner, and would never be for me even if I were thirty years younger.

As the heat soars in the room, I hang out of one of the double-glazed windows to try and get cool. The immediate view is of a mishmash of bright orange, fluorescent yellow and green buildings on an industrial estate framed against a vivid blue sky. For a moment, it is all too bright. My two litres of water have vanished into nowhere and I take my leave dreaming of lemonade with ice tinkling in the glass.

13

PROFESSIONAL DEVELOPMENT

On a hot, summer Saturday in June 2015, I am back in Kelly's gym, this time as a paying punter. I am investing my hard-earned cash and deciding to give it a real good go. With a little trepidation, I have booked a private training session with Jamie, one of the professional boxing coaches whom I have met briefly before.

Kelly's gym has many advantages but is a longish drive from home or work. The drive does not bother me, but the real fly in the ointment is that I have to drive past the abattoir which less than a mile east of the gym. This causes me real distress as I am a lifelong vegetarian. My vegetarianism has not been an arc of perfection, but a genuine attempt to eat no cows, pigs, sheep, chickens or fish. I really don't see why I should have a prima facie right to cause them to suffer and be killed, just so that I can eat them – especially when there are so many alternatives which would be so much better for both for me and them. My only regret is that I have never managed to become totally vegan, although there is still time to make this noble transition, but I am well on my way, battling cryptic food labels and finding that dead animals are outrageously insinuated into the most benign-looking of foodstuffs, clothing and household items.

The vile workings of the abattoir go on largely unseen and, as yet, largely ignored, underpinned by a rapacious, moneymaking machine. This peddles harmful fast food to hapless humans and causes unimaginable suffering to millions of animals whose only crime is to be themselves. On hot days, such as these, noxious smells from the abattoir hang faintly in the air outside, but never quite go away. For the time being, I hold my nose and carry on. As I put on my wraps and boxing gloves, ready for Jamie's training session, I gulp down a glass of water to quell my nausea from the faint abattoir smell outside, grab a skipping rope and start to skip.

I notice that the boxing ring has a soft and spongy American-style floor and the skipping ropes are super-heavy. This drags energy from the body – a deliberate ploy in the training of professional boxers. As I skip in the ring to warm up, it feels very weird, like jumping on a feather mattress while holding dumbbells. The boxing ring is positively gleaming and there is no spit-and-sawdust feel here. I try some shadowboxing as part of my warm up routine, moving rather woodenly round the ring and feeling at odds with the upmarket surroundings.

I think that Jamie is surprised by my reasonable level of fitness but taken aback by my lack of boxing technique. Clearly, I am a novice with low skill levels, and I can see he is finding it hard to come down to my level. Nonetheless he is terribly encouraging, which puts me at ease. Apart from the jab and the right hand, which are solid, the other more complex shots are not great, but as I relax, I throw them better.

I try a few hooks. I know in theory what I must do but the body will not obey. Jamie can sense that I am keen, and he is quick to pass on useful nuggets of information. He suggests a much more open stance for the left hook, with my left shoulder abutting straight onto the bag and right foot almost turned outwards. He tells me to throw a straight right first to set up the pendulum swing required for the left hook, and to drop and turn in my right knee. After months of sideways standing, this more open stance feels very vulnerable, but you need to be up close and personal to deliver the hook. The trick is to deliver the hook super-fast in your opponent's blind spot and then to retreat very quickly. This works for a fleeting moment when the slap of the gloves on the bag is suddenly converted into a sharp and satisfying crack.

The professionals have a very different way of doing things and I discover that the trainers and coaches are hypercritical but in a super-nice way. It is strange not to be sworn or shouted at for once. Jamie points out a lot of basic errors but teaches me one very important lesson: that I am experienced enough to do some valuable training on my own and to correct some of my own mistakes.

He suggests that from time to time I should adopt a southpaw rather than an orthodox boxing stance. Now that I know the basic moves, adopting the opposite stance will give flexibility and strength to my default position and will reduce the potential for lopsided injury. It will also improve the muscles for a range of other punches. He warns me that this will feel really strange at first and it does, like suddenly putting on two left shoes. (This reminds me that, decades earlier, in a fit of efficiency I decided to buy two pairs of identical shoes. I must be one of the few human beings on the planet who actually managed to turn up for work one day wearing two left shoes. Ah well...)

Next, Jamie encourages me to think less along tramlines

and to try to be more creative and experimental with various shots and manoeuvres. This is difficult as I still feel that I am trying to grasp the basics.

Jamie also makes the heretical suggestion that I drop my hands. Due to the laws of physics, the body can twist and weave more easily with the hands down because they are closer to the body. I protest, as this contravenes everything I have learnt so far. Jamie replies: 'Anything is possible, as long as it is within the rules of boxing.' And it is.

I carry on with a fitness session after my formal boxing session is over. There are other grafters in the gym: Ceri, who says that she has done some boxing previously, and Derek, who is a beefed-up management consultant from Warrington. Unlike me, Ceri has a great left hook, but all her other shots are to pot. She has speed and a good hip swivel for the hook, but, surprisingly, her body remains resolutely stiff when she tries a jab or right hand. She ducks and weaves really well, but is a serial hand-dropper, which is never good. If we could both be mysteriously combined, together we would make not a bad boxer. I get the pads out and Ceri is a worthy assistant.

I ask Derek if he will hold up the pads for me, but I can see that he is genuinely fearful. For one so beefed-up, he is worried and even a bit shaky. Eventually, he holds up the pads for Ceri and then for me, first a bit hesitantly. Eventually he is convinced that we are not going to make mincemeat out of him, merely practise some shots. I leave feeling the satisfaction of a good two-hour session, but feel overwhelmed by the amount there is still to learn and whether the old body will hold up long enough for me to be able to learn it.

The following Saturday teatime I fetch up at the same venue. The gym car park is stuffed full of Mercs and BMWs and I suspect that the gym will be full of Sloane rangers. Instead, there is a wedding in progress in hotel next door. I notice a low-slung, white sports car tied with a lilac ribbon right outside the gym door, and I think immediately of Morrissey's song 'Will Never Marry'.

The gym is deserted and, after a quarter of an hour of skipping with a few embellishments, I unselfconsciously practise hook after hook after hook, no doubt making many mistakes. I crane my neck time after time to try and view my efforts in the long mirrors which line the gym, grading each punch out of ten.

At the eleventh hour two professional boxers appear. They spend a few minutes inspecting my shots on the bags. The jab and right hand are judged as near-perfect, but my attempts at a hook are just not right. One of the boxers demonstrates the left hook again and again, punching up and down the bag in a furious barrage of piston-like shots. His bent left arm barely moves – all the power comes from the hips, feet and floor. He reassures me that there is no mystery to the hook, just practice, practice, practice. He also tells me to move in and out from the bag more – I am loitering again in that dangerous punch zone. The truth is that I don't have the right musculature for throwing the hook. The elbows need to be glued to the hip bones and alternate knees need to be turned in at lightning speed using muscles that I just do not have (yet).

When I get home, I consult the oracle that is Cornelius Carr's online compendium of 'boxing tips for dummies'. There are hooks, hooks and more hooks, low hooks, high hooks, pivoting hooks, looping hooks. I study each, but I just want the economy, no-frills version. Eventually I find a no-nonsense version, and discover that, unlike the jab, I need to move my front foot forward more, sort of bend forward and crouch down, drop the right knee, turn the left knee inwards, before turning my head to the right. I am told that the rest of my body will automatically follow, like magic, with a weight shift and the delivery of a hook. I try and try, but actually fall over, as my feet swivel into an unsteady straight line.

In July 2015, my life is enhanced by watching a thrilling TV boxing match live from El Paso. The experienced northern Irish boxer Carl Frampton attempts to defend his bantam-weight title against a younger twenty-two year-old Mexican challenger, Alejandro González Jr. González Jr is an inscrutable underdog, fighting on home turf with the roar of the Mexican crowd behind him. He makes an excellent start, and unexpectedly knocks down Frampton twice in the first round for two standing counts. González has a great right hook, and as soon as Frampton tries to box on the 'inside' (or close-up) he gets hooked.

Then Frampton's experience shows, as he changes tack, moves back out of the punch zone and instead employs his jab to very good effect. The match goes the whole twelve rounds, with both boxers giving it their all, except for a few sneaky low punches by González which are conveniently ignored by the Mexican referee. Frampton simultaneously retains his title and breaks into the American market for the first time. Bizarrely, he is disappointed with his performance, as he has expected this bout to be a pushover, blaming his wrongly allotted weight category and the spongy floor of the ring as contributory factors. By any measure it is an impressive display of technical excellence by both boxers.

Also in reflective mood, I decide that I am now pretty strong and have reasonable stamina, but that my flexibility could be vastly improved, and yoga seems like a good option.

Yoga sessions are held in the gym of a brand new primary school in the local town. In the modern way, the school is a veritable fortress, designed to keep the children in and the outside world out. This means that those who are new to the sessions (like me) can never find their way into the building.

Once inside you can look through a magnificent curved picture window which frames the local hills, immediately inducing calm. Sonia, who runs the sessions, bends into the most impossible poses and in a wonderfully soporific voice entreats us gently to do the same. Most of the participants are much older than me, some in their seventies and eighties – yet I am always the only one hugging the wall, feeling as stiff as a board or toppling like a skittle as my balance fails. I career helplessly to the ground for the umpteenth time.

You can arrive at a yoga class on a Friday night, with the blood flooded with cortisol and sky high with adrenaline, fresh from the trials of the working week, but leave feeling as if ice and barbiturates have seeped gently into the veins. This is all due to Sonia's magical yogic powers. I muse on the past words of a sage-like physiotherapist who reminded me that, unlike boxing, yoga could likely be pursued well into old age. I certainly think that gently slipping away in a comfortable, crumpled heap on the floor in Sonia's yoga class, with the faint tinkle of Eastern music in the background, would surely be a good way to go.

Jamie is away on holiday and therefore not available for a training session. I am £25 better off, but cannot throw a hook for toffee, and spend a listless Wednesday night at the Kelly's gym. In frustration, I punch the bag really hard as all technique goes out of the window, and for a brief ten minutes this feels good, but I know it is a cop out.

Slightly worried, Ceri asks me if I ever imagine that my

boxing bag is a real person. Without hesitation, I say, 'Michael Portillo,' a sheep in wolf's clothing whom I regard as dangerous, Thatcherite right-winger, who has reinvented himself as your benign great-uncle. (At least Margaret Thatcher was a wolf in wolf's clothing whom you could clearly hear howling at the moon).

Ceri chips in, 'I think the Tories did great things for this country.' Well, I *don't*. In my imagination I vomit into my boxing gloves, and I note that Ceri and I can never really be friends. Just for good effect I throw in a few baiting remarks, concerning rock-bottom public sector pay, dancing on particular graves and the like, before returning to the bag.

I believe that I am qualified to hold such opinions as I witnessed at first hand the laying to waste and subsequent abandonment of Northern England in the early 1980s by Mrs Thatcher's Government for ideological reasons alone. This catastrophic loss of industry and jobs caused massive destruction of communities and families in northern towns. There were riots on the streets as unemployment rose to horrific levels.

So-called Job Centres were objects of derision, as there were no jobs. As I recall, the dole office was a dehumanising place, where transactions took place from behind a screen, as if the staff might become contaminated by the jobless and feckless. Hours were spent in pointless queues shuffling about from desk to desk. The poor were blamed for their own destinies, over which they had no control. Prosperous mining towns in Lancashire, South Yorkshire, Nottinghamshire and Derbyshire went to rack and ruin as mines were shut down, even though many at that time were still profitable. (A group of miners in South Wales pooled their redundancy money, bought an 'unproductive' mine and ran it profitably for many years.) This all culminated in the miners' strike, which caused a further schism in mining families.

I visited a huge range of factories in Northern England as part of my job from 1987 to 1991: steel rolling mills in Sheffield, paper mills in Lancashire, dye works in Manchester, textile mills in Bradford, coal mines in south Yorkshire and Lancashire. I estimate that around 40 per cent of the coal mines were shut down over that period. I witnessed the very last gasp of traditional British industry as the tumbleweed rolled through. Globalisation was on the way, but there was no real attempt to replace anything with anything, as had happened in more far-sighted countries such as Germany. Anyway, back in the gym, punching conveniently drowns out further speech before I say something that I will probably regret.

The following Friday, Kelly's gym is almost empty, except for a largish, ripped bloke, who is toiling away. He tells me that he is preparing for a Tough Mudder challenge. This is a sort of grown-up SAS-style egg-and-spoon race. Of course, it is easy to be facetious about these events, which I personally find herd-like and unappealing, but I genuinely admire his determination as the course requires mental courage as well as physical endurance. Each to their own, I think.

He tells me that part of his training regime is skipping which he cannot do. He says that he has been a boxer in the past, but has lost the skipping art. It is the one thing that I know I can do. I grab a rope and give him a few tips, as I show him my full, gleaming repertoire of four separate skipping tricks: alternate fast and slow skipping rhythms, crossed and uncrossed arms in a quarter of a second, swooshing the feet from side to side and finally running forwards and back, as if on hot coals. He is suitably impressed, and (secretly) so am I.

A delightful ex-potholing friend of mine, Rob, took up serious fell running aged forty, and, as it spiralled out of control, he found that he was a natural. He began to undertake longer and longer runs, some in the 'Tough Mudder' style. Some endurance events lasted several days and nights, including the famous round of Mont Blanc. Rob told me that if you manage to complete this you are given a standing ovation by the Chamonix mountain guides, as Rob deservedly was. Closer to home, Rob was astounded to find a strange scattering of leaflets on the ground at the start of an overnight fell running event in the Peak District. They were SAS recruitment flyers. Presumably Rob's simple enjoyment of night time solitude on the Derbyshire fells meant that he could kill someone with his little finger, and would of course have no hesitation in doing so.

⊙

One Saturday night our off-duty boxing coach, Dai, unexpectedly rings to announce invitations to his fiftieth birthday get together in early August. All his boxing, footballing and army friends and family will be there. As usual, I can hardly make out a word he says as he mumbles into the telephone. I hopefully make the right noises of approval, and just manage to make out that the location is The Buick Hotel on the Lancashire coast. I truly love Dai, but at times I cannot understand a bloody word he says, and we normally communicate only by punching. However, it will be a pleasure to go along.

That same Saturday night, instead of sweating in the gym myself, I watch several bouts of boxing vicariously from the safety of an armchair. This time it is the clash of World Super

Middleweights, an underdog challenger pitted against a title defender. As usual, the boxer with the good jab is the rightful defender of his title. His challenger is taunted, boxed mercilessly into the corner and is then finally demolished with a demon right hook.

14

HOOKS

With the hook in mind (again), I book a training session with Jamie for the following Monday. That day, I have had a long and fairly tiring session in the laboratory supervising students undertaking various summer projects. With the crash, tinkle, tinkle of test tubes ringing in my ears, I look forward to blocking it all out with an hour of hooks.

I drive through the torrential, Lancashire rain. Knowing that I am running close to late for my gym session, I find that the slowest vehicles possible have been assembled in an infuriating convoy on the road, including a hay wagon, a concrete mixer and a quad bike without lights, travelling at glacial speed. I stop at the local garage as I have nearly run out of petrol. At the counter, a woman dressed in high heels and a fake leopard skin coat is undertaking a complex set of negotiations. This lasts all of ten minutes and concerns a ten quid prize lottery ticket prize. That's one pound per minute, I think. Surely she has been brought out of hiding just at that exact moment to add to my despair.

Still, I get to the gym with five minutes to spare, racing in through the reception area at the speed of light. Jamie looks puzzled, and I later find out that he mistakenly thinks his training session is with a male, Polish boxer who shares my name. Regrettably it is me. I imagine what Dai's choice comments would be as, red in the face, I skip frantically to warm up.

In truth, I am actually a bit nervous, as I have not had any kind of formal boxing tuition for a good three months. I am psyched up for a full on sparring session, but instead, much more constructively, Jamie and I stand in the boxing ring, facing each other, completely static.

He holds up the pads and I throw my best jab and straight right, while he makes an assessment. The punches snap onto the pads with a perfect crack. It is good to have someone facing me who knows how to hold up the pads – a severely underrated skill. I know that the shots are good, and Jamie concurs, saying that the jab is totally solid, and the straight right is very powerful. Jamie tells me that the upper body part of the punching mechanism is really good, but I really need to concentrate much more on the feet to throw a really good hook.

The hook is still proving too much of a challenge, and to my surprise we spend the next ten minutes doing a repetitive yoga move which I find really tricky. It is simply standing in a square on pose and the twisting the upper body through 180 degrees with the torso remaining totally upright, the chest out, but with both feet swivelling alternately to the left and right. A lunge manoeuvre is dropped in on either side for a more exaggerated effect. Using the same basic motion, the right knee is dropped and turned in, as the hips are twisted sharply, and the straight right is thrown, setting up the momentum for a perfect left hook.

If executed correctly, the momentum in the twist keeps going, allowing the hook to be thrown and then snapped back very quickly, with the body weaving from side to side in perpetual motion. The left arm feels almost static, but is pulled back then thrown forward like a bolas by the elastic torque of the body. To make me crouch right down with a deep lunge, Jamie drops to his knees and holds the pads three feet above the floor, as I throw a passable straight right. Jamie tells me to pull back the left hand in readiness for the left hook. Surely this constitutes the sin of telegraphing – pulling back a shot for a split second, and giving your opponent a wrongful insight into your intentions – but no, it has to be so fast, and the pull back is so minute the opponent will not even see it coming.

For the very first time I can see the art of the deconstructed left hook – in theory at least. Finally, I see how the hook should be set up and thrown, the value of the twist in putting punch combinations together and of all the wasted momentum and energy in single shots. Jamie says that the left hook can be a great reply to a straight right, as the hook can loop round on an opponent's blind (right) side, bypassing their shot and largely out of view. The twisting and lunging motion should be easy, but it is not. I think of all the missed yoga sessions and the eighty-year-olds in my yoga class who could do this without even stopping to blink while I teeter and fall. Jamie tells me to widen my stance, to provide more stability for the hook, as I swerve unsteadily from side to side.

My biggest sin is still leaning forward into my opponent's punch zone as I drop the right knee. Jamie also tells me that although I have been previously programmed to always have my hands up, I am actually bringing my head down towards my hands, further into the punch zone, and therefore I am not quite standing tall enough. At only five feet two inches tall, I need every ounce of verticality that I can muster, so the hands must go up to the head and not vice versa. I have always imagined that the hook is a shot on the inside, close to one's opponent, but Jamie shows how, if the rotation is right, you can rotate it in and out of the punch zone, essentially boxing safely from an outside position. I learn that there is hook for every occasion, presumably including births, weddings and funerals.

The hook will be weakened by outwards or inwards deviation from the vertical due to the laws of physics that govern rotation and moments of inertia: anyone spinning giddily in an office chair with their legs stuck out can tell you that. Since the power of the hook comes ultimately from a twist of the feet, the up-on-the-toes stance that I have been previously taught for the hook may not be correct. Instead, I should be digging both feet into the floor to get maximum power in the twist.

There is controversy about the exact foot placement for hooks. Some say flat, some say up on the toes, but I say the former. The right heel should be slightly raised to start with, but as the rightwards turn is completed the left foot should twist rightwards, and the left heel should lift automatically.

I desperately try to think through the plethora of moves and tense up as Jamie tells me to do anything except think. After purging all thoughts from my mind, I start to loosen up. What a difficult business this all is, and how unaccountably I love it! Just a handful of times the twist comes out perfectly, and I throw two or three great left hooks. The motion is like throwing a discus. The hooks fall on the pads and snap back immediately as if drawn away by invisible elastic. It is not only the fact that they are good that gives me satisfaction, but mainly the fact that I can recognise them as such. At last, I am a hooker of sorts.

⊙

The following morning at work confirms that even after nearly two years in the boxing gym, I have managed to find a set of muscles that I have not yet used. I hobble along the pavement towards my laboratory and a colleague shouts unhelpfully, 'Been in the wars?'

The next week continues with the hook obsession. During the following Sunday, in early August, I toil in another almost empty local gym. The afternoon sun streams in darkly through sheets of summer rain. A smart girl with blonde hair piled on top of her head tells me about her failed bodybuilding career, and how difficult it was to find a suitable coach in a rural area such as ours.

Matter-of-factly she reveals the reason for her swift move to the Yorkshire Dales as she points to a small scar over her left eyebrow. 'Abusive boyfriend,' she says without emotion. 'The scar's still there after a year, but now at least my daughter and I are safe.' I feel a healthy dose of boxing spite rising to the surface.

At Kelly's gym the following Monday and Wednesday, I see Frank, Jamie's protégé, in the car park. He seems to live at the gym and I admire his dedication. Somehow, we get onto the subject of motorbikes and Frank reveals his history as an ex-biker. I ask him if he is one of the middle-aged men who rip along the snake-like road past my house at weekends, TT style. These are older men, dads who can afford their Ducati racing bikes but should know better, with their exploits often ending in tears and whose loss is keenly felt.

The expression on his face tells me that he has been one of these. Frank confesses that he sold his bike fearing the same. I say that thirty-six bikers have been killed on local roads within the last five years. Twice in the last month I have had to abandon my car and walk over the fields to my house, as the police have closed the road due to fatal motorbike crashes. For a whole month I have had to drive past a heartrending memorial sign held up by a rain-sodden teddy bear stuck on the grass verge only a few hundred yards from my house.

Suddenly, Frank asks me if I think there is life after death. I want to sugar the pill as he is clearly contemplating the tragic ex-bikers and their families left behind. I use an expression coined by my late father which covers most eventualities, and say that indeed many people indeed think that. I am too kind to state what I think is the real truth about the blood-streaked road.

15

ROVER'S RETURN

On a Saturday night in mid-August 2015, I make my way to The Buick Hotel, Morecambe. The occasion is Dai's fiftieth birthday. Still slightly unsure of the location, I check the pub's details online and ring up on the Saturday morning to see that I have not misunderstood. It becomes obvious that this is Dai's local and that the landlord has had equal difficulty understanding his requirements. However, the landlord says that food will be on and he will be the DJ with the help of The Clash, The Jam and various Northern soul singers.

I arrive fashionably late at around 9 p.m., having parked down a dark alley round the corner, where kids wearing hoodies are prowling about on mountain bikes. The pub is a traditional millstone grit building clamped defiantly onto a street corner. There are around sixty or seventy people inside, a mixture of ex-boxers, footballers and ex-servicemen and Dai's family and other friends. The warmth is palpable. The friendly landlord greets me, uncannily stating that he can always put a face to a voice.

Dai is smiling in the midst of a clump of footballing friends and is already rather the worse for wear. He is obviously very pleased to see me as I hand over my paltry offerings. As you can never have too much of a good thing, these are CDs (you may have guessed) of The Specials, The Clash and The Jam, and I sincerely hope that they will be played to destruction.

I sit at a table with the landlady, her daughter and friends, and we laugh immediately and heartily about nothing. We dance round our handbags, imaginary and real, brushing the dust off our antiquarian Northern soul moves. Unwisely, I have bought Dai a double whisky on the rocks, and as the karaoke gets going Dai gets up unsteadily to rap. I am struck by Dai's sense of rhythm, not quite totally extinguished by the alcohol, as out-of-tune expletive after expletive magically hits the beat, accompanied by the beautiful voice of the landlord's daughter who later tells me (wrongly) that cigarettes have permanently ruined her voice.

A very ancient man gets up and does a passable and enthusiastic hip-swivelling Elvis impersonation, crooning 'Peggy Sue', to loud cheers. I suggest 'Mercy' by Duffy, which has us all on our feet and the landlady dancing on the furniture. However, the *pièce de résistance* is a drunken Dai, accompanied by his mum, tackling a karaoke duo as we look on helplessly, rocking with laughter. At around 1 a.m. I bid Dai goodbye. He is clearly at the crying-into-beer stage as he crushes me in a hug that takes northern hospitality to new heights. I wonder what kind of state he will still be in on the following Monday, never mind Sunday. I leave the pub reluctantly. It is a cliché, but I feel that I am leaving behind a host of brand new old friends whom I will see again very soon.

◉

I have been doing some hip-swivelling of my own over the previous two weeks, and in a training session the following Monday Jamie tries to explain the notion of hooks as body shots, and how the crouching lunge and twists that I have been practising underpin the body shot hook. This is a hook delivered at a lower level than the hook to the head.

My only past experience of delivering body shots is of trying out the rather visceral and nasty liver shot under the ribs of my old boxing coach Gerard. This shot, if delivered correctly, will totally floor an opponent, but in general the body shot hook is a new and complex idea.

Like any new boxing shot, there is far too much to remember. The brain immediately goes into overload, then freezes and I suddenly cannot tell my left hand from my right. Not this again, I think. Like a pregnancy of two years which has come to fruition, I have had to go through all this with the jab, right hand and left hook, and now I need to forget all the pain and grief and go through it again with the body shot hook.

To satisfy my own obsessive approach, I will record exactly what needs to be done. First off, mostly forget about the arms except that they should be merely positioned, and then later whirled round by an excessive body twist. The arms should be held at eye level, elbows in an L-shape, with palms of the hands orientated towards the face, like pistons waiting to be cranked. The knuckles must be flat and vertical. The hands may be held horizontally, but the default hand position for the hook is a vertical orientation. For orthodox boxers, such as myself, the front foot is normally turned in at an angle of about 45 degrees rightwards. For the hook-as-body shot, the stance is much more opened out, and the front left foot can even be pointing forwards. The back foot should also be pointing at 45 degrees, as normal, but with a slightly wider stance to aid stability.

For any boxing nerds out there, the next bit is crucial, so listen up. For the left hook body shot, the right knee must be turned inwards, and both feet must be driven into the floor, with the heels ever-so-slightly lifted, but not usually on the toes. The chest must be pushed outwards and the torso must be upright. The overall body position must be crouched down, more at first than you might imagine, with the knees bent, but relaxed. The back foot is then rotated rightwards and ground into the floor. This should rotate the torso rightwards, as the front foot is swivelled rightwards also. This should create a whiplash effect where the left arm then swings automatically rightwards, and the hook should just keep going, according to Newton's first law of motion. If not stopped by an intervening body, the shot should end up in the air somewhere near your right shoulder. The gaze should be rightwards at the finish of the left hook, but your eyes must still be on your opponent somehow.

I have read that experienced boxers manage to somehow keep their gaze straight ahead while executing a hook, but I decide not to burden myself with this refinement for the moment. Jamie also suggests that it can make the shot easier if the glove is angled upwards almost in a semi-uppercut orientation, rather than being plumb-vertical, as it is then easier to get the body weight behind the shot. (Jack Dempsey also recommends a 45-degree angle).

I get into my stance and crouch down and twist. For the first time in almost two years, I can see at last that, as well as being the set-up for the left hook body shot, this is the elusive defensive slip move, which also avoids an opponent's straight right hand shot. This is the slip move that I have previously watched and tried to emulate, but that has somehow eluded me.

I try a couple of shots. They are poor as I have suddenly become the Hunchback of Notre Dame. I have not crouched down enough or too far or I have totally forgotten to shift my feet. Then, just for a few shots, I get it right. In a slick, slapstick routine, which looks like it's been taken from an old Buster Keaton film, I simultaneously duck and twist, elegantly avoiding Jamie's straight right, while setting up a perfect left hook onto the pad. The pad shots ring out as I hunker down, and I manage to put a nifty little uppercut angle on the hook. They are sweet shots. Jamie suggests throwing a left hook, then a straight right, but I am so concentrating on the hook that I leave my right hand simply flailing around in the air somewhere near my right ear, where it is not in a position to do anything useful. After twenty-five minutes of left hooks I am drenched, drenched, drenched in sweat. I gulp down gallons of water, and wonder why I didn't bring a towel.

The right hook is next. This should be the converse of the left hook, but somehow it isn't. It is much less of a natural shot, and Jamie suggests that I throw it as a much wider shot to get more power into it. Wrongly, I am also artificially 'pushing' the hook with my hooking hand rather than letting the right arm crank around machine-like after the body. The arm should be automatically dragged round, not forced. After a further fifteen minutes of sweating and throwing right hooks, it is not really the body but the brain that gives out. Once the left hand/right hand confusion kicks in you know you are finished, but the session is over anyway. I thank Jamie for unfurling the mystery of the hook and I am gone.

I arrive late on a Friday night for another solo session at a Kelly's gym. I skip for the obligatory fifteen minutes, before a round of side jumps and shadow boxing moves, hooks, left and right. I am feeling excessively tired and heartily blame my GP. I suffer from hypothyroidism, and the GP has recently reduced my daily dose of thyroxine, believing me to be over-treated and fearing the potential long-term complications of heart arrhythmias, fragile bones and other deficits. The truth is that no one really cares if your hormones have gone to pot just as long as it is not life threatening and you can still feed and wash yourself.

In the preceding week, despite plenty of sleep, I wake late and exhausted with telltale black circles beneath puffy eyes, signs that my thyroxine levels are way too low. My endocrinologist thinks that my dose should certainly be higher and a plethora of tests indicate strong bones and a fantastic heart, but until the GP is convinced I will have to morph into a slug. Anyway, various bits of me will give out long before the snapping of bones, I think.

⊙

A busy weekend just allows a lovely Sunday evening cycle ride in the upper reaches of Kingsdale, near Ingleton, not too far from home. Summer mist hangs in the valley, and there is the barest chill in the evening air. The cycling is perfectly lovely in itself, but it has a knee strengthening benefit which also pays off in the boxing gym. My old boxing coach, Gerard, advised that cycling helps to develop a good range of muscles in the knee which aids skipping, and this certainly seems to be the case.

The cycle route starts with a steep climb past a little wood, where I once saw a long-eared owl swoop out silently at dusk.

Then the road bows over a series of giant rocky steps as the view opens out like a wide, frozen limestone sea, with distant views of the Howgill Fells gradually opening out. The hormones are still raging but not in a good way, as I pour with sweat despite the cool air. Worse still, I have left my water bottle behind. The water levels in the mountain becks are low, and a deep pool at Swere Gill Bridge which is normally a mini-cauldron of swirling water is no more than a puddle. I think of the poor, pudgy semi-Arctic fish that usually inhabit these waters being hot and stressed (like me!).

I am similarly afflicted at Kelly's gym the following night. The dry summer heat has turned humid, and at the end of the session I feel as if I have been lightly steamed in a pressure cooker. Despite overcooking, I throw some great left hooks. Three or four make the heavy bag quiver like jelly. I just know that they are good. As I leave the boxing ring, I notice a T-shirt of mine that I have not seen for a while is hanging over the ropes at the side of the boxing ring. I realise that it has been there for several weeks without me noticing, and it feels like the grey matter is diminishing in a middle-aged fug.

16

LEARNING TO WALK AGAIN

The foreseeable future is clouded with a terrible pain that cannot be ironed or beaten out even in the boxing gym. I can cope with any human tragedy, but the slow demise of my beloved twenty-year-old cat, Penny, is more than I can bear. As well as being very arthritic she has been steadily losing weight over the last few months. Her slow decline is monitored by our dutiful vet.

The cause is unknown and even the simplest investigations cause her immense stress. The vet and I have decided that, because of her great age, the kindest course of action is to do nothing but administer steroids and painkillers for whatever it is. Various blood tests are theoretically on offer but all would require a general anaesthetic, which she would almost certainly not survive. The vet is an exceedingly kind man of good judgement, whom I have known for many years. As he starts to tell me what I know already, I politely reassure that him that I do not expect any miracles, but just at that moment that is exactly what I would like him to do – perform a miracle.

A welcome distraction comes in the form of an unexpected phone call from a representative of the local pet rescue charity

– the origin of our two feline residents. The woman at the end of the phone asks my permission to use a photograph of my other cat, Tigger, now aged a mere sixteen years old, in their annual charity calendar. I agree at once and she announces proudly that he will be 'Mr August'. Mr August basks on the windowsill in the sunshine, snoring loudly. He is a picture of rude, gingery health, with four legs in the air, unaware of his burgeoning pin-up career.

A further short session in Kelly's gym, late on an August Saturday, gradually improves the hook, as the benefit is seen from all the crouching and lunging of the past few weeks. Outside it is the hottest day of the year. The air is heavy and humid, poised and ready for end-of-day thunderstorms. I decide to build up some stamina, and box the bag in a relentless 1-2, 1-2 series of shots, throwing 6 x 4, 4 x 6, 4 x 8 and 3 x 10 punches in continuous two-minute rounds, finishing off with my own special version of the Board of Death. There is nobody around as I hang around intermittently in the car park, trying to cool off in the baking air, head bowed and chest heaving, but nonetheless feeling good.

A week later, I have a training session booked with Jamie. I always try to second guess what he has planned for me, but never can. We both warm up in the gym then start with some easyish side steps towards either side of the ring with a lunge at either end. Jamie adds a further embellishment as, with each lunge, I must raise my arms high to one side, and then low down on the opposite side, as if unstacking invisible high supermarket shelves.

Next, Jamie tries to encourage a more natural movement when throwing a 1-2. We stand side by side in front of the mirrors and I throw a jab and right hand. I am getting enough hip swivel in the jab, but not in the straight right, which I am leaving out far too long. Jamie tells me to turn my right foot in more, and think of throwing each punch as a chopping karate move with each punch completed only when alternate arms are fully extended or retracted. This should bring about a more fluid delivery with no stop–start jerkiness, and should use the momentum inbuilt into the system to strengthen all the shots. Next, we do the opposite in a southpaw stance.

Then I am given the apparently simple task of just following him around the boxing ring, but keeping a constant distance between us of about half a metre. The difficulty of course is in maintaining some kind of punch-ready boxing stance while doing this and not expending too much energy. I manage to follow him at speed as he changes direction. Instinctively, I feint some shots and cut off his exit from the corners of the ring, trying to get him on the ropes. It is funny that this is not in the brief, but it is what I do twice over without even thinking – the rare emergence of a bit of boxing intuition.

My footwork is all over the place. I am also springing off the floor and wasting precious energy. I am in and out of my boxing stance like there is no tomorrow, and it is clear that I have momentarily forgotten the basics. I seem to be sort of hopping, putting in extra steps and simultaneously dragging my feet – this is a quite a spectacularly bad achievement.

In my defence, I have been told so many conflicting things about simply moving around the boxing ring in various different gyms. If moving backwards, some say the back foot should be moved backwards first, others are adamant that to move backwards the front foot should work like a spring, pinging the whole body backwards. To move forwards, some say to step forwards with the front foot first or others say to spring off the back foot. Like a machine that has malfunctioned with too many switches, I wrestle with the conundrums of which leg to activate first.

Jamie points out that the manoeuvres I have described are in fact the same thing, when moving in any one direction, and the easiest thing to do is just to actually step backwards with the back foot and simultaneously spring off the front foot, and vice versa for going forwards. This is just walking of course, but mysteriously I have forgotten how to do it.

Jamie makes me exaggerate the movement for good measure. I have a tendency to wheel round in a leftwards direction, which is the natural tendency of all orthodox boxers and this has to be curbed, so Jamie makes me throw a jab, then walk backwards along a straight line, then forwards again, then backwards again.

Bizarrely I am still putting in a little extra running step each time and both feet are ending up too much in line. JUST WALK! I think. Then I think, DO NOT THINK! Then I find that I am trying to walk and throw the punch at the same time, which is not working at all. Jamie also points out that I am concentrating so hard that I am not breathing either, which is also not good. I think of Spike Milligan's 1970s Christmas novelty hit: 'I'm Walking Backwards for Christmas' and as my head fills with nonsense. I finally relax, walking forwards and backwards in my boxing stance, and throwing some not bad jabs in between.

Next, it is crab-like sideways walking. Here at least the experts agree. To go leftwards you move the front left foot leftwards first, let the back foot follow. To go rightwards you step the back foot rightwards, and the front foot follows. The key is to take small steps, as this helps with stability, and not to cross the feet, and this causes terrible toppling.

The penultimate exercise is for me to throw a straight right, duck under Jamie's straight right, take a small, but distinct step to the right, BREATHE, and then regain my stance, which I should be in anyway, and throw another right. The first part of the manoeuvre goes OK. I manage some good right knee dropping and manage to duck and step right, but I step too far right and lose my stance, ending up with both feet side by side. My knees are also straight, instead of bent, which is absolutely no use to anybody, as I have become a boxing sitting duck. I am then in no position to throw any kind of right hand shot. As a result I am wrongly leaning forward to get power in the straight right, and moving in too close. Jamie suggests that I slow the whole thing down. He indicates that my left foot should end up just to the left of his front foot, and no further right than that. I get the hang of it eventually, and get into a sort of rhythm, finally managing to set up two good straight rights.

The final stage is to repeat the crazy crab walk, but moving leftwards with jabs substituted for right hand shots. I deliver a jab, Jamie throws another, I duck under his left arm, step left, but not too far, BREATHE, get into my stance, and throw another jab. This feels more natural, but I hit the buffers again by moving too far left, and end up so far from Jamie that I am out of his punching range. He is also out of mine, so we have prematurely ended the boxing match. He suggests that my finishing position after the step should be with my right shoulder beneath his opposing left arm. I try again, and I am not sure why but he is wheeling round in a circle, forcing me to maintain my position as I creep continually leftwards.

When I get home, I read an excerpt from the American boxer Jack Dempsey's boxing primer *Championship Fighting*. His book is always right, and when in doubt recommends going back to the basics.

At last I can see Jamie's strategy. This is exactly what he has done over the last three sessions, teaching me knee drops as the basis for various hooks, and improvement in the strength of the straight right shots. He has tried to improve my flexibility in the knees and hips to facilitate the twisting and lunging required and along the way, has retaught me how to walk again in the boxing ring. This has effectively laid the foundations for the two most basic defensive manoeuvres, the slip and roll, and all of this without either of us shedding a single tear.

17

UNDER THE COSH

After Jamie's Saturday training session, I feel good. I dither around for most of the next day, finally heading out for a Sunday cycling trip in the evening sunshine on one of my favourite Dales routes. My route ascends the snaky 1-in-6 road out of the mediaeval Yorkshire village of Arncliffe, and ends at the remote Darnbrook Farm, where the road continues to Malham Tarn beyond.

Beautiful Arncliffe is as solid and unchanging as ever. Over the last thirty years, I have noticed that the trees are a little more luxuriant, and some of the houses now have bold and brassy name plates. I hope that it will look the same in 500 years and I expect that it will.

I park in the familiar layby not far from the church, close to the footpath which leads west to the head of Littondale. Near the layby, there is a signpost which points the way to a tiny Viking settlement at the head of Littondale called Cosh, consisting now, I think, of only one renovated dwelling, Cosh House. There used to be no vehicular access to Cosh until fairly recently. In years gone by, a trail of ruined Saab cars that had been driven to destruction on the rough footpath between Cosh House and the roadhead. There are two ancient pastures close to Cosh House, known as Cosh Inside and Cosh Outside: one consists of enclosed land and the other comprises the wild fells beyond. The latter contains some of the remotest caves in the whole of the Yorkshire Dales, including the mysterious Lante Shop Caves.

After Cosh House was abandoned for a while prior to renovation, someone had helpfully scrawled something like 'The Devil Lives Here' across the front door, giving the whole place a distinctly edgy feel. At that time, there appeared to be no electricity or running water inside the property, except the beck flowing immediately outside the front door over a miniature clapper bridge. Lord alone knows what it was like living there through the winter or even summer with a two or three mile walk, past the dead Saabs, to the nearest road head, and a further fourteen miles by road to the nearest shop. In this remote land of the curlew and sheep rustler time stands still.

I start my cycling trip, already relieved that I am not going to Cosh. Instead, I follow the steep road which leads from Arncliffe towards Darnbrook Farm. I have inched my way up this hill on and off over the last thirty years. It feels as testing as ever, as my bicycle and I sweat our way up each chicane-like bend, hemmed in by drystone limestone walls. Each telegraph pole beside the road is a mark of success or failure, and I make it to the second cattle grid above Brootes Barn, before finally hopping off and pushing like mad. This is not actually bad going considering the antiquity of both the bike and me. Even though I am in my early fifties, the recent boxing training has allowed me to reach a new highpoint. The road crosses a cattle grid and breaks out into unenclosed land, where there are splendid views of Britain's finest limestone scenery, white and shining in the gloaming.

I can just make out the spectacular Yew Cogar Scar, a striking limestone cliff, visible in a deep, green ravine to the south of the moor road. This edifice rivals any Alpine scenery, and the ravine carries Cowside Beck, with its whirlpools and glorious theoretical summer swimming spots, blighted with black clouds of midges.

For reasons which I cannot adequately explain, I have spent many enjoyable hours alone in Cowside Beck, unravelling the geological mysteries of a particular brand of blue limestone right at the bottom of this ravine. I look south to the high ground above Cowside Beck which includes a remote area of landscape known as Hawkswick Clowder. A clowder is the ancient name for a collection of wild cats and this reminds me that the youngest place names on the map are a thousand years old.

The moor road then undulates over a series of giant limestone steps, before dropping down a series of steep switchbacks to the next landmark which is Darnbrook Farm. For the bold, trained and well-equipped, this landscape also promises a unique caving experience. It is here that I recall an unusual caving trip to Robinson's Pot in the 1990s. I suppose I can now regard caving trips such as these as some sort of general toughening-up phase which has served me well in life, including latterly in the boxing ring.

The entrance to the pothole is directly under Darnbrook Farm's kitchen window, beneath a manhole cover. Any trip begins with gaining a special permit prior to the trip, and, on the day, asking the farmer to move his Land Rover off the driveway to allow access to the cave. Underneath the manhole cover there is an unlikely twenty-five foot abseil, skewed under the stone slabs of the farmhouse kitchen floor into the blackness below. At the bottom of this drop is an accumulation of items which accidentally fell into the cave over many decades: old, abandoned teddy bears; Lego pieces; baked-bean tins and pop bottles with ancient labels from the 1960s; and old kitchen paraphernalia not seen for fifty years.

A few hundred feet into the cave, you nervously steps over a yawning chasm in the floor (best not to look down), gaining access into the first chamber where you can stand up and view some conspicuous nineteenth-century graffiti. The cave passage continues for several miles underneath Darnbrook Fell, in parts very low and constricted, and partially full of water. I remember a rather miserable, long cold spell towards the end of the accessible parts of the cave, slithering along for a few hundred feet on wet, ice-cold gravel, which only seemed to lead to more of the same. Further in, the cave is entirely flooded and therefore accessible only to cave diving specialists, who push the improbable exploration limits within permanently flooded caves, making them at first possible and then familiar.

As I turn the bike round and return to Arncliffe, I muse on my past trip down Robinson's Pot. The detritus at the bottom of the cave entrance could be regarded as characteristic of the Anthropocene: this is the official name for the geological era which will record the coming and going of human beings. According to environmentalists, this will be marked by a rock layer that will record biodiversity loss, pollution from plastics, chemicals and man-made radioactive materials. Apparently it will include rubble from generations of crumbling modern buildings that have not been built to last. It will be dominated by chicken bones: as a race we have bred and eaten more (unfortunate) chickens than any other creature. In effect, KFC will be our legacy. I return home with this negative thought lodged in my mind, as the black sky falls like a blanket over the landscape.

⊙

The next day I realise that this cycling trip has been an enjoyable mistake, as I wake up feeling as if I have been on a rack, the combined effects of this and of Jamie's training session being felt in every muscle fibre. Jamie has managed to work me very hard indeed, but in an entertaining way, without me noticing. I find that boxing creeps up on you in this way has an uncanny knack of doing this.

I have planned a day out, so I take the train to Manchester, but my legs buckle slightly as I alight onto the platform at Oxford Road Station. In a rather pathetic way, I manage to stagger only as far as Waterstones' bookshop on Deansgate. This is a dangerous zone of temptation, and in my weakened state, I know with certainty before I enter that I will buy books that I don't really need. As the Manchester singer Morrissey rightly said: 'There's more to life than books you know, but not much more, not much more.'

I manage to restrict myself to buying just one book: it is Joe Frazier's guide to boxing: *Box Like the Pros*. This book has a chatty, colloquial style, telling you simply all the things you should and shouldn't do in the boxing ring. A Brit could never write in such a direct and easy style, with its cheerful home-spun philosophy, which extends to respecting one's parents, God and just about everybody else, while simultaneously battering your opponent to a pulp.

My eyes are also drawn to the Peak District and North

Wales rock climbing guides, which bring back both happy and traumatic memories. In my twenties and thirties, I hauled my way up various rock faces in the UK and abroad. Few who haven't done this can see its appeal, but to me each climb was just a vertical walk, marked out by different companions, rock architecture and perspectives. Looking back now, I can still very much see the attraction. As with the caving scene, the climbing scene was populated by eccentric, non-conforming outsiders who refused to do as they were told, and with whom I and my climbing companions certainly identified.

Climbing was also appealing to me in that had an essential simplicity, with only a very few rules and requiring only rudimentary equipment. I find a similar appeal in boxing. Climbing is said to have begun as a UK sport in the late 1880s after first solo ascent in 1886 of Napes Needle in the Lake District by Walter Parry Haskett Smith. Modern boxing came into being in 1857 at around the same time with the drawing up of the Queensberry Rules, by the 8th Marquess of Queensberry.

I can see that both sports share appealing elements of style. Each has a set of basic moves and manoeuvres that can be learned and then adapted into an individual style, allowing for a degree of creativity, but also having a basic framework. As ever, my companions and I take climbing to extremes, slightly beyond the bounds of our own capabilities.

Many of the so-called classic routes in the Peak District listed in the guide were climbed for the first time in the 1950s and 1960s by Joe Brown and Don Whillans. Both hailing from Manchester, Brown and Whillans were the first to put up some of the hardest and boldest rock climbing routes of the day in Britain and just about everywhere else. They relied on skill, nerve and sheer brass neck rather than any fancy gear, pushing the technical limits. They changed the face of British rock climbing, snatching it from the domain of privileged public school types who had dominated the earlier climbing scene. Both Whillans and Brown went on to have distinguished Alpine and Himalayan mountaineering careers.

At the peak of my rock climbing powers, I climbed some of Whillans and Brown's easier routes, finding them dreadfully difficult as they required the strength of an ox and the delicacy of a ballerina. Suicide Wall at Cratcliffe Tor in the Peak District stands out in the memory. (The clue is in the name, though it is not to be confused with Suicide Wall in North Wales, which is technically more difficult.) Graded an Extreme rock climb, Haydon and I climbed it on a summer evening when rain threatened. It is a beautiful climb, around a hundred feet high, which demands a particular skill known as 'jamming'. Here, the hands are made into fists and stuffed into various cracks in the gritstone rocks, effectively acting as chocks. This gives rise to a temporary affliction known as 'gritstone rash', where the skin is torn off by the rough rock. The top part of the route demanded extraordinary strength, and I remember sitting in a small peapod-shaped cut-out in the rock, about twenty feet from the top of the route, shaking out my arms to try and propel them into action, before launching out onto the final gritstone headwall.

Whillans was a genius, anti-athlete and also a technical innovator. In photographs he appears wearing a flat cap, paunched, laconic and often smoking a fag. Apparently, he was a pugnacious and abrasive character, famous for not being nice. I spent a good deal of time as part of the rock climbing scene in North Wales in the 1980s, and was honoured to meet someone who had been sworn at and then punched by Don Whillans in an after-the-pub fight.

Whillans designed a climbing harness, the eponymous Whillans Harness, which was fine until you turned upside down as then you immediately fell out of it. He also designed a more successful boxlike tent, known as the Whillans Box. This could be erected and anchored to the sides of high altitude mountains in very high winds more easily than a traditional ridgepole type tent. I visited a mountaineering exhibition in the Lake District in the 1990s, where there was a Whillans Box tent on display. Visitors were allowed to crawl inside, as I did, trying to imagine the whirling Himalayan snowstorm outside.

In the 1980s Haydon and I, plus a trusted climbing companion, Ewan, became obsessed with vintage accounts of Victorian and Edwardian rock climbs. On the way to North Wales or The Lakes for weekends away, the two out of three of us who weren't driving would read aloud from past accounts of derring-do in the mountains. Our Victorian and Edwardian climbing heroes, George Mallory, Siegfried Herford and John Menlove Edwards – in whose steps we were sometimes ill-fated to follow – put up various classic rock climbing routes in Snowdonia and beyond. Not content with just climbing, Menlove Edwards would row single-handedly across huge bodies of water often as a prelude to his climbing endeavours, once rowing over The Minch to the Isle of Harris in 28 hours. It helped that he was an obsessive genius with a superhuman strength.

The eccentricity of the climbers captured our imagination. As a treatment for frostbite, the Victorian Lake District climber Owen Glynne Jones allegedly plunged his hands into a vat of boiling glue, permanently deforming one hand into a clawed shape, which he later claimed was a beneficial climbing asset. In 1927, Ivan Waller made the first ascent of a famous rock climbing route on the mountain Tryfan in North Wales which became known as Belle Vue Bastion, taking a wind-up gramophone to the base of the route, as he favoured some musical accompaniment.

A favourite vintage day out was a compendium of routes known as 'Avalanche, Red Wall and Longland's Continuation', put up by J. L. Longland in 1929, on the Eastern Buttress of a crag called Y-Lliwedd, which forms part of the Snowdon Massif in North Wales. These routes were strung together in a vertical chain on the massive alpine face of Y-Lliwedd, whose top forms part of the famous walk known as the Snowdon Horseshoe. It was one of only a few routes in Britain which could truly be described as Alpine in nature and scale, involving a sheer 1100-foot vertical climb on the rock face.

Remembering this route, my eye glides to the current Snowdonia rock-climbing guide on a nearby bookshelf. As I leaf through it, the modern guide it warns that it is on 'Avalanche, Red Wall and Longland's Continuation' that 'The consequences of being caught out by the elements can quickly reach epic proportions.' I concur, as the photograph of the rock face brings back a specific day in my mind's eye in glorious technicolour.

On just about the shortest day of the year, 12 December 1986, my climbing companions and I set out late, walking along the Miners' Track from Pen-y-Pass, and arrived at the base of the crag at around 10.30 a.m. On reflection, I am not convinced that we correctly located the start of the climb. Once on the rock, we immediately lost the route, drifting onto much more technically difficult ground than we had expected. The route is now graded Severe (actually a relatively easy climbing grade), but we soon found ourselves clawing our way up a morass of vertical vegetation and extremely loose rock graded Very Severe or Hard Very Severe which was (as it sounds) hard.

As we were roped up, with my partner acting as lead climber, our escape plan was to find a series of anchor points and abseil off the crag if it all became too much. It did, but with so much loose rock around, abseiling was not an option, and we were forced to continue onwards and upwards, further and further out of our comfort zone. It looked like the crag had not been visited by climbers since Mallory's time, and the occasional, solid belay points, fixed pitons and iron pegs that we were expecting, as described in the historical accounts, were no longer there.

Around 4 p.m., as it went dark, we made it onto a grassy, horizontal terrace, where we thought we might have to spend the night. The light was fading fast, the sky had turned an ominous yellow-grey colour and it had begun to snow. Wet, heavy snow flakes muffled any sound. Before it went dark, I caught sight of some Welsh mountain goats, which I could just make out as dark spots with horns on a neighbouring crag. They looked much more at home than us in their vertical world, chewing calmly on vegetation and bedding down for the night.

In our favour, we were young, fit and strong, and in the preceding few years had been doing an awful lot of climbing. Despite our naivety, initial poor decisions and late start, we were well equipped with plenty of food, drink, warm clothing and bivvy sacks, and crucially we had Petzl head torches, then a relative novelty.

It was in the days before the mobile phone. Nobody knew where we were and in any case, out of pride and shame, we definitely did not want to be rescued. At the very worst we would have a cold, but survivable night and would finish our climb the next day.

After a mini conference, we made the decision to try and climb the last 200 feet in the dark. Small circles of yellow light from our head torches pointed up tiny hand and foot holds buried in the slush, vegetation and loose vertical rock. The snow froze, remelted and froze again on the outside of my Helly Hansen furry jacket and salopettes into a makeshift suit of armour which trapped the air and was surprisingly warm.

After an eternity, we dragged ourselves up and up and eventually onto the Snowdon Horseshoe path. Later that evening, we met up with our North Welsh friends in Deiniolen whom we regarded as proper climbers, with respectable Alpine credentials. Windswept and freaked out, we confessed to them where we had been. They were aghast. 'Nobody climbs there now!' they exclaimed. That much we had come to know. Feeling that we had just climbed the north face of the Eiger, we slugged back too much homebrew to blot out the memory of the day.

Anyway, an hour or two is whiled away shamelessly in the bookshop, looking at Peak District and North Wales rock climbing guides and remembering past triumphs and errors of judgement.

As I walk back through the streets of Manchester towards Oxford Road Station to catch the train home, I ask myself if I have really learned anything useful from past caving and climbing exploits? I decide that there are no real earth-shattering answers. Sometimes things have gone well, sometimes not so well. Usually I know why. The question pre-supposes that there is some great sum total of experience or magical formula that automatically translates directly into progress or betterment. I find that this is sometimes, but not always the case. That is not to say that there isn't good sense in preparing for and being disciplined about any intended activity: going down a cave, up a climb or trying your luck in the boxing ring. But the outcome is never guaranteed, and I conclude that the best thing of all is just to get on with it and enjoy it while you can.

18

UNLUCKY FOR SOME

I have two medium-weight boxing bags set up in a stone outbuilding at home (Jack Dempsey-style). One is surplus to requirements and one Thursday night, I take it to Kelly's gym for Jamie's protégé, Frank. I am unthinking as I wrestle the bag out of the outbuilding at home and into the car. There is a telltale twinge in my lower back. Aargh! is followed by another Aargh! I then spend what I think is a productive hour moving round the boxing ring, shadow boxing and stretching, as the endorphins conveniently drown out anything nasty, for the time being.

On the route home, at Long Preston village there appears to be a cat, lying stationary in the middle of the dark road. Other drivers are passing around it, either not bothered or assuming it to be already dead. I have a really good look as I pass by. The cat is very much alive, in an awkward sitting-up position, but not moving and appears to have been hit by a car. I pull over as a passer-by telephones the vet's emergency number in Settle, which is ten minutes' drive away. We bundle the cat as gently as we can into my car, and I rush to the vets at top speed. I am delighted to find out the following morning that it (actually he) has survived the night. He owes his life to the late night attentions of the on call vet, Kirsty.

Friday is not a good day at the outset, and only gets worse. I find I have ricked my back good and proper, and head out fairly late in the evening for a walk along the Occupation Road at the head of Kingsdale to try and loosen up. This is an old drover's track running parallel to southern Dentdale and is an open gateway into the high and lonely fells of Gragareth and Great Coum. Its name refers to the time when the land was enclosed by walls or 'occupied' in the late eighteenth century. It is the domain of the plover and lark, where the wind never drops. There are impressive views of Rise Hill and the Howgill Fells to the north. Rise Hill wins my prize for The Most Boring Hill in The Entire World, as it has the most concentric contours on the map of any hill I have ever seen.

The summer colours are fading and greyish browns are fast replacing the green rushes and sedges. A small herd of dappled fell ponies is silhouetted against the parasol-pink sunset. There is a striking harvest moon low in the sky, and I find that the gentle walking has improved my idiotic, self-imposed back problem. For the moment all seems right in the world.

Life turns on a sixpence, and when I get home at around 9 p.m. I discover that my aged cat Penny is not at all well. Her arthritis has suddenly and dramatically worsened, and it looks as if she cannot move her back legs. I ring the vet for the second time within two days. My cat is clearly in some pain and difficulty and I arrange to meet Kirsty at the local veterinary surgery at 10.30 p.m.

After the trials of the last few weeks and months it is clear that my cat's suffering cannot be relieved, and the vet and I both agree that euthanasia is the kindest and best thing. She is a delightful cat who was fortunate enough to have known only love, something we humans cannot always claim. Although I am a bit tearful, her peaceful demise is also a blessed relief.

With a kind attempt at black humour, Kirsty says: 'I'm on call again tomorrow night. Please don't bring me another cat.' As I exit the building I promise I won't.

The next day, feeling tired and emotional, I bury my cat alongside all the other ex-cats in what I regard as the family plot, which is the quiet edge of the long field next to our house. I am totally resigned to events as I finish washing the soil off the spade and head out to Kelly's gym for an hour of perfect distraction, wishing my back problem away.

Later that evening, feeling like I have totally earned it, I slouch on the sofa in front of the TV with a massive bowl of spag bol. I am also helpfully distracted by the TV, watching a mesmerising set by The Libertines at the 2015 Reading Festival. The band landed direct from their own planet as a peculiarly British noughties indie/punk outfit that had their fair share of troubles. I realise that I cannot imagine them rehearsing at all, as the music just pours out of them with a faultless naturalism – all crazy rhythms, unexpected riffs and witty music hall lyrics.

The two charismatic front men, Pete Doherty, forever on his way down but never quite reaching the bottom, and the Jim-Morrison-like Carl Barât, unaware of their own brilliance, do not even appear to be trying. Only the drummer seems to be present in the moment, healthily stressed and aware that he is actually playing to a paying crowd.

I have read in the media that, at a particular low point, Doherty apparently broke into Barât's London flat, stealing some of his possessions to buy heroin. Amazingly they pulled their friendship back from the brink and went on to create sublime and original music. Pete Doherty manages to wear his heart on his sleeve without embarrassing British sentiment too much.

⊙

Well, my back is still complaining a bit, as I take to Kelly's gym again on an autumnal Wednesday in early September 2015. I am not really pushing the limits but just trying to move. Saturday teatime brings on more of the same, and as I jab, duck, step to the side, BREATHE and jab again, I feel like a duck bobbing on choppy waters, but the feet are no longer paddling manically under the surface. I repeat the same with the straight right, and throw a few left hooks to boot. One or two ring out nicely, as I compare my boxing stance with that of two MMA fighters, who are weightlifting in the same room.

I ask them if they think that MMA fighting is a bonkers enterprise. They say 'no', but their bashed-in faces tell a different story. They have a much more open stance, as they have to turn and kick. I am a novice pianist, whereas they are already thudding out on the organ foot pedals. We discuss which groups of athletes are the greatest of our age. In no particular order we plump for Tour de France cyclists, Olympic wrestlers and boxers, but we decide that dancers and prima ballerinas, who are as tough as old boots, trump the rest.

YEAR THREE

YEAR THREE

19

GETTING THE HANG OF IT

Who will appear out of the woodwork on the first Wednesday of the new boxing term? It is mid-September 2015, and Dai is not there, and I find out that he is not scheduled to appear again until the following Monday. We are all just a little bit relieved about this, after the inevitable slacking over the summer. Peter is absent, which means we do not really have a quorum, but those that do appear are Mark and James, the two brothers, and Bob, diffident and quiet. Mark and James confess to a massive Sunday afternoon drinking session from which they are still recovering. I am not against drink and remember its uses, but I'm now boringly teetotal as I can no longer take it.

I slip into the boxing store just off the main gym, with its familiar musty smells: my favoured orange skipping rope is still there, and better still someone has repaired it. I grab it and skip effortlessly for a good ten minutes. The Board of Death is propped up benignly in the corner of the boxing store, but, as sure as the sun rises and sets, it will come alive next week.

As we start the bag rounds, Mark and James comment that my technique has improved, which it has. Mark puts on a body protector, and tries to teach me a shovel hook/liver shot, which is basically a cross between a hook and an uppercut. I try a corkscrew body twist and try to angle my glove upwards and at 45 degrees. It does not work. Among other things my knuckles (and therefore everything else) are in the wrong place.

Mark takes my best fatal liver shot under the ribs as if I have tickled him with a feather duster. This is a bit dispiriting, as it is the supposed to be a knuckle duster shot which has him rolling on the floor and out for the count. The truth is that I cannot manage any fancy hybrid variations on the hook, as I have not yet mastered the simplest versions of the shot. My sessions with Jamie have confirmed what I already know – that I do not learn anything quickly.

I go right back to basics on the bag, not pushing it fitness-wise, but just stepping forward and back throwing a steady 1-2 in and then out of punching range. Then I try a few more hooks. They sound and feel better as I get much more of a throwing action. It is great to stand at a proper heavy bag once more, as I decide that others have been too lightweight. James is throwing some great shots, but his body seems to hardly move at all at the other heavy bag. It is an education watching him, as he effortlessly wrangles every atom of power from everywhere and concentrates it into his shot, without telegraphing his intentions. However, I notice when he is sparring with Mark he is wasting huge amounts of energy by just leaping about.

Bob looms round the hook bag to my left like a silent jungle animal stalking an invisible prey. Bob is quietly confident. He is in relatively poor shape in terms of fitness but is every inch a boxer. He moves really well without actually appearing to move. Despite the impressiveness of Mark and James's shots,

I think that Bob would be a much more formidable opponent, with his steady, relentlessness, considered shots and calm economy of movement. Moreover, he has a totally solid and consistent jab, and great timing. It is half-past eight already, and as is nearly always the case we lack the time for the stretching that we really ought to do. We therefore probably suffer irreparable damage, which none of us cares about, and saunter out stiffly out into the cool night, bidding each other goodnight.

It is Monday night and the proper start of the boxing term. Dai looks a bit wasted and I worry that another drinking session has taken its toll. We laugh about his birthday party, but he confesses that he cannot remember most of it, even after three full days' recovery time. Although we laugh, there is an acknowledgement that the jungle juice will have to be ditched, otherwise Dai's liver will expire not from a nifty boxing shot but from third-degree pickling.

Peter is not there, and Dai and I surmise that he must be seriously ill or worse as he has never once missed a session in two years. A very slight, young Chinese woman, Kam, appears for the first time, demonstrating exactly what it is to be a super-efficient kickboxer. We marvel at the volley of thrown legs as well as arms on the heavy bag. A tall rangy lad, who is a bit shy, is also new. He huffs and puffs but stays the course. As we race round the gym, I note that I am not as fit as I was and the eight rounds on the bags interspersed with step-ups and various jumps and jerks on the benches seem like quite an effort. At the end of the session I am anxious to show Dai my new improved shots. Like a child vainly attempting a magic trick, I fumble around for my best jab as he holds up the pads. Dai immediately says that it is much, much more solid, but then the inevitable fly in the ointment … I am still too tense and too slow.

The following Wednesday, after the usual skipping and jumping, Dai holds the pads up for me again and again. I move in, throw a 1-2, and then rush backwards at the speed of light, in and out of Dai's punch zone. Dai manages to hit me in the face about three times, but remarks that I am moving much better. I have concentrated so much on the jab over the last year that my straight right is no longer so good. I am losing my stance again and again, as I transition between the jab and straight right, stepping and leaning forward as I throw the right, and not turning in my right foot enough.

In a further training session at Kelly's gym, Jamie simplifies everything – telling me not to bother about extending the left hand, but snapping and turning in my left shoulder as fast as I can, while snapping back the right. This is the most basic stuff and I am still getting it wrong – just as I think I have perfected new shots, cracks appear in the old ones. I see for the first time that boxing is really like tending a car, with routine maintenance required to keep the boxing repertoire oiled and functional.

Jamie tries a new and apparently simple tack. For the last fifteen minutes of the session he says he will give me no technical direction whatsoever, but just call the shots on the pads and ask me to throw a long sequence in the most naturalistic way that I can. This is an experiment to see what kind of impulse takes over, if any.

This is different from all the usual neurotic, microanalysis of every shot. The boxing equivalent of method acting must take over where the heart rules the head and the body rules the mind. I secretly think that this may also be designed as a test of stamina, as Jamie calls the first of a sequence of shots – jab, right; double jab, right; jab; jab; 1-2,3-4, left hook;1-2;1-2;

double jab, right; 1-2, left hook; and so it goes on … and on … and on.

To my amazement, I do really start to relax as shots slap on the pads. A stuttering engine is called into rhythm. There is a definite kind of swing and sway in the hips and shoulders. There are obvious defensive weaknesses. My stance for the straight right is still far too square on and forward, so in a real boxing match I would be in trouble. I am also leaving the jab and right hand out in the same dangerous zone for too long. Nonetheless, I am getting momentum (and therefore power) into the shots quite effortlessly. This speeds everything up, including the snap back in the shots.

Jamie throws a straight right. At first I hesitate, but then duck under it swiftly, step right and throw a right of my own. He throws it again – I duck and respond with a jab; then he throws it again, and I duck straight down without the right-ward step and throw a right. These different responses feel quite intuitive. There is a temporary halt, when Jamie calls a right uppercut, as I have never really been taught how to throw one, but apart from this my shots come thick and fast. The left hook that I have struggled with over the last few months is starting to take shape, and I am managing to deliver it quickly in among the other shots, with its proper whipping action.

As I throw shot after shot after shot, I notice that Jamie has a widening smile. The shots are not technically correct, but this might indeed be boxing, transmuted into my own peculiar style, for the very first time. I can see that Jamie is really pleased, as we have both witnessed something that neither of us thought I could ever do.

As usual, my half-hour session has been generously extended beyond the allotted time. Jamie finishes with some prophetic words: 'Just remember – not every shot can be perfect. In most boxing matches most boxers throw mostly imperfect shots. You cannot consider each of these at the time – you just have to get the next shot out as best you can. Perfection is the enemy, and the art of the possible is king.'

I knew it all along.

20

FAMILY VALUES

My elderly Aunt Marion, who lives in Broughty Ferry, near Dundee, has suddenly become much more frail and needs me by her side. On the journey up to Scotland I make a point of listening to the latest pop music that BBC Radio 6 Music has to offer. This entire radio station attempts to substitute for the musical engine house that was the late, great John Peel.

Over the previous four decades, John Peel's evening radio slot showcased the music of several generations of youth in an unpretentious and non-silly way, championing various musical genres. The rise of indie music in the 1980s, brought the cost of pressing vinyl within the grasp of many embryonic, aspiring bands, as small independent record companies sprang up everywhere. In the late 1970s and early 1980s it seemed like every teenage band in the land would put together a demo tape, package it up in a Jiffy bag, marking it for John's attention and praying for it to be played on his show. A record deal would often follow if there were sufficient interest generated. I remember several such packages being passed round the school bus with pride before being posted off to John. Each offering was accompanied by a moody promo photo.

John Peel became an unwitting king of cool – critical, but never negative. It is true that some of the records he played sounded like dustbin lids being banged together. These he merely described as 'interesting'. Various gems and iconic bands were unearthed, for example The Fall, fronted by the late Mark E. Smith, whose unique artistic vision was totally championed by John Peel.

Mark E. Smith was a unique Manchester poet and singer who set his drawled, half-mumbled, half-swallowed alcoholic words to music. Mark E. Smith hired and fired at will, with over sixty members of The Fall coming and going over the years according to his whim. Mark was an avowed enemy of healthy eating, or indeed of healthy anything. He was famous for allegedly firing a band member for eating a salad sandwich.

He was a notoriously difficult man to interview, as he was by turns deliberately taciturn, hateful, drunk or dismissive, but somehow John managed it, because Mark knew that he and his barbed wit were truly loved. In Mark E. Smith's last gig, which was televised, he appears defiant, his body wasted by cancer, unapologetically propped up in a wheelchair. As always, Mark continues heroically spewing and 'wowling' out his poetry to the very end.

Courtesy of John Peel, the Northern Irish band The Undertones also came to the fore with their hit 'Teenage Kicks', reputedly John's favourite song of all time, which also made him cry. The song tells of a tragic teenage love affair and it became a national anthem for doomed youth. John Peel singlehandedly galvanised and harnessed what is now officially known by sociologists as 'Bedroom Culture', celebrating popular music which was conceived and produced in teenage bedrooms across the land and elevating it into a recognisable and respected art form.

Perhaps it is just age on my part, but the modern stuff on BBC Radio 6 Music seems overproduced, derivative and lacking in verve. Radio 1 is a travesty. Radio 2 is not much better. The up-and-coming artists sound like less-polished versions of what is surely to come, and few bands have an identifiable style. Lack of money prohibits the emergence of music from the ground up. Musical pap gets blurted out on most other radio channels. Bands do not understand their place in history because they have none. This so-called music industry is mostly cash and tax driven.

I plonk myself at the very pleasant Hotel Broughty Ferry for the Saturday night. My aunt tires very easily, so I plan to see her for a couple of hours in the middle of Sunday. The hotel is very clean, the staff are friendly and the clientele appear to be mainly golfers and retirees, substantially divorced from real life.

The empty gym in the basement of the hotel beckons, but Jamie's recent training session has totally finished me off, and feeling like I have been put on a rack I soak in a very hot bath and retire to bed, undisturbed by the traffic noise, the heat in the room and Saturday night revellers who holler in mangled Scottish accents in the street below. Every few minutes the room turns red, orange and green from the dim glow of the traffic lights in the street below, but nothing stops me from twelve hours of uninterrupted sleep.

Early on Sunday morning, I take a slow walk along the beach at the side of the Tay Estuary, staring out at the green-grey sea then sipping coffee, bought from a mock art-nouveau café caged in glass on the sea front. It would be heaven, except for the tiredness that I feel from the long journey and various recent slightly inadvisable boxing activities.

My aunt is really delighted to see me and this alone makes everything right. I take her out on a shopping errand, manhandling her in and out of the car as gently as I can, her arthritic body as creaking and fragile as glass. We have the same conversation that we have had for fifty years. After a hearty meal and endless cups of tea, I take to the road, waving her goodbye, with both of us secretly wondering if this will be our last meeting, but never alluding to the fact.

21

EYE-WATERING SPEED

The art of the possible, and therefore also the impossible, is explored again in the following Monday night session with Dai. The muscles are recovered and ready for anything, but my back is giving me a bit of gip from too much Scottish driving, and I wonder if it will bear up.

Dai has set up a circuit of exercises around the gym on green laminated cards dropped onto the floor. The gym is set out for a cast of thousands, who never appear – in the end only James and I turn up. As we pick up the cards, Dai tries to hide his disappointment at the dwindling numbers, and we worry again about Peter's continued absence. Well, there is nothing to do except set up an imaginary ring in the middle of the gym, and do some sparring with Dai. This is what James and I like best, as it is a chance to hone our skills, and for Dai to showcase his.

Dai means business as he gets ready in the corner. I move to the opposite corner. I still have very few defensive skills and once again this excursion will be a test of boxing intuition. To start with, Dai does not wear any boxing gloves, but just holds the pads up in a sequence, and my make-do-and-mend punches do their best pitted against Dai's lightning speed. I have to throw a 1-2 or a 1-2-left hook, and then levitate backwards as fast as I can to avoid a clip round the ear with the pads. I manage pretty well, and as Dai speeds up I manage some very passable shots; my arms relax, and I feel the torque of the body really throwing the shots. We stop for a breather and Dai says, 'That's the best I've ever seen you box, Marianne.' Yes ... for once I do seem to be putting it all together in my head *somehow*.

Next, Dai spars with James. They are both very fast, but Dai's superior speed is apparent, as he tires James out with effortless little runs and side steps. I shout to James to step rather than jump round the ring as he is wasting precious energy. Dai is dominating the ring, standing resolutely in the middle, with James tiring as he whirls round and round the perimeter. Suddenly Dai pelts out his favourite signature shots, four jabs in very quick succession. James is not expecting this battery and is pushed back immediately onto the ropes, but he recovers enough to parry Dai's jabs out of the way twice, and to deliver two really good jabs of his own.

Then it is my turn again. Dai attempts and succeeds in looking slightly menacing as he jumps up and down with mock impatience in a southpaw stance in the corner of the ring, but as soon as the bell rings, he changes to an orthodox stance – a nice little trick to confuse your opponent, I think. This is overkill, as I am confused anyway from the off. Dai is on my side, but he also means business, saying that he will get me on the ropes as he moves forward. I deploy my best 'Dunn family' look and say that I am having none of it.

I throw my best jab and right hand, but fail to get out of his punch zone quickly enough, and my gloved hands in front of my face take a battering. I step back and redouble my efforts. Then I duck down and deliver some good body shots, but as soon as I stand up Dai is on my case again. I am just not fast enough. I decide to stand up again, and try to push him back with a 1-2, 1-2 sequence, but know that if I try this I may well take a hit. I stand up and move forward, and just for a second I push him back.

I am too square on and take a few body punches. Then Dai begins his assault. I am ducking down, almost rooted to the spot, hands up and taking a battering again, and unable to think. I feel that I do not have any strategy for escape, as every option appears theoretical. Rather bizarrely, Dai shouts instructions to me throughout the steady thud, thud volley of his own shots: 'MARIANNE! PARRY MY JAB OUT OF THE WAY – THEN DELIVER YOUR JAB!'

We stop for a moment as Dai shows me the parry manoeuvre, again. I have tried this before and mostly failed. The secret is to watch your opponent's hands like a hawk. The parry only works if you wait right until the last minute, when your opponent's gloved jab hand is almost on your chin, before shoving it away. This is quite unnerving, but if you attempt it any sooner, the wide sweep of your arm will expose your body as a target.

We start again and immediately I remember that this sequence of shots exposed a chink in Dai's armour in his previous round with James. I try my very hardest as I wait, wait, wait for Dai's jab. Sure enough, it arrives on cue. As I shove it out of the way, I almost simultaneously deliver a perfect, hard jab to Dai's chin. I do this twice to good effect. James shouts encouragement – they are two really good shots – and I notice that a small crowd of bespectacled kids has gathered at the side of the ring: they start to clap furiously.

However, there is pride only before a fall, and after a minute's rest Dai and I take to the floor again for more of the same in a second, third and fourth round. In the fourth round I am definitely tiring as I make one final attempt to push Dai into the corner. I fail to catch him at all, but I stand up to full height, determined not to be beaten. Once again, I am too square on, but as I try to launch another jab Dai gets me full in the left eye with a stinging jab.

He does not really mean to do this, and it is not that hard a punch, but my eye is wide open, as I am trying to eyeball him and second guess his moves, so it hurts like hell. I double up in pain for at least ten seconds. If this were a real boxing match, I think, this would be a humiliating standing count.

But it is also hilarious, and Dai, James and I are suddenly gripped by a bout of hysterical laughter. Dai comes over and gives me a hug, saying: 'I'm so sorry, Marianne – I really didn't mean to do that!' I know that he didn't, but this just makes it all the funnier. Dai can hardly get the words out for laughing. I can hardly reply, as I am simultaneously wracked by side-splitting laughter and pain. I can feel my eye bruising and swelling. Dai peers at me with a small amount of his own eye-squinting concern and says, 'It looks like your eye is closing.' 'Yes,' I agree, as my eye closes.

The following morning, I notice that I also have a cut lip. I think of the words of my previous coach Gerard, who was fond of telling us all how he remained so 'beautiful' after enduring sixty-eight amateur boxing matches. 'The reason that I am so beautiful ... the reason that I have kept my youthful good looks ... the only reason ... is that I am a good defensive boxer.' I reflect now that beauty is not on my side.

⊙

The following Wednesday I arrive early in the evening, while Dai is still training the youth boxers. He grimaces at me from the inside of the gym, through the small internal window, and points to my eye, which is a delicate shade of black. I give him the thumbs up sign and we laugh, but in reality my eye is still sore from the clout I received on Monday.

I do not know this but this session will be really hard as Dai tries to lick us into shape after the summer recess. The tall, rangy lad appears again, and also a slim boxer, Calum, whom we have not seen before. Dai recognises Calum, who has clearly been a boxer in past times.

Calum irritates us a bit by assuming the role of secondary coach and pointing out our mistakes. Calum also tell us for nothing that he has boxed for Britain. He may have done, but somehow we doubt it as the 'bullsh—t bell' starts to ring and ring. Unfortunately, over the months and years, we have seen a small procession of irritating, macho men claiming this and that but never quite staying the course, and we are naturally suspicious of them.

I have to say that Radio 3 listeners and teachers are the very worst, as the size of their egos generally outstrips any skill. They are also very hard to box simply because they cannot box, and annoyingly they often assume the role of self-appointed coach.

James – who is actually a really good boxer – catches my eye as Calum gives him unwanted instructions, and we both pull a face and giggle out of sight. The truth is that we are all sufficiently experienced to know what we are doing wrong:

putting it right is the difficult part.

Dai takes no prisoners as we warm up by skipping for ten minutes, and the heat soars in the gym. Then it is six two-and-a-half-minute rounds on the bags, interspersed with bench exercises of various types – press-ups, 'mountain-climbing' in a press-up position, step-ups and step-downs, pike jumps and tuck jumps. We have a minute's rest after each round. This is really exhausting and there is no doubt that all of us are struggling a bit.

Dai growls: 'You are all making this look *hard*!' I certainly am. I have a sneaky ten-second rest, and Dai immediately adds an extra minute onto my rounds. My legs burn and burn. Then it is the same in minute rounds. All technique goes out of the window, as I just totally focus, focus and focus, trying to stay punching the bag without actually stopping. Next we plummet to the ground with a series of dips, tucks and stomach exercises, then against the wall in a mock-sitting position until we can take it no more. I manage two minutes of this torture before my legs shake and buckle. Perhaps Dai is secretly training us for the SAS.

We finish in silence, as there is no energy left to speak, and then slowly regain our composure. I survey the various pools of sweat which have flooded onto the dusty, gym floor. High as kite, the endorphins shunting round the system, I wonder if I will be able to sleep that night. My fears are unfounded, as I watch the ten o'clock news from the safety of the sofa. This is the last thing I remember, as I wake up at 7.30 a.m. the following morning, totally knackered and fully clothed. Tigger is fast asleep at my shoulder. I make a race for the shower and a double-shot coffee as my cat looks miffed.

22

THE HAPPIEST DAYS OF MY LIFE

The following weekend I have a proper rest in which I feel fully justified. On the Saturday, I attend my secondary school reunion at Bolton School, which is celebrating a significant anniversary. The school has a grand building, erected in 1924, funded by the Lever family – a set of philanthropists to whom I am ever indebted. They believed that girls were individuals entitled to an education. The school is imposing and square cut, built out of Pennine millstone grit, and lies in pleasant woodland on Chorley New Road on the outskirts of Bolton.

I have not been back for five years, and the first thing I notice is the plethora of black iron gates and fences which now surround its perimeter. When I was a pupil there, almost forty years earlier, the school grounds and woodlands opened out right onto the street. It was possible to go directly from a den you had built in the woods to the local corner shop without being missed, but now a proper plan of escape would be required.

New, artsy buildings have been constructed and the large stretch of open, grassy ground, known as 'The Levels', which was used as a sports field, has diminished in size. The Levels were the main location for burgeoning romance, as this was the only common ground shared with the boys' school built in a mirror image next door. The Levels were patrolled by spinster teachers, wreathed in tweed, who all seemed to have been to Girton College, Cambridge and knew nothing of the opposite sex (or indeed of any sex).

In the 1970s, the matriarchal headmistress who presided over us all was the towering five-foot-nothing-with-her-arms-up figure of Miss Margaret Higginson, a.k.a. 'Hig'. She was a dyed-in-the-wool suffragette with genuine credentials, who understood the benefits of stout boots and a diet of mashed potato, and who slightly pitied men.

We were terrified of her, but yet she also had our respect. Her message to us was simple: you can do anything you like, but along with the privilege of a good education (which we were assured we were getting) went duty and responsibility. It is easy to see those schooldays through rose-coloured spectacles, but the mantra of social responsibility that was preached ran deep, and much of the charitable work that was encouraged was undertaken simply because it was the right thing to do, and not merely to adorn a thin CV.

Long after she retired, Hig continued to be a practical support and benign influence on thousands of 'grown-up' girls. After I left university jobs were scarce, and I spent five soul-destroying months on the dole. Although I must have been a single face in thousands, Hig was the only person who offered practical help, suggesting a number of sensible contacts who could help me find a job. Another ex-pupil aged only twenty went deaf overnight due to a stroke, and suffered with terrible depression. Even though Hig was in her late seventies by then she was there like a shot, immediately on the scene, taking her for days out to boost her mood and offering practical help.

☉

On reunion day I meet my old contemporaries in a new classroom, which we do not recognise. I am struck by both how similar and how different each person looks. We catch up on news and have a laugh. Our lives and career paths are picked over. Veronica says that my mannerisms are just the same and as quirky as when I was at school. This is funny as I am not aware of having any mannerisms.

Quiet, thoughtful and bound to religion, Veronica is employed as a Church of England school educator in Cornwall. She damns modern society and blames Thatcherism – as I do – for the death of social responsibility, perhaps seeming pious, but not meaning to.

Cecilia runs a one-woman hedgehog rescue society somewhere near Hereford, and Barbara declares that she is unhappy, as a lawyer's wife marooned in the south-east of England, burdened by too much convention and incessant childcare duties. She was an intellectual tour de force bound for Cambridge University and set apart from all of us by her massive machine of a brain. Now she battles suburban boredom, escaping into books and solitary walks.

We remember our hilarious sex education lessons, which were initially taught only in science in relation to frogs by Miss Curzon. She talked at a very high embarrassed speed while fiddling with a pen and staring out of a laboratory window. My dear friend Marjory Tasker would delight in asking her the most awkward questions.

Later on, Mrs Clatterbridge, a woman of some importance, advised us never to marry a cyclist as his wedding tackle might be severely compromised by too much cycling. Despite these faltering starts, we discover that our contemporary Stella has become a sex therapist, a career path as unimaginably un-British as could be imagined. We shrink back and prostrate ourselves before her in awe, as it is something-that-we-could-never-do.

We also remember our old music teacher Miss Fott, who certainly seemed to us at the time to be mad and certifiable. She had a loud whooping voice. Someone recalls that she was confined only to a single downstairs classroom like a wild beast chained in a cellar.

Old classmates Ellen and Alma have a proper family day out, as they have their ancient dad with them, an old boy at the school, and also their sons and daughters who are present as current pupils. Although exhausted, Dad rightly refuses to go home as he is having such a good time. Most touching of all is our old classmate Jenny, a larger-than-life character who has recently split up from her partner. Jenny is bravely on course to adopt two children, while caring also for her ninety-year-old mother who lives next door.

The light falls as I say goodbye to my companions and I race round my old school for a final time, drinking in the unique, slightly gaseous smell of the science laboratories corridor. The gymnasium, which seemed huge and Dickensian in the past, is small and ancient now. I almost hear the terrifying clickety-clack of the heels of Miss Evangelista along the parquet corridor floor, as she swept from the smoke-filled staffroom into classroom B9 to teach us mathematical mysteries to no real good effect. I creep through the woods alongside the old rounders pitch and past various long-gone woodland dens, then navigate fences and security gates in the darkness back to my car.

After the excitement of Saturday, Sunday is whiled away with various tedious domestic tasks. I finally make it out of the door in the safety of relative darkness and head out to the tiny hamlet of Halton Gill at the head of Littondale. I cycle up the hill towards the southerly watershed Dale Head, expecting no one about, pedalling like mad and humming a tune. A dramatic blood moon illuminates a lone green campervan at the edge of a field close to the snaking road, producing a striking space-ship effect. The van appears luminous in the dark grey foggy atmosphere, framed by a few surprised looking sheep. By the time I turn the bike downhill the blackness obscures the way ahead, my puny torch making little impact. I make it back to the car without incident, as the homely, yellow lights of Halton Gill twinkle and twinkle.

23

GOOD AND BAD

On Monday night, Peter is absent again, and worryingly Dai says that he has called round to his house and got no reply. It is a mellow, late summer evening, and the good weather has tempted away all but a few boxing inmates. Thankfully, Mr Cocky-know-it-all has not reappeared, as I predicted. Only James, a new lad and myself are towed along in Dai's wake. Wales have beaten England at rugby over the weekend which allows comment from Dai, mainly in the form of a ska-inspired dance of triumph for a moment or two.

Henry, a new recruit, also appears. He has passed the first two selection procedures for joining the paratroopers and wants some intensive boxing training from Dai. This is to help him pass a boxing assessment which will form part of his army training. Henry is fit, has a very positive attitude, and we all agree that he is quite a natural puncher. Still, Dai will have his work cut out trying to embed the boxing basics in only a month or two. Rather embarrassingly, without even really trying, I burn Henry off in the gym, and his attempts at the Board of Death are almost as pathetic as mine. Dai growls at him, saying how he will be trashed in the paras, but I am not so sure. A woman at my workplace whose son is a Royal Marine says that the paras are regarded as wimps, so perhaps I should submit my application form.

In the gym we discuss a television programme where hapless members of the public have volunteered for SAS-type training. This mainly involves harsh physical activity, being shouted at by Russian soldiers and occasionally downing shots of vodka. The gear that they are supplied with looks terrible, as their camouflaged clothing turns into a heavy sodden mass of wet canvas at the slightest suggestion of rain. This self-selecting group are tough, deluded and willing to push themselves into physical and mental zones so exacting that they could never simultaneously fight a battle. If we must go to war at all, I can't help thinking that there must be a more intelligent way of training soldiers.

I remember reading a vivid and disturbing account of the training endured by the Apollo mission astronauts in the US in the 1960s, some of whom went to the moon. There was no model for training astronauts as they had never previously existed. In lieu of anything else they were brutally trained like the US special forces. This daft strategy was completely unnecessary as these men were mostly test pilots or scientists, thoughtful, resourceful, obsessive types, already perfect for the job.

Apparently Buzz Aldrin, who became the second man to walk on the moon, was terrible company at any party as he wanted to talk only about spacecraft rendezvous. Gordon Cooper was sufficiently chilled out to actually fall asleep at the controls of his spacecraft during launch. Neil Armstrong was to be found coolly shuffling papers in his office only minutes after ejecting from a crashed and exploded mock-up of the *Apollo 11* Lunar Lander spacecraft, which had been nicknamed 'The Flying Bedstead'. Even during the stress of lunar launches, astronaut John Young's heart rate famously never went above 70 beats per minute. As he sat atop the mighty *Saturn V* rocket, he quipped laconically in Texan drawl: 'I told 'em my heart was too old to go any faster.'

Some of these men had tremendous difficulty returning to any kind of normal life after going to the moon, the enormity of what they had seen and done, plus the media attention, was just too overwhelming. Some became religious, seeing Earth for the first time as a whole, fragile entity which needed protection, mainly from its human population. They saw the futility of human conflict in the widest possible perspective, but could do nothing to prevent it.

Only Buzz Aldrin's father seemingly put things into perspective. He was unimpressed, and allegedly gave the following fatherly advice: now that Buzz had gotten all of this 'moon business' out of the way, he had better start looking for a 'proper job', which Buzz interpreted as meaning a doctor, lawyer or accountant.

⊙

Meanwhile, back on terra firma, we skip and sprint, then endure another punishing fitness session with six two-and-a-half-minute rounds on the bags punctuated with two minutes of step ups, press-ups, pike jumps and tuck jumps, and a round on the pads. My jumping capabilities are severely tested. Then one-minute rounds, with the same, again and again and again. I am cross because I am making daft mistakes, largely due to tiredness. Old demons suddenly reappear, the hands dropping and the boxing stance too square on. Aargh! Aargh! and treble Aargh!

I make it home, looking forward very much to reading Morrissey's new novel *List of the Lost*, recently published by Penguin either as an expression of faith, hope and charity or as a cynical marketing ploy. He really can write, and I am all agog for an imaginative masterpiece, bristling with witty, Wildean epithets which stick two fingers up at the Establishment. After all, apparently Morrissey did once say, 'To see a man buying strip plywood in a mall on Sunday is to look directly into the eyes of human suffering.'

The book is a surprise and this is the best thing about it, but it reads as a long, genuinely tragic, drawn out suicide note. It is a thinly disguised autobiography, in which character, plot and narrative are all desperate but not defective. Embedded in the text are tiny shining diamonds of brilliant writing.

Wrongly, the book gets terrible reviews, because none of the critics understand that it is a modern day fable. I think that each character in the book represents aspects of the protagonist's troubled psyche, rather like the characters in Wagner's *Ring*. It reeks of awkwardness and hubris, and so within a day of publication the prurient press makes sure that it is in the front-running for the Bad Sex in Fiction Award. Morrissey is a clever writer, fond of allegory, and my guess is that he has deliberately written certain cringe-making scenes in an excruciating style to evoke pity and revulsion, which they do.

One review says that it is like the literature of William Burroughs, but without the anodyne effect of heroin: this is a totally fair assessment. Like the critics, Morrissey is beyond help, but his book is totally original and deserves to be published on grounds of originality alone. As I close the covers with a feverish sigh, I weep for Morrissey's mental health and, right on cue, a searing toothache starts.

⊙

As soon as can be imagined, it is Wednesday. Just when we all thought he had died, Peter suddenly returns, casually saying that he has been busy over the last few weeks and has been unable to attend the gym. We all think this odd, as he never, ever misses a session. In a quiet moment between boxing rounds, I ask him if everything really is alright, and he assures me that it is. I have to take him at his word, even though I secretly remain worried.

Two older teenage girls, Jackie and Jane, attend our session for the first time. Without any concessions to them, Dai puts us all through the mill, with skipping followed by six two-and-half-minute rounds on the bags and then six one-minute bag rounds interspersed with various bench exercises, finishing off with a quick session on the pads.

Having never boxed before, Jackie and Jane make a very valiant effort on the bags and pads, as Dai spends a good deal of time mumbling at them. I can see that they cannot make out a single word. Luckily, Dai also gives them a vivid version of his own one-act play, which demonstrates every conceivable boxing shot at lightning speed within about twenty seconds encapsulated in a sort of dance routine, so they sort of get some idea of what to do.

I try some hooks and uppercuts on the hook bag. Finally, it is the Guantanamo Bay prison torture positions which are supposed to strengthen the legs, and the calf raises, which leave me feeling as if I have had a stroke, but apart from this it all goes well. Fortunately, I am codeined up to the eyeballs because of my toothache.

At the end of the session, Peter and I have a serious discussion about hooks, and we compare angles and elbow heights and foot swivels, and decry standing too high on the toes.

Dai is off on holiday the following week, so while he is sunning himself in Spain listening to The Jam we are appropriately instructed to make our own entertainment.

⊙

Anxious still to improve my boxing stance and get some proper 1-2 swivel into my hips, after a frantic Saturday of cleaning I drive to Kelly's gym for an indulgent hour on the boxing bags. Win, a pleasant young woman, is also training and we compare our meagre boxing arsenal.

She has also been having some training with Jamie. She is me eighteen months ago. Her orthodox stance is all wrong. I think to myself that at least I can see what is awry. Her front left foot is far too straight, so she is really square on. The whole of her body is completely undefended – in the ring she would be no more than a target. Her hands are almost dropped to the floor, and there is no momentum built up in the shots, as her stance is all wrong. Her foot placement is also too linear so she has no stability. However, she is enthusiastic and determined, and after saying that she cannot skip, I give her a few tips, and she instantly looks better. The truth is I am only a tiny amount ahead of her in terms of technique, but the incremental differences translate into my shots being much more powerful and defensively superior.

The following Monday, Henry appears again. In terms of boxing accomplishment, he is me two years ago, and it is odd to find that I have actually learned something as I again pass on a few very basic hints and tips. If I can continue with these small improvements, perhaps I can make the odd quantum leap of my own.

Wednesday sees more of the same, as James tries to teach me uppercuts again for the umpteenth time. James's left elbow is almost at his hip bone as he swivels up suddenly high on his left foot and delivers a massive thump to the poor old hook bag. I try and reproduce this, with some difficulty. I discover that my hand has to be exactly vertical with the palm facing my face or it will not work. The slightest deviation seems to cause a reduction in power, and I sort of get it.

⊙

A morning visit to the dentist has necessitated driving past the abattoir near Kelly's gym in broad daylight. This is even worse than in the dark, as I know that the killing is actually going on unseen as I drive helplessly past. There is a death wagon of unfortunate sheep at its gates. Whether I see it or not, and whether I approve or not, these animals will be needlessly dead by the time I drive past again in two hours' time. They will be killed in the presence of vets, professionals in animal welfare who, perversely, are supposed to represent their last line of defence.

That night I meet Frank, who is on his way out of the car park at the gym. He describes his latest boxing trick: this is a wide, looping hook, angled downwards at imaginary opponent's jawline. We agree that it is a thoroughly nasty shot, of which we both heartily approve, and cannot wait to add it to our miniature boxing repertoire.

Frank is very tall, whereas I am short, and the truth is that I cannot imagine angling a punch downwards on anyone – they would have to be unfeasibly short. I suppose it might come in handy if attacked by a street gang of dwarfs, or whatever politically correct term we are supposed to use now for people who are just very short. Once inside the gym, I skip for a frantic ten minutes, then take it all out on the boxing bag, trying a few hooks and beyond-range back stretches and so on until the gym closes and I am turfed out, which is probably just as well.

It is late when I get home, and although the sofa and the quiet company of Tigger beckons, I decide instead to drive out to a local vantage point in search of the northern lights. Living out in the sticks without the immediate dazzle of sodium streetlights, I can sometimes make them out. I go north towards Newby Head Pass, a lonely road junction, where all ways lead nowhere, and the only sign of life is a farm that sometimes sells cakes.

The night is so still and moonless that the sound of sheep chewing grass is deafening because I cannot see them. Looking south towards Skipton and Bradford there is the faint orange glow of a thousand streetlights, but on the opposite horizon a faint green glow, with shimmering splashes of pink, is the prize possession.

⊙

On Monday we are expecting Dai to put in an appearance at the gym, but his Spanish holiday is unexpectedly extended by bad weather and presumably cancelled flights. While he is still sipping sangria, we do our own thing, which in my case is The Board of Death. Peter is as always wedded to the boxing bags, but I notice that he is leaning too far forward, so for better or worse I point this out.

The following Wednesday sees Dai's return. I arrive early and help him out with the youth boxing session. The kids have so much energy and enthusiasm that it is almost impossible to get them to stand still even for a minute, let alone for me to give any useful instruction, but so what – we all run about madly for an hour and everyone enjoys themselves.

In the adult boxing session, we shy away, as without warning Dai exposes more flesh than is normally allowable to proudly show off his holiday sunburn. Unabashed, mildly jetlagged and probably hung over, he grouchily cracks the whip: eight rounds on the bags and pads are followed by another cycle of The Board of Death, from which there is no mental or physical escape. Jackie and Jane appear again, making a second heroic effort.

There is good and bad in the boxing ether. I drop my hands and get a clip round the ear from Dai, but I also throw a couple of miraculous and stylish straight right shots, the sound of which ricochets around the gym with a satisfying whip crack. These are underpinned by a perfect right knee drop, which cranks surprising power into the right hand. We both smile at this rare bit of boxing perfection, as Dai's hangover and mood momentarily lifts.

When I get home my partner thrusts into my hand a free boxing fitness guide out of a men's magazine. Perhaps unfairly, I suspect it is the sort of magazine written for beerswilling, gym-hating men, who sport pink shirts, pointy shoes and Brylcreemed hair, who ogle busty women and want a raise from their boss for doing no extra work. These are surely the cohort of Audi drivers who will never do the washing up, but will make a lot of noise not doing it.

I discover that over the past two years I have covered every conceivable recommendation in this bumptious pamphlet, which assures me that I am now fully ready for ten rounds with Joe Frazier. Well, that's a relief, I think. Completely fulfilled, I can now get on with the rest of my life, as long as I don't have to wear the pointy shoes.

On Friday I take the afternoon off work for a session at Kelly's gym. It is empty except for Mr Kelly, its owner, who is also the chief trainer. He is wiry, unassuming man, pumping iron in the small heavy weights room. His competitive days in the ring are over, but he is far from disinterested and at any one time trains a couple of professional boxers.

We agree how genuinely sad it is that a large proportion of the youth today is hunched over computers, with virtual sport over-taking the real thing. I point out that my nephew watches various exciting skateboarding videos, but is surprised when I suggest that he has a go on a real skateboard. Ruefully, Mr Kelly says that he cannot get enough amateur youth boxers to graduate to professional status because of the training commitment. I agree out of politeness, but we both know that the required sixteen or so training sessions a week need an almost religious devotion.

I while away a lovely hour on the two bags in the weights room, reflecting on how unnatural the hook still feels to me, and wondering if it will ever become committed to muscle memory. Eventually, a couple of genuinely good tight hooks emerge without the usual arm-waving.

A large man with a black beard, who looks like an extra in the film *Gladiator*, lumbers into the weights room with his tiny girlfriend in tow. Wrongly assuming that I am a total novice, he immediately gives some unwanted hook advice. What is it with these men who must continually advise, advise, advise?

I watch his hook – admittedly it is quite good, but when he comes to set it up with the jab and right hand his stance is all wrong, and his front foot is far too forward facing. Consequently, he is majorly off balance for the most basic shots except the hook. This is just not right, and he pulls a face as I tell him that his feet are all wrong. He is far too square on, and would present a very large target area to an opponent. It is true that the feet have to be slightly differently placed for the hook, but he claims that his adopted stance is part of his own finely honed individualistic style of boxing. This I have discovered is a well-worn excuse for those substandard boxers who have not yet ironed out elementary mistakes. I leave him to his mansplaining and say nothing, as I really can't be bothered.

24

DON'T MENTION THE WAR

It is October 2015, and the Cave Rescue Organisation's eightieth birthday party at the Falcon Manor Hotel in my local town of Settle. For over twenty years I was a minor cog in this cave and mountain rescue team in the southern Yorkshire Dales, and on Saturday night around ninety beloved friends from past and present crowd into the hotel dining room. I am used to seeing them in their oldest clothes, but instead they appear dapper in new suits or diamond necklaces. Stanley Lockwith, a stalwart team member who is also my window cleaner, is transformed by a pinstripe three-piece suit with yellow tie and matching handkerchief. He looks like an aging Mafia boss as he holds court in the hotel foyer.

Short in stature, but stout in heart, Stanley was a key member of a pioneering caving expedition to Iran in the 1970s, and is still potholing overseas in China over fifty years later. Cavers of Stanley's generation and before would never think of themselves as athletes or pioneering explorers, yet they truly wcre. In later years, Stanley's delightful companion was a black dog called Svalbard, an improbable cross between a corgi and a Labrador, resulting in very short legs. Unfortunately, in a highly controversial decision, Svalbard was banned from attending rescues as he used to bark loudly and chase the RAF rescue helicopters, causing a major distraction to the pilots.

Some much older members of the team who are present can only communicate using metaphors which relate to Second World War aircraft or steam-driven coal mining equipment. Fearing this as the major topic of conversation over dinner, I sit next to Ted Winstanley, an ancient potholer of eighty-four years with a glass eye. Ted remembers cave exploration from around the post-war period, and is an easy and humorous conversationalist whose fascinating life speaks for itself.

One of life's innocents, Ted seems strangely unaware of the concept of danger. He cheerfully recounts being caught underneath a huge boulder collapse some forty years earlier, in a pothole called Lost Pot on Leck Fell on the Lancashire–Yorkshire border. His main concern was not that he had nearly died or was left in a coma for three days in the local infirmary, but that he had lost his glass eye. Ted was a kingpin of the rescue team in the mid-1960s, as was another friend of his, Charlie, who happened to have a wooden leg. There was a famous incident where they both turned up simultaneously to rescue the same casualty, who was heard to remark something like, 'If this is the f——king rescue team, then kiss my a——e.'

In 1970, Ted was an eager participant in a caving expedition to the mountainous area of Shimla in the Indian Punjab, the main expedition vehicle being a Lancashire Corporation double decker bus. This had been bought on the cheap and was lovingly renovated by the twelve caving participants. Though completely unsuitable, the bus was driven from the UK all the way to the Indian subcontinent over high mountain passes of up to 16,000 feet, well above the snowline, but all the while showing 'Morecambe' or 'The Beach' as viable destinations. (There was also a 'Not in Service' option, which I suspect was never used.)

However, on one fateful day the bus was found to be too tall to negotiate a small archway on a remote mountain road. To no avail, the tyres were let down, then someone produced an angle grinder out of nowhere and cut off the roof.

The bus continued on its roofless journey, but Ted's team returned home by other means, having finally found the crushing Himalayan winter too vexatious. Apparently, it had become too cold to cook on the bus's lower floor, as an icy blizzard blew continually down the stairwell from the open upper deck. There were days of digging the bus out of massive snowdrifts. Moreover, the bus tyres, which were designed for suburban Lancashire, could no longer cling to the snowy and precipitous roads.

Ted's deadpan account of the entire proceedings, with expressions of mild surprise at the most outrageous and trying circumstances, and the incongruous image of the Morecambe bus later photographed next to the Taj Mahal, causes me to stifle laughter for a full thirty minutes. Eventually, I escape into the hotel foyer for a breather. Speeches follow by various old farts and I briefly wonder which century I am in, but overall the evening passes off well, and all the drunks are finally shepherded onto a taxi bus. I love them one and all.

⊙

Monday comes around as the wheels of the bus finally come off. Dai puts us through our paces, with the usual skipping then six two-and-a-half-minute rounds on the bags, punctuated with a minute of tuck jumps, burpees or whatever followed by thirty seconds' rest; then six one-minute rounds with ten seconds' rest, then collapse; then the Board of Death and collapse with knobs on. Old friends Peter and Mark are present and correct, together with Henry who is still honing his boxing training for the paras assessment. Henry is due to undergo his proper boxing initiation with Dai on Wednesday, and so Dai recruits an old boxing colleague of his, Santos, whom he trained for ten years, to take on Henry. He tells us that he will set up the proper ring in the corner of the gym.

Wednesday is upon us and, true to his word, Dai has put out the gilded and hallowed hemp ropes of the ring, levered and stretched on ancient stanchions embedded into the gym walls and floor. There is a sense of history unfolding in these old ropes and ironwork, and I wonder how many others' fortunes have been made or lost within their confines.

Henry does not show up. In fact nobody does, apart from Dai, Santos and myself. I have met Santos before a couple of times. Stocky, affable, aged around thirty and of Hispanic extraction, Santos has a shaved eyebrow and a slight air of menace. I watch him out of the corner of my eye as we skip and warm up on the bags. He struggles with the skipping, and is clearly a bit out of condition, but for sure there is some boxing magic there: I hear the bang, bang, bang of hooks ratcheting up and down the bags.

'Well, there is only one thing for it,' Dai says nonchalantly. 'Marianne – you will have to go head to head with Santos in the ring.'

I silently gasp. Feeling like I am about to make the short walk to the executioner's block, Dai advises me to wear a gum guard and headgear. I am in the red corner and Santos in the blue. I trust Dai, and therefore I expect that Santos will be no psycho, but nonetheless I do seriously wonder if his sparring will really be pitched at my level, since I still have very few defensive skills.

Earlier in the evening, Santos has confessed that he had a 'brush with the law' when he was young and foolish. It is honest of him to say this, and I mumble something about us all doing something silly we regret when we are young, but I would secretly like to know what form his transgression took before I get in the ring.

In the following few minutes I try to focus very hard on what I intend to do, but my mind is an apprehensive blank. I have only five lines of defence: block, parry, duck (if the shots are slow enough), pivot (if the shots are slow enough), and last and most importantly run away – preferably backwards at lightning speed, but not in a straight line.

Boxing a person is very different from boxing a static bag, and making the transition is difficult, as various habits have to be unlearned. It is easy to stand close to the bag and dither around before throwing the best technical shots that you can muster. With a person, once you are in range, as sure as eggs are eggs, they will punch you. On the bags and pads, you are throwing the shots onto a target area which is essentially static, or at the worst slow-moving. With an opponent, you are trying to hit them in the target zone. Your eye must not be lured onto the target as it is with static work: the only thing you must do is watch, watch, watch their hands. The second your eye wanders, bang – there is another jab; crash – there is another hook; wallop – there is the straight right.

As Santos comes out of the corner, we touch gloves in the time-honoured way, and then I move forward with the hope of delivering a 1-2. All hopes are dashed. I am far too static and I take a bashing, but I do manage to keep my hands up and avoid a punch in the face for all three of the two-minute rounds.

This alone is a significant achievement, but in the second round Dai shouts to me that I am panicking and have forgotten everything he has ever taught me. This is not actually true, as in fact I feel quite calm – I just do not possess a wide enough range of defences. Not being a boxing natural, I genuinely need some strategic help in the form an actual battle plan. I need a bit more instruction than the usual old-school See One, Do One, Teach One approach.

I do manage to parry a few of Santos's jabs out of the way and deliver two really good jabs straight to his chin, but mostly my shots are pathetic non sequiturs. Through the barrage of shots, Dai shouts approval at my two good jabs, which are followed by a marvellous knee-dropping straight right, but in general I am much too far forward, treating Santos like the static boxing bag he is not.

As we get to the end of round two, we are both tiring. I try, try, try to move forward, but I cannot get past the barrage of Santos's continual rain of shots. I never, ever give up, but my arsenal of jabs and straight rights are merely shots-in-waiting, a never-plundered hoard. What is the point of being able to throw these on the bag, if I can never get past any of my opponent's shots?

Santos throws some great hooks. These are his forte and, unusually for an orthodox boxer, his right hook is better than his left. One almost knocks me over – it is not that hard but I just do not see it coming as it looms out of left field. I whisper a silent prayer of thanks to God for my choice of headgear, the best that my bank balance will allow. Then, I lose my stance and stumble forward. Dai groans, as well he might.

At the end of round two, I have, have, *have* to get some water. I signal to Dai, but he will not let me take my gloves off, so he force-feeds me the water at the side of the ring, then shoves me back into the fray after a mere thirty seconds. Santos is really tiring now and for the shortest of intervals I get him on the ropes.

Once again, in round three, I am much too close, and fall victim to his final assault of weakening hooks, hooks and more hooks, from which I have no idea how to defend myself. I think about parrying them away, but that will surely leave my face vulnerable to a jab, so I do nothing except hunker down. Even though it would be obvious to an observer, I do not even think of making a simple step backwards.

As Dai calls time he looks incredulous as I lean over the ropes, breath rasping. Between gasps I say, 'The really frustrating thing … is that … I know what I am doing wrong.' And I do, up to a point, but somehow I can't put it right. Dai gives as Gallic shrug as a response, and asks me if I would like to go another round with Santos. 'No!' we both simultaneously shout a bit too enthusiastically, as Santos looks up blankly, red in the face.

Well, I think to myself, at least I have tired him out a bit – that must count for something. Santos says that when in the ring I am trying to do too much all at once and he is right. On the bags you can just toil away without a worry, but in the ring you have to bide your time before throwing the shots, a skill which I have yet to learn.

Dai hands me the stopwatch, as he dons his own inferior headgear to take Santos on. They will be boxing for two two-minute rounds. I am ref and timekeeper. As Dai bolts out of the corner, his lightning speed and relentless jabs are immediately apparent. They wear Santos down again and again. In the first round Dai is almost static in the middle of the ring, lord of all he surveys, dominating the space. Santos is whirling round and round the periphery like a dervish and getting ever more tired. He is fading fast, even as I call time on the first round.

In no time at all I shout time for the start of the second round. Santos throws a killer right hook and Dai is momentarily put off his stride, but the hook is no match for Dai's signature shot, the quadruple jab. Just as no one expects the Spanish Inquisition, no one expects the quadruple jab, especially not Santos, and especially not in triplicate. He is pushed back, back and further back onto the ancient and creaking hemp ropes. This round is just as full on, as Santos is boxed repeatedly from the ropes into the red corner.

It is an astounding display of speed and skill by Dai, but I feel that he is getting too aggressive. I shout to him in my best no-nonsense voice to rein it in, as he unleashes a whirlwind of perfect hooks to the body. If he does not heed me, I will stop the round. It makes me think that Dai is just not doing enough boxing and the urge to showcase his skills is just too strong. Like riding an ancient bicycle, all the muscle memory is there as Dai makes the ring his own. I call time on the second round. Santos bows his head, bent double, and Dai grins.

We are all totally knackered, even Dai. We agree how much harder the sparring is than anything else we could possibly devise. Even the Board of Death momentarily looks a soft touch. Santos has managed five rounds, me three and Dai two. I muse on how it is humanly possible to expend so much energy in so little time. I know it will take me at least two days, possibly three, to recover from this paltry six minutes. It is a type of exhaustion that it is also impossible to convey unless you

have experienced it yourself. (In a reality TV show, the actor
Idris Elba trains for a full year in 40-degree heat in Mexico to
prepare for a one-off professional kick-boxing fight in the York
Hall in London. Even months into the intensive training he is
still exhausted after a couple of rounds of sparring.)

Brain fog reigns as Santos says that he can no longer tell
his left hand from his right, a condition with which we are all
familiar. Anyway, that is that, and Dai says emphatically that we
should do more sparring. I make a mental note to force Jamie
at gunpoint to teach me more defensive boxing. As I wring the
sweat out of my T-shirt, Santos lies motionless on the floor,
his expressionless, beetroot face turned skyward. Even Dai,
forcing a smile, looks like another round would kill him. We
all agree what fun we have had and how we can't wait to do
it again.

25

SLIPPING BELOW THE WATERLINE

I fetch up at Kelly's gym on both the following Saturday and Sunday, desperately trying to instil the defensive instinct into some bag work, practising moving in and out of a theoretical punch zone. I throw one or two good hooks, and at last they are becoming a little less clunky.

On Monday night I am full of a cold, but also with a restless energy, as Dai puts us through our paces. Mark, James and Peter are there – the old guard out in force. Dai jokes that Santos will no longer put in an appearance as I have warned him off with my three punishing rounds the previous Wednesday. It is kind of Dai to say so, but we both know that this is not true, as my sack-of-potatoes demeanour in the ring is apparent. Dai, Mark and James genuinely applaud my guts for having a go. Dai mischievously admits that he put me in the ring with Santos to wear him out before his last two fateful rounds. A fine boxing tactic, I think – with friends like Dai who needs enemies?

The following day, someone from Kelly's gym texts me to say that Jamie has broken several ribs. Obviously, I hope that he makes a good recovery for his own sake, but I selfishly hope that he recovers so that can also teach me the rudiments of defensive boxing before it is too late.

Since only the old faithful have appeared on Wednesday, this gives Dai a licence to push us really hard. Ten minutes of skipping is followed by five two-and-a-half-minute rounds on the bag interspersed with a minute of tuck jumps, bench jumps of three different types, one of which defies description, and with a thirty-second rest in between each couplet of bag work and bench exercises. Then the same again, with one-and-half-minute rounds, one minute of bench exercises and a ten-second rest in between. Hallowe'en is approaching and the whole of the youth club is decorated in fine style. This provides a bit of distraction from all the pumping iron, as we whirl round and round the gym with the ghoulies and ghosties looking on.

The only one of us to give up is Mark. He tries very hard indeed, but cannot quite finish the last round. I get very close to throwing in the towel as my hands feel like an invisible, heavy rope is pulling them down to the ground. My hands are so sweaty that the sweat actually runs out of the gloves and onto the bag, so that the shots slip and slide unsatisfactorily for the last round or two. Finally, it is the stomach assault, with sit-ups straight and twisted, leg raises, and my exercise of choice the plank, followed by its little brother, the side plank. Dai tells a series of very funny jokes which disrupt our concentration, causing our legs to drop to the floor like felled logs. Well, we surmise that the jokes are funny, but can only guess, as only the expletive-laden punchlines can be made out and we have to imagine the back stories.

Then, like crumbling buildings, we totter and fall weary and supine into puddles of sweat. I feel by rights that Dai should stay there and read us a bedtime story. When I get home, I eat a massive bowl of spag bol, followed by two bowls of muesli, and still feel hungry.

I slump down on the sofa and watch the trashy SAS-type training reality TV programme. The contestants are continually shouted at by a nasty little man who looks like a cross between a brick sh–thouse, a careworn gym monkey and aging gigolo. In one scene a ten stone man is given the task (twice) of carrying his fifteen stone colleague up a long, steep hill in an exercise known as 'The Sickener'. Well it looks pretty sickening to me. I think of all the physiotherapists in the land averting their gaze in horror as the carrier's vertebrae threaten to break. He manages to finish, but all I can think of is the irreparable damage to his spine.

I am reminded of a mountaineering story from the 1980s concerning Andy Kirkpatrick, an outstanding Alpine mountaineer of his generation. Apparently he had been suffered with a bad back, and was hobbling around at a party where an orthopaedic surgeon happened to be a guest. Andy had mentioned his back trouble in passing, and the surgeon asked if he had been doing anything recently which might have contributed to his condition. The surgeon was aghast when Andy casually mentioned that he had been ferrying 50kg rucksacks on remote expeditions for the past few months. On further investigation in his clinic, the surgeon found that Andy had actually compressed his spine with the extraordinary loads he had been carrying. This is surely a reminder that we are all fallible human machines, with mechanical limits.

I sink into a deep, deep sleep, dreaming that I have inadvertently joined the SAS, plunging a hundred feet down a cliff into the ocean in full military gear, then falling a further hundred feet through the briny deep, before actually touching the bottom of the ocean, which is vividly covered by a population of ugly, black flatfish. Thankfully at this point I wake up with a start, without having to bother about swimming the lungbursting journey up to the ocean surface. The dream probably means something deep and unfathomable, but instead it is 7 a.m. and I find myself sweaty and cold, on the sofa at home, with my hands still swathed in red boxing wraps and the blue autumn light creeping under the curtains. Tigger is fast asleep at my shoulder.

Wednesday brings more of the same, as Dai jibes at Santos in his absence, saying that he has been scared off by another bout in the ring with me – *if only*. Dai commends me once again for having a go. The story of my life, I bleakly reflect, the ability to have a go, but with *no real lasting effect*.

The old guard crawl out of the woodwork, Mark, James and Peter, the latter rushing in late and apologetic as usual. We simultaneously cheer as law student Will reappears for the first time since May. A new college term has started, and we all wonder if his friend Donny will also appear. Will and I catch up on news and agree that we are both ready to try some sparring, perhaps the following week if Dai will officiate. Will and I trust each other, as we both know that there will be no psycho-killer punching. Mark, who is mild mannered and polite, also offers his services as a sparring partner, but in the nicest possible way I decline: his punching volume is permanently turned up by default due to years of kick-boxing and hard sparring with his brother. I fear this could be too much for me.

Two determined Eastern European girls appear, having never boxed before – Julia and Anna. We rocket through our usual skipping and bag punching, and then a round of the Board of Death. I box quite well on the pads, really trying hard to move in and out, but lose some punching power, as my hip swivel is too speeded up. I am not getting clocked in the face by Dai, so this is progress.

⊙

Colleagues tell me that I am suffering a bit from a bout of Fresher's Flu, an unwanted gift from the university. I dismiss it as no more than the common cold. I have virtually lost my voice and when I speak a comical croak results, which makes me laugh, causing me to sound even worse. Everyone sympathises, then laughs, then tells me to go home as I sound so terrible. In the gym, Mark tells me sagely of the dangers of training while suffering from viruses, citing marathon runners who have dropped dead after a night on the Lemsip and a day on the running track. I think of the dangers of Weil's disease, caused by rats' urine, which kills in a mere twelve hours. I wonder if I will cark it on the way home, but miraculously I do not.

However, I really have overdone it this time. I wake up on Saturday morning, ears blocked and the sound inside my skull of my own chest wheezing with the crackle of a chest infection. An enforced rest on Sunday and Monday and miserable skulking indoors restores equilibrium. I feel guilty at letting the side down, as I think of Dai's voluntary efforts on my behalf, but I know it is for the best.

I hit the sack early on Monday night, dreaming of a lively comeback with all sparring guns blazing. I wake up with a start at 5 a.m., and while away an hour with a cup of tea in the company of Joe Frazier's compendium of home truths about boxing before falling back to sleep. Joe Frazier says that there are two things that you must never do in the boxing ring. I find that I am doing both. These are stepping backwards in a straight line in response to any opponent's shot: this is the boxing equivalent of walking the plank, as it leads directly to the ropes or corner, where humiliation and death are certain. The other is raising your chin after taking a hit, which invites your opponent to throw his best uppercut.

⊙

I slave away in the laboratory for twelve hours on a sunny Friday and still have much to do on the following rainy Monday. Being sensible for once, I again miss my Monday boxing session with Dai as I am still shaking off the horrible virus.

Instead I take the afternoon off on Tuesday. It is a quintessential grey, late autumn Lancashire day, as I head down the M6 and then the familiar bypass to Kelly's gym. Part of this route evokes distant memories of the Friday night excitement of travelling to the Yorkshire Dales when I was much younger to meet up with my potholing friends. The promise of underground exploration to some of the remotest bits of Yorkshire caves was our lifeblood entertainment. Those days seem distant, but part of my plan is to keep fit enough to repeat some of this when I retire. I kid myself that then there will then be more time for rest and reflection.

As I walk through the door, I see Jamie and ask about his ribs. He says that the message has been scrambled, and that it is in fact shoulder problem, brought on by holding up the pads for some very powerful six foot four professional-hitters. He looks really tired and genuinely fed up, and I worry that there is something else going on apart from his injury. In typical British fashion, I can only express mild concern.

I have a full hour of glorious stretching and mooching around the hook bag and light bag, trying out the unfamiliar southpaw stance, and trying the defensive slip, duck and roll. My reactions are far too slow and Jamie suggests just throwing a ball at a wall and catching it as a means of improvement. He also suggests that I practise on a double end bag.

Jamie and I discuss a new generation of boxing pads and headgear which contain a shock-absorbing 'smart' material known as D3O. This is a British formulation made with cornflour powder and water, based on the principles concerning the behaviour of thixotropic liquids, where molecules in the liquid spontaneously coalesce if hit hard with a localised force, almost forming a solid impact-absorbing surface. The material is used to good effect in bulletproof vests, motorbike gear and walking boots.

Please do not try this at home. There are hilarious videos on YouTube which show someone wearing a slab of D3O paste on his head concealed under a beanie hat, being hit over the head with a shovel by his best mate: the victim looks completely unphased. My headgear contains D3O at the sides and I remember that I never really felt the impact of Santos's hooks even though some of them nearly knocked me over. I do some work using the D3O pads. They are more impact absorbing than the usual kind, but also feel slightly stiffer, but somehow not quite right.

At home, I set up a simple double end bag arrangement in the outbuilding. The bag is basically a green rubber tennis ball strung between floor and ceiling on two very strong pieces of elastic. Jamie says that hitting it as it rebounds helps with hand–eye coordination and I find that it does.

⊙

Jamie's shoulder has improved sufficiently for a Saturday training session. I warm up with skipping as usual. Skipping now seems like a gentle stroll through sunlit meadows and I cannot imagine how it once felt like wading through treacle.

I throw a confident 1-2 and 1-2-left hook as Jamie holds up the pads. I have been practising assiduously on the bags, and this really shows up in the emergence of a much more fluid movement which even I can see.

Having had the rudiments of it laid out about six weeks ago, it is time to revisit the slip, the first real line of evasive defence that I will ever learn. Jamie says that this is the best and most indispensable form of defence, as it translates immediately into an attack manoeuvre, whereas blocks and parries do not. It also changes the punching angle, allowing for an input of extra momentum. The slip forms the basis of the other important defensive manoeuvres, the duck and the roll.

The secret is to have a slightly more open stance, with the front foot almost pointing forwards (which feels wrong), a bit like the hook stance. If evading a left jab from an orthodox opponent you must turn the torso to the right, as if throwing a jab, but instead keeping both hands up, and knees bent, tilt your head slightly rightwards, as (hopefully) their jab swooshes past safely. Having been trained on the bag, at this point it is mightily tempting to lean forward and look at your opponent's face, as a potential target area, but this will tell you nothing and you must not do it. Instead you must keep your eyes forward even though your head has turned a bit, watch their hands and return to your stance, ready to throw your own jab.

I try this again and again and again. The main problem is that when my head turns a bit, not unreasonably my eyes follow, and I end up facing slightly to the left, no longer eyeballing my opponent. This is incorrect, as the eyes should still remain in a forward-looking position as much as possible, even though the head is slightly turned. Also my stance is not quite wide enough so there is a delay in the middle of it all – when I awkwardly adjust my stance, after having slipped the jab, I am not yet in the correct position for throwing another.

Jamie comments that I am also throwing the punches so hard that they are causing me to go off balance. This is a very difficult habit to break, as we are taught in the amateur gym to make every punch count. This is underpinned by two years of conditioned hard punching on pads, and the heaviest of heavy bags that feel as if they have been fashioned out of the finest poured concrete. In a way which I do not quite understand, when I am in the slipped position to the right my left shoulder is not protecting my face enough. Also, I am not breathing, but can manage it all without turning blue, so I decide to worry about that later.

The first and most elemental thing is as ever to get my stance right, as there is no time for any readjustment. The slip and response in the form of a jab to Jamie's pad must be at lightning speed, possibly faster, and I have the eternal difficulty of snapping my jab back quickly enough, before Jamie's second jab comes out, which I must also slip. To try and speed things up I am mistakenly throwing my response jab too soon, while I am still coming out of the slip, and consequently I am not in a position to throw it, and therefore off-balance on two counts. I am sometimes not returning properly to a neutral stance, leaving my head behind in the slipped position as a ready target for my opponent. As all these sins begin to crowd the brain the historical scourge of hand-dropping restarts.

This makes a total of nine mistakes to be corrected before I can perfect the slip, but the worst one is the eye rolling.

Jamie shouts again and again: 'Hands up! Eyes in!' First of all, I manage stop my eyes from turning to the slip side, and manage to fix my gaze into a central position, even when my head is turned. However, instead of eyeballing the pads, I find myself staring blankly at Jamie's face.

Then, as ever in life, things are complicated and speeded up. Jamie forces me to slip to the right then left, with a funny little transition in the middle. I slip to the right evading one jab, get back to a neutral position, then throw a jab of my own, immediately throw a straight right, then slip to the left to avoid Jamie's straight right, throw another straight right of my own, slip Jamie's right and return to a neutral position. We do this about ten times before I sort of get the hang of it. As ever the real solution is practice, practice and more practice, probably in the form of lone shadow boxing.

The real secret of the slip is to slip just enough, but not too much, so that no one notices, nobody important gets hurt and valuable resources are conserved. This was the very successful strategy of Joe Louis, who slipped punches by imperceptible amounts, leaving him in the perfect counterpunching position. Finally the brain fog takes over, and I find that I can no longer follow the simplest of instructions.

Next, Jamie and I discuss the duck, as we quack and quack about its merits. I have never understood how boxers can duck so quickly to avoid lightning-speed punches. Jamie explains that the duck is not really a mere articulation of the knees. It is instead a fully fledged freefall with the knees saving you from a crash to the ground. Jamie demonstrates his suicidal knee drop. I try it, but it seems clunky and wooden. I wonder if my ancient frame will ever be up to the job.

I have plenty of time to reflect on genuflection the following day, when I truly find out how much energy I have expended in the boxing ring. Sunday is indeed a day of rest. It passes in a haze of sleep on the sofa with Tigger, who speaks to me in his own special cat language. My good intentions for the day start with staring out of the window at the lashing November rain, considering (and ignoring) my tax return, and end with the dulcet tones of Jarvis Cocker on the radio accompanied by Ukrainian piano music, with no intervening constructive activity whatsoever. I scoff industrial amounts of spag bol and nut bars, caffeine fed in by a drip direct to the brain, and read a good book as the room darkens. Ah, heaven indeed.

26

ANYTHING IS ALLOWED WITHIN
THE RULES (OF BOXING)

The following Monday, only me, Peter and Dai appear. As usual, Peter will not be budged from the bags, and after the usual skipping Dai times two-minute rounds. Peter says that he is far too inexperienced to do any sparring. He has said this in every single training session that I can remember. Perhaps it is just as well, as now his thunderous punches would be a match for any person I can think of.

I explain to Dai that Jamie has been trying to teach me the slip. We reflect on its positives and negatives. Dai thinks that the slip, duck and roll are consigned to the foreign country that is professional boxing, and knowing how difficult even a basic slip seems to be I am inclined to agree. Even though it is not his thing, Dai immediately conjures up a brilliant slip from nowhere, his boxing instinct taking over.

Anyway, the default setting appears to be just me and Dai sparring. After my semi-black eye a few weeks earlier, I hope that he will be a little kinder, mainly so that I can learn something. I am in the red corner, Dai in the blue. The bell tolls for us both as we touch gloves. I sincerely hope that my gum guard is firmly in place.

Dai tries out his jab on me and instead of being the static lump that I was a fortnight earlier, I do actually move, even managing a pivot. I try with a couple of feinted jabs and straight rights, the only shots I can conjure out of the air. I parry Dai's jab out of the way and throw a couple of great jabs myself. I see Dai's chin tilt upwards and away under their force, and I know that they are good shots.

Dai moves forward and puts the pressure on. He forces me backwards into the corner. Perhaps this is my Final Judgement, or so I think, until we take a breather. Dai demonstrates an exit strategy. If you find yourself marooned in the corner, as long as you keep your hands up and your elbows tucked in, no harm can really come to you, except that you are pinned and disabled there for what seems like an eternity. While your opponent pummels away you are not in a position to win any points, but usually they are so preoccupied with your apparent submission, and their apparent supremacy, that they forget that you are in a great position to deliver a straight right into the solar plexus and shove them straight out of the way. This avoids the embarrassment of any clinching and can knock them clean over.

In the second round, Dai forces me into the dreaded corner. I lull him into a false sense of security, deliberately delivering some weak left hooks, which will make him think that I have long since given up and gone home. Then Bang! A killer straight right really does shove Dai backwards as he stumbles, just a little.

Round three sees a few minor successes, as I manage to slip a couple of Dai's jabs, and deliver some good right body shots. I feel that I am slipping by far too much, and if this goes on for any length of time I will run out of energy. Also, I fall victim to various blindside hooks, and take a couple of nasty body shot right hooks. I need to shimmy out of the way of these, but somehow can't and don't. I manage not to panic though, realising that I have a precious microsecond to think. Instead of whirling round and round, I wait for Dai to come to me and waste his energy first. He smiles, as he recognises my little strategy, but he is tempted to come forward nonetheless, thinking it worthwhile.

In the fifth and sixth rounds Dai puts on the pressure for real, as the quadruple jab and triple right come out of the closet – his not mine – with astounding jack-in-the-box speed. I hunker down and manage to avoid getting punched in the face, which I still regard as progress. I then make the fatal mistake of staring at the floor and not my opponent, so I can do nothing against a barrage of constant shots, as I cannot see them.

Dai tells me that I am panicking, but I am really not – it is just the inevitable brain fog taking over. I am glad when the sixth round bell rings. I begin to come back into the room, registering other sounds in the gym, including Peter's thwacking bag punches. I express frustration at my lack of progress, but Dai brings me right back down to earth: 'For God's Sake, Marianne, you are a woman of fifty – what do you expect?' It is a really good question, as I wonder what I do indeed expect, especially as I am actually fifty-two. The truth is that I do expect more, as I know in my heart that I am capable of more and that is that. Anyway, Dai has no room to talk as he is already beyond his half-century.

All three of us spend the last ten minutes on the benches doing various ups and downs, and I show off a few fancy stretches that I have learned in the professional boxing gym.

Although I do not feel at all tired, I know that I will have to eat like a horse later to replace lost calories.

As I drive home, I try to assess whether I have a headache or indeed any other sparring injuries of note, which the imminent adrenalin drop will soon expose. This is an essential self-assessment ritual, which with all its nagging doubts must still be gone through. I park under a particular streetlight, not far out of town, simultaneously staring into the driver's mirror and craning my neck to search for bruises. I decide that I will remain as nature intended, for good or ill. My little bit of boxing defence has worked.

⊙

On Wednesday, old hand Peter and determined newbie Jade appear. Mark appears in fine form but his brother James is absent again. I am still wretchedly tired from the sparring on Monday, which seems to have reached further into the body's resources more than any other activity I have yet found. I am slow, clunky and slightly bored on the bags and pads.

Dai lays out a combination of other activities, one of which includes running on the spot at extremely high speed. He makes us laugh as his running is so comically fast that his feet blur, like the wheels of a departing train. I persuade Peter to abandon the heavy bag for a moment, and as he throws jabs and straight rights I practise a few slips. I get them mostly wrong, but a few look and feel right.

Peter laughs at my attempts to look straight ahead while my head is slewed uncomfortably to one side. I throw some good right body shots, but Peter returns a couple. I think that my left side has been rendered too vulnerable for too long (by me) and I must slither eel-like out of the way.

Peter says that you are not allowed to duck at all during a slip. I disagree and say that you are allowed a tiny movement down and forward like a small nodding toy, but you must not stray into your opponent's punch zone. Like all the lovely boxing tricks, I sense that this new, cranky one will soon be added in to my repertoire. Unaccustomed to giving or receiving praise, Peter tells me that my boxing is massively improved when sparring. I don't know why, but I secretly feel that this inexplicable fact is true.

⊙

It is easy to get hung up on minutiae, some of which are important, but the truth is that you can do anything you like as long as it is within the rules of boxing, and Jamie reminds me of this from time to time, as I pointlessly obsess and fuss over every damn shot. We observe that alternative influences in boxing often bring out creativity.

Travellers and gypsies include boxing within their culture from an early age, and are often highly skilled and stylish fighters. However, there are others who lack style but still seem to be effective. Everyone hails Tyson Fury as a great fighter, but I wince at his wide, sweeping 'haymaker' shots.

I watch two memorable boxing matches on TV, which showcase different boxing styles. As a storm rages outside, I curl up in on the sofa with Tigger and a lukewarm cup of tea. In the first match, Nick Blackwell from Trowbridge defends his British Middleweight title against Blackpool's Jack Arnfield, who has only had a few weeks' notice of the fight, due to the scheduled challenger becoming injured.

From the off, Blackwell just looks more powerful and just has the right combination of bounce and menace to put off his opponent. He has a killer jab, and seems to be a volume puncher, slugger and good technical boxer all in one. Arnfield tries long jabs but these are always too slow – he continually falls prey to Blackwell's over-the-top roundhouse right hook, as the left side of his face remains undefended for far too long. Again and again he is hooked and thrown off balance, as Blackwell pushes him back onto the ropes, where he is hooked and hooked and hooked again.

Arnfield the underdog never gives up and has a great right uppercut which he employs, together with a straight right. This gets him out of the corner time after time when combined with a deft leftwards pivot of the feet. Despite being exhausted he resorts to the clinch only a handful of times to get out of the corner. I notice that he is moving leftwards too much, the default movement of a right-hander, and I hope that he will start moving to the right, just to fox Blackwell for a second, but he doesn't.

In round five Arnfield is hooked by Blackwell, and a cut opens up above his right eye as he endures a standing count. Arnfield has never gone more than about eight rounds with anyone, so he brings a new definition to digging deep as he goes the full twelve rounds with Blackwell, looking occasionally unsteady on his legs, but rallying magnificently again and again.

The crowd are on their feet. The final score cards show what a close match it has been, and although Blackwell is chipper at having defended his title, Arnfield is the real hero, whose grit and mettle are apparent. One commentator instantly moves him up from number twenty-eight in the world rankings to somewhere near the top. Blackwell gives a little bow of respect and the orange Blackpool scarves wave.

The next televised contest is for the title of British Flyweight, and twenty-six-year-old Lee Selby, a Brit from Barry, South Wales, defends his title against a very diminutive and fast Cuban, aged eighteen, who weighs in at under eight stone.

Selby is a boxer of considerable style, tipped to be The One of his generation. The commentators state that he has had the uncanny ability from a child to slip seamlessly from an orthodox to southpaw stance without a second thought. His movement around the ring, with effortless taunts to his opponent and flagrant showboating, reminds me of Muhammad Ali. Throughout the short contest he brims with energy, having the time and energy to pull a series of funny faces at the Channel 5 commentators in between the shots.

The ref sensibly stops the match in the second round as the more inexperienced Cuban crumbles, incapable of delivering any meaningful response at all. The Welshman is very gracious in victory, as he smiles and holds his opponent's hand aloft. He is clearly destined for greatness, no doubt built on years and years of respectable slog in amateur gyms. Selby is predicted to win ten more professional fights and then become World Champion.

27

DEATH SLIDE

In ways that cannot be fathomed, any boxing skill that I have managed to build up drains away in a single week. As the poet Stevie Smith once *nearly* said: 'Not boxing, but drowning.' Unaccountably, I find that I cannot throw a jab or even a right hand. I try changing gloves for a smaller more nifty twelve-ounce pair, but nothing is better. I have the reactions of a whelk and the less said the better.

One Wednesday night, exhausted after achieving nothing, I slump in front of the telly and watch whatever is on. It is *First Dates*, a morbidly compelling TV reality dating programme for the too beautiful, too prissy, too vacant and too deluded, some falling blindly into all four categories.

One unfortunate is a portly housewife who mistakenly thinks she looks good in latex, and tantalises her date with this apocalyptic vision. His tongue visibly hangs out and his jaw drops to the floor. He drools in anticipation as his brain registers absolutely nothing on the dial. It is a degrading, freak-show spectacle of the pepped-up, prepped-up and tarted-up, thrice-divorced looking needily for a fourth, desperate throw of the dice. Well, this is the free market gone absolutely mad.

The week continues badly. Late on a Friday night, my colleague spies me working in the laboratory. My boombox churns out 'I Stand and Face the Rain' by the Norwegian 1980s band A-ha. 'That is a sad song,' he says, emphatically, with a touch of pity. 'Yes,' I lie sagely – to me it sounds ecstatically happy.

Once he has gone I put on 'Asleep' by The Smiths and vow to read the collected plays of Sarah Kane (again). The following day, Jamie has not appeared at the appointed time for my Saturday training session which is at 1 p.m. This is another bad sign.

⊙

It is December 2015 and there is snow on the ground. Tigger has grown an impressive ginger winter coat which makes him look like a Canadian Forest cat. While we shiver indoors, he is totally at ease. He slinks through the coniferous undergrowth close to the house, in search of something that he cannot explain to us; entirely of his own volition and called by a force that is not human. He goes out at night and returns covered in frost, none the worse for sleeping in the icy greenhouse, despite my numerous attempts to call him in to the fireside.

One Sunday, I lurk at Kelly's gym, as the black winter sky descends and shimmers with a few flakes of snow. It is a rare occasion where, from a boxing point of view, everything goes right. Afterwards I repair to my favourite cosy café nearby. The salad sandwich which I order is a melee of fresh leaves, the perfect diet for any right-thinking chimpanzee. I sip a cappuccino for an hour in silence reading Morrissey's *Autobiography* without the interruption of anyone. Part of the book describes a drive out across Saddleworth Moor near Rochdale in vivid

Gothic prose and the witnessing of a phantasmagorical vision. I doubt the presence of the vision, but the book recalls the publicity surrounding the Moors murders, which loomed large in my childhood imagination.

These unspeakable child murders took place in and around the poorer streets of Manchester in the late 1960s and sent a paroxysm of horror throughout the whole community and country. Many of the victims were poor, latchkey kids, charmed by the perpetrators who assumed the roles of surrogate big brother and sister, and lured the children away with the promise of days out in the country for picnics and frolics. Some of the children were buried on Saddleworth Moor. Cruelly, the perpetrators never revealed all the burial locations, tormenting grieving families for an eternity. Every few years, some new information would come to light prompting policemen in grey overcoats with comb-over hairstyles to grab shovels and dig behind cordons on parts of the moor; a flurry of futile activity.

My parents spoke of these evil acts in hushed, anguished tones. They tried to shield my sister and I from the worst excesses of the media coverage at the time. In the early 1970s I went to school with a girl whose father was an ex-police inspector who had worked on the case. From my girlish perspective, he seemed perfectly ordinary, except perhaps slightly more jolly and humorous than normal. His daughter had told me that he had been pensioned off sick as a relatively young man due to the trauma of working on the Moors murders case. Somehow, I found the knowledge that this humorous and decent man had been inwardly transformed more shocking than anything else.

I remember Saddleworth Moor vividly in the early 1980s. As a podgy schoolgirl, I struggled across it on a failed attempt to walk the Pennine Way. In particular I remember Black Hill, a landmark reached after hours of trudging across and sliding helplessly into peat bog, which had the consistency of treacle. The summit of Black Hill is a tiny, high circle of grass with a trig point – a green island floating in a sea of black. I see Saddleworth Moor now, in my mind's eye, transformed as a benign place with ramblers strolling, the cotton grass waving and the skylark twittering. Nature and Time are ultimately bringing about some kind of redemption.

On the run up to Christmas, local events and planned celebrations of every kind are dwarfed by insane and dreadful international events as Islamic terrorists' bomb and shoot at so-called soft targets in Paris, and Mali and Brussels go into lockdown. Hundreds die at concerts, football matches and in hotels, as the French flag flies in international solidarity over my local town in place of the Union Jack. At international events the 'Marseillaise' is sung in place of any other national anthem. This senseless violence achieves absolutely nothing, except hardening the resolve of right-thinking people whom abhor it, as France declares open warfare on the Islamic State.

Britain also says that it is going to war, but in reality it has probably already been at war with the Islamic State elements in Syria for many months, even years, it is just that the government did not have the courage to announce it. How can anyone decide whether it is best to take out these elements or not? So-called experts disagree about what to do. Who can predict the outcome and decide what will be better or worse in the long term? The World is a lighted tinderbox, and seems dangerous all over the place, but it would be wrong to be scared.

28

SEEING STARS

Knackered from a week of hard work, where I have walked the extra mile across the laboratory floor, I sleep in on a wet Saturday, with Tigger the cat and The Kooks crooning in the background for company.

I have somehow previously dismissed The Kooks as lightweight, because their lead singer has a very annoying, yet beautiful voice and the lyrics make no sense to me. I have to concede that he can actually sing, and their music is in fact a sublime mix of rockabilly, acoustic guitar brilliance and hypnotic beats that I have temporarily fallen in love with. They sing all their usual songs, but in slightly different keys, tuned up or down a tone or semitone for different effect.

I sing out the songs at the top of my voice in the empty house. This probably annoys the neighbours, and causes Tigger to raise his catty eyebrows: he looks at me, baffled, then joins in, miaowing along. I think highbrow artistic thoughts as the music drifts dreamily along, and I suddenly remember that on the previous day I left a very large bag of potatoes that I have already paid for at the local supermarket checkout.

The telly blares out and I recover myself with the help of a pint of Italian coffee. The programme on offer showcases four very silly men who claim to be chefs, but are more in love with themselves than food or anything else. They dally around a professional kitchen, tinkering there, chopping here, marinating this and that with an array of ingredients that are far too expensive for most ordinary people, their red-faced bravado, designer shirts and hairstyles quite ludicrous. I wonder what Lord Reith, the first director general of the BBC, would have made of it. His idea was that TV should showcase the best of endeavour and achievement. Now these worthy ideas are light years away. He must turn in his Presbyterian grave at the lowest-common-denominator reality TV pap that is force-fed on a 24-hour loop. I am so knackered, that I don't even have the energy to get up, find the remote control and turn over the TV channel.

◉

My hands are hurting, I think from too much heavy bag punching, and I am in a constant state of anxiety about whether my boxing gloves (or hands) are worn out or not, or if the gloves are too heavy or not. I punch better with smaller gloves, but they provide less cushioning, so I decide to stick with a heavier pair, but double-wrap my hands.

It is happy hour at Kelly's gym on this Saturday afternoon, as I move round and round the bag achieving some kind of sensible motion, head movement and all of the rest of it, as I try hard to imagine the bag as my opponent. I throw some heavy, satisfying punches for a whole energetic hour. Even normally taciturn gym addicts remark on my improvement.

The following Monday, I am tired from a long day in the laboratory and do not feel up to much, but an eventful evening awaits. Christmas is approaching and Val, one of the youth workers at the youth club, is making a Christmas tree out of paper cutouts of a thousand green handprints turned upside down. The kids are supposed to have done it, but they do not really have the dexterity, so Val valiantly wields the scissors for hours on end while we toil and sweat in the gym. When the creation is finished, I suggest that it needs a fairy on top with a pair of boxing gloves, and Dai pulls a face.

Two new faces appear: Amy, a student of nineteen who says that she is very sporty and that her friend has taught her some boxing at home, and Javed, an Asian man, probably in his late thirties and greying at the temples. He has the look of an ex-boxer as he warms up on the bags.

Javed is fit and determined, and huffs and puffs, never giving up. He is pushing himself too hard we all think, and something in his macho frame must give. He could never survive in the ring as he is just expending too much energy. Moreover, there is absolutely no need. We know these types and have seen them before now a thousand times, and it is hard not be cynical about the trajectory their training will take.

Amy tries very hard but a lifetime of study and recent sofa-dom means that she lasts only twenty minutes into our usual one hour session. She is clearly very embarrassed, almost tearful, and Dai and then I try to put her at ease. At least she is actually present and genuinely trying her best, the minimum requirements for entry into the boxing gym – this automatically counts as a very good start. Amy crumbles into a sweaty heap at the side of the gym, head bowed. It is the system that makes young people unfit like that. It is not her fault, and I admire her for turning up at all and giving it a go.

Will, the law student we have not seen for some time, unexpectedly reappears. Affable and dedicated, Will is still part of our trusted team. His life has been overrun with essays and assignments, and he has suffered with the college virus that is going around. Like two hypochondriacs, we both agree that we have had the same thing and are not up to much, except, of course, a couple of rounds of sparring.

Our morbid self-assessment reminds me of a passage from one of my favourite books, *Three Men in a Boat* by Jerome K. Jerome, where three world-weary Edwardian men take a constitutional holiday on a boat on the River Thames. They are accompanied by Montmorency, their dog, who proves to be the most sensible member of the party.

One of the men, Harris, who is the most practical of all of them, forgets the tin opener, and all three try various desperate measures to open a tin of succulent pineapple that they have brought along as a treat. Using hammers, chisels and other inappropriate tools, they do not manage to open it, but instead beat the tin into a shape which takes on the appearance of a demonic face. Spooked, they throw the tin into the river. On reflection, I am sure that this episode is designed as some kind of morality tale, which I do not get. Their travels are precipitated by a visit to the library, where, on seeking advice on world weariness from a medical dictionary, they agree that they have all the ailments in the book apart from housemaid's knee. As we put our gloves on, Will and I go compare notes from a similar list.

I square up with Will for three two-minute rounds of inevitably unequal sparring, which we both agree will do us good. Dai is ref so anything could happen, and it does. Will is lean, rangy and about six feet tall. He has a very long reach. It is an acknowledged fact that it is hard to box someone taller than you are, so I know that I am going to struggle. I do not really have an appropriate strategy, but I try and think sensible thoughts.

Will and I put on our headgear. Will's is the most elaborate, space-age creation that I have ever seen – all black, with a series of black straps which almost entirely cover his face. Dai buzzes about unhelpfully while we get ready: 'What the hell are you wearing, Will? What do you think Marianne is going to do to you? You look like f—king Darth Vader!'

Dai then turns to me, grinning: 'I bet you didn't realise that you'd be boxing f—king Darth f—king Vader tonight, Marianne.' Dai then does his best Darth Vader impressions, with rolling eyes and sharp, hissing intakes of breath. This is so funny that Will and I collapse double with laughter, but this interlude also breaks my concentration, and while laughing till I cry I am also ever so slightly annoyed.

In the first and second rounds I try to slip or parry Will's series of continuous jabs. It's like someone has turned on a water cannon which just consists of jabs. These are manoeuvres that previously worked quite well with a shorter opponent, but once I have parried or slipped the odd one, I find that I am miles away from Will, and even my planned body shots fall aimlessly into the air. I try to push forward, but I am just met with a further stream of jabs.

I know I should really be ducking under Will's jabs and trying to box him on the inside. But I can't seem to find a break in the action where I can propel myself forwards and just deliver some good shots.

My reactions are too slow and when I try and throw a jab it is retracted far too slowly. Will immediately sees the chink in my armour and delivers a couple of strong right hook counter-punches. In the second round, I get punched once straight in the face as I am undefended for a fraction of a second too long. This results in a standing count for five seconds which just gives me time to thank the Lord (again!) for my quality headgear.

Dai is shouting and shouting encouragement, but it is to no avail. His voice trails off behind the thud, thud, thud of Will's jabs. Will's defences are very good, including a Muhammad Ali type backwards-twisting slip, which is very impressive and totally resistant to breakdown.

In round three, I vow to try harder. In a risky manoeuvre I shove myself forward into Will's punch zone. I manage to parry one of his jabs out of the way, and immediately throw a great head shot with my jab, which catches Will's chin – the only decent shot that I will get through in the entire bout. As a consequence of an ill-judged decision to trade punches at close range, I immediately trip over Will's right foot and fall flat on my face in the middle of the boxing ring for another ten-second count. I find that I cannot get up because I am now laughing too much and the bout turns into a comedy Carry On Boxing sketch.

At the end of the round, Will and I are both spent and enough is enough: at least I have managed to keep going. But I feel that have been too hesitant and need to take a few more risks, instead of waiting to throw the perfect or indeed any punch without loitering in my opponent's punch zone at the same time.

Will tells me that I should have been boxing much more on the inside, and praises my one good jab, which he says was a quality shot. How easy it is to be wise after the event, I think, as I instantly dream up all the things I should have done in the previous six minutes. Still it is worthwhile, and I add the experience to the sum total of other experiences, under the filename: 'What not to do when boxing a tall boxer'. Will and I remove our headgear, and Will apologises, saying that he has been punching too hard, but I really don't think so, as for once this has forced me to correct my cardinal hand-dropping sin. I have managed to keep my hands up mostly for a full three rounds.

We finish off with a round of the Board of Death, and I am surprisingly untired as I crank my way through the familiar exercises. Javed leaps and shouts, but Will and I take it at a steadier, quieter pace, as I feel the recent benefits of recreating my own version of The Board in recent visits to other gyms. Dai joins us in silent suffering until the bitter end and finally the gym door clanks shut.

⊙

Wednesday arrives, but Amy has not put in an appearance, sadly humiliated into absence but not by us. Javed pummels the bags with more than maximum aggression. I arrive late, delayed by work in the laboratory. Dai tells an unrepeatable joke about what I have allegedly been getting up to in the lab. Everyone laughs and I feign deafness, making the others embarrassingly explain the joke (though no explanation is needed). I have the last laugh as they squirm and blush. I secretly hope that I do not have to spar with Javed: I sense in him a killer instinct which I do not like. Instead, vegetarian, cat-loving Will appears, and he will be my sparring partner again. Dai puts his cunning plan into place, where I will spar with Will for two rounds and conveniently wear him out, leaving others to appear heroic in a further two rounds.

Due to the group dynamic, the atmosphere in the gym can change in an instant. Sometimes it is light hearted, sometimes serious, usually the latter when sparring is in progress or when we have been worked so hard that we do not have the energy to speak. On this occasion, Will has his Darth Vader headgear on again, but no one is laughing as I put on mine. Our faces are set and unsmiling as I check my gum guard, and an air of seriousness descends. I am in the blue corner and Will is in the red.

In round one, I feel that Will is pulling no punches. As before, I am at the mercy of his continual long-reach jabs, which land with muffled thuds through my headgear, sounding like underwater mortar fire. Everything else is blanked out, even Javed and Peter's thunderous punches on the nearby bags. At least I am moving backwards, now, trying some pivots and slips and just about avoiding getting pinned on the ropes. All my jabs fail, as Will is just too fast. No sooner have I slipped one of his jabs then there is an uppercut or another set of jabs immediately on their way. Valiantly, I keep my hands up and eyes locked onto my opponent, taking no undefended punches in the first round, but delivering a disappointing zero myself.

In round two, I am under further pressure, and respond by taking some risks by trying to box Will close up, on the inside, as Dai shouts and shouts for me to move forward. I throw couple of jabs, and just one jab and a body shot get through. Will delivers a great jab straight into the centre of my face, as my hands drop for half a second, and I feel my nose flattening, a strange feeling like a nosebleed about to start. I bend double as Will puts further pressure on, and I am felled by a giant left hook, which stings my right cheekbone, just missing my headgear, but I immediately straighten up and throw the best jabs that I can muster. Thankfully, Dai calls time and commends me for trying so hard, but I feel that I must speed up my reactions somehow.

I box a further, fairly uneventful round three with Dai, delivering a couple of great jabs and body shots, but the truth is I feel that Dai is pulling his punches a bit, no doubt mindful of his two impending rounds with Will, but also intent on building my confidence. I am a bit grateful as I finally flop over the ropes. The instant I get out of the ring, I can see in my mind's eye a rerun of every mistake, like a high-speed video clip. As Dai takes off my headgear he says, 'I can't fault your enthusiasm, Marianne.' And he can't, but lack of enthusiasm is not my problem. Will says there has been dramatic improvement in my boxing over the last six months and this is fantastic to hear, though I do not really see it myself.

I am now the ref for Dai's further four rounds with Will. I know that they will both get carried away, so I warn them at the outset. In both rounds I see that Dai is put under pressure by Will. Dai tries and fails to push Will back and is starting to see all my difficulties first hand. I feel a bit vindicated as Dai takes jab after jab. Will's long reach and side shimmies mean that unusually even Dai's jabs fall into thin air. Will moves back and is impossible to reach.

In round two, Will changes effortlessly into a southpaw stance, forcing Dai to jab with his right, which he does not like. In the end, it is Will's lack of fitness, not technique, which allows Dai to finally push forward with his signature quadruple jabs and quickfire body shots. At the end of the fourth round, Will crumbles and cannot move. He looks like the better technical boxer, but is now wasted after eight minutes of dishing it out. They touch gloves, and Dai claps Will on the back.

I am glad that they are not boxing any more rounds as I feel that someone might get hurt. Dai says that apart from a lack of cardio fitness, which can be easily acquired with hard work, Will is ready to go into the ring. I definitely agree, and Will beams. We all enjoy the sparring, and Dai says that we must do it more often. But we are doing it often, I think. Often enough for *me*, anyway.

Peter and Javed have already gone home without us even noticing, and we pack up the ring. I feel that it is rude that we have not bid them goodbye, temporarily lost in the microcosm that is the boxing ring.

Dai says of Javed, 'He's just done ten years' time, but is on the straight and narrow now.' I want to think the best of Javed, who has dispensed with his old life and associates, but I somehow I cannot. I remember the look in his eyes as he squared up to the bag, and strangely no one appears to want to spar with him, not even Dai.

I drive home, going through my usual injury-checking protocol under the favoured streetlight. I decide that there could be a bruise on my cheekbone and one on my chin, but these turn out to be only shadowy tricks of the light. I do not have double-vision just yet, so I feel that for the time being all is well and my boxing addiction can continue, as long as I proceed with caution. Starving hungry, I eat an entire malt loaf, wishing instantly I had bought two or even three.

Although I am in a general state of denial, I do know that this is probably the most risky phase of my boxing endeavours – my defences are still very poor, yet I am sparring twice a week against much better technical boxers. I also know full well that two or three days' rest will be required as a forfeit for my recent efforts.

29

WHEN THE LIGHTS GO OUT

When the nation is on its knees anyway from a surfeit of manic consumerism and patent exhaustion, catastrophic floods hit Carlisle, Cockermouth, Kendal, Keswick and Lancaster and the lights go out. Civil servants in the Environment Agency, who should be protecting us from floods, fail to realise that one-in-a-hundred-years events now happen every decade.

People's cherished homes and livelihoods become temporary prisons as climate change rails at the front door, and neither insurance nor respite can be found. Beloved cats looking frightened in baskets, heirlooms and elderly relatives are all carried out at eye level or on boats, and nothing will be the same again.

The Tory government, which continues to hate The North, pledges a paltry £5,000 per household, on application *of course*, so that the poor and needy will be speedily disenfranchised and dispensed with. The North reminds the Tories of the things they can never achieve and have no intention of achieving, and so is hated forever.

At work the electricity is on, then off, then on again, in a merry-go-round. Laboratory equipment breaks down without a thought for anyone. The generators come on and go off again. The fire alarms are not working, so we are told that fire marshals will operate air horns to warn us if the building is on fire. I wonder how they will know where we all are in the vast building. The lunatics are finally in charge of the asylum. I am called into work, then sent home, then called back in, and so on. We are cast into darkness, some of our precious equipment and experiments gone to ruin.

There is a massive graduation ceremony at the university which must go ahead at all costs. I volunteer to line up 130 students in a special crocodile queue, so that they can have their glorious moment on stage, collect their degree certificates and put some letters after their names for ever more.

Blocking out the trials by flood, I swarm into Kelly's gym on both Saturday and Sunday. The spirit is willing, but the flesh is weak. On Sunday Jamie is there, and I explain my difficulties in boxing Will. From my description, Jamie tells me that Will is almost certainly using the eponymous Mayweather Defence, where the head is tucked into the right shoulder, and the left arm is placed across the front of the body. We agree that there is very little that I can do about this apart from some bold boxing on the inside, where I will certainly take a few hits. I am suffering from the occasional very heavy hook, and Jamie says that it is permissible to move the hand to position outside the opposite cheekbone to repel hooks, but this requires speed and must be practised. The other thing that I am not doing is tucking my chin behind the top of my shoulder.

Jamie also suggests that I should try and control Will's punching pattern by drawing him into throwing certain punches, which I may have some hope of countering, for example by throwing my right shoulder forward, encouraging him to throw a jab. I must say that in a specific sense I do not see how this will work, as he is already throwing a thousand jabs and I really do not want him to throw any more, but the general idea might work in another way with thought and practice.

On the following three days, I rediscover why I cannot go boxing four times a week at my age, and for once I am glad that the routine sessions are cancelled on both Monday and Wednesday due to floods and no electricity, as I am truly all in. Two sparring sessions the previous week plus another two training sessions are really too much, and in the evenings after work I fall asleep with Tigger on the sofa to the background burble of *The Archers*, not remaining awake through a single episode. Note to self: REST, REST and MORE REST.

While I am resting, like an actor temporarily off the stage, I do some boxing homework, and look up ten of the best Mayweather boxing tricks shown as tantalising video clips on YouTube. The clips are just too fast and furious for me to even take in, and I replay them at impossibly slow speeds, trying to deconstruct the action. Many of Mayweather's tricks just look like adapted forms of grappling. He is certainly pushing the boundaries in terms of boxing style. The least complicated manoeuvre is a slick shoulder roll, and I decide that this is at least possible, so I put this one on the starting blocks. In the same week, Tyson Fury, fresh from winning a World Heavyweight boxing title, brings all boxers, and indeed humans, into disrepute by making a series of ridiculous sexist and homophobic comments. In an impromptu interview his face leers out from the passenger seat of a white van, as, caught in his own time warp, he cites God as his excuse.

⊙

One Saturday, it is Jamie's impossible task to teach me some proper defensive boxing. He rises magnificently to the challenge, while I am the major stumbling block.

We talk about sparring and all its benefits and difficulties. I now have a decent jab, but am incapable at times of getting it anywhere useful into my opponent's punch zone. This is because I am far too slow at getting it out, after employing either a block or parry. In the amateur gym, I have been used to blocking and parrying shots without much precision, then with the shortest of delays throwing out my jab. Blocking is simply putting your hand in the way of the punch, and parrying involves a short pivot of the forearm or hand inwards or outwards to knock it out of the way. Jamie says that I must not use the parry at all, as I am just too slow, and must not block first then jab, again on grounds of speed. Instead, I must simultaneously block my opponent's shot and throw out my jab. This takes a bit of getting used to, as it feels like the childhood game of patting your head and rubbing your stomach.

Jamie throws jab after jab, which I manage to block. He tells me to get into the habit of bringing my right hand facing outwards over the front of my face to block his jab, while throwing out my own, but then moving the right hand back immediately to the side of my face, far enough back so that it protects my right cheekbone from a sly left hook. Also, I am still not tucking my chin well enough behind the ball of my left shoulder when throwing my jab, so I need to work on this too, otherwise I will be vulnerable to a right hook.

Jamie speeds things up a bit, and throws a mixture of single and double jabs. I manage to block most of his shots, but have to remember to keep my right hand block in place for two shots if he unexpectedly throws a double jab. Then we try the same thing again, but this time I touch Jamie's forehead with my glove, instead of throwing a jab to his glove, making him a more realistic target. Then things are further complicated by him moving round the ring. His hands are deliberately quite low, and this wrongly tempts me to lower mine, as I try and catch his jabs, which appear to come from below. I manage some good, naturalistic blocks at reasonable speed.

We talk about the ideal height to hold one's hands. Jamie's hands are low, because he has the speed and confidence to move them up into position. He says that it is not a bad idea to leave your left hand drifting in space at half punching distance and height in readiness for a jab, as this confuses your opponent, making their eyes drift in different directions. This is a brilliant piece of advice. This also means that your jab is already 'halfway there', or you have a feinted shot waiting in the wings, ready to spring out from behind the curtains. Will certainly used this tactic a fortnight previously to good effect, as I did not know what to do with his drifting left hand. I had decided that the best thing to do was to totally ignore it, unless it appeared suddenly in my face – any other response represented a level of sophistication that I was not yet ready to embrace.

Jamie starts to teach me a lovely manoeuvre that I have longed to learn. Initially I do not even know its name. It looks to be a quick lean backwards to avoid the forward thrust of a punch, but is nothing of the sort.

This clever trick is called a swayback. You need to first get into a stance where the feet are slightly closer together than usual but, of course, not in line. Then you must taunt your opponent by pushing your right shoulder forward a smidgen, appearing to lean forward, but not really doing so. This is to encourage them to come forward into your punch zone to throw their best jab. The instant your opponent's jab comes off the starting blocks, you must take a small step backwards with your back (right) foot. Then, keeping the torso upright and the front left leg ever so slightly bent, the back right leg must be cranked down *as far as possible* with the knee at an impossibly acute angle, until it *really hurts*. The right leg acts as a repository of as much potential energy as it is humanly feasible to store in the knee joint and muscles.

As your victim comes in to jab, the crank in your knee will just keep your head positioned out of danger, and you are then in the perfect position to uncrank the knee, twist the hips and unleash the perfect jab. I try this about thirty times. I forget to step back about twenty times, sometimes managing to convert my mistake into an awkward duck, nonetheless missing the jab, and just for three or four throws of the dice I get it right.

'Empty your mind,' says Jamie, as I try to abandon a lifetime of over-analysis. Jamie's full-stretch jab falls aimlessly into the air, and I return a beautiful slapped jab onto his glove. I try a return with a right hand, but I am telegraphing the shot too much, rendering it useless. Jamie says that there should be enough crank from the knee to throw a jab or right hand straight from my cheekbone without any unnecessary pulling back. He also shows me how the cranked-knee position is also the perfect precursor to a left hook, but this is just too much to take in. After a whole hour, brain fog starts to take over, as I forget to step back or do anything, signalling that it is time to stop.

Jamie tells me that I will have to develop much more explosive power in the back right leg, as it is all too slow. There are specific impossible-feeling exercises that will develop this attribute. The first one is like walking off a diving board – in this case the edge of the boxing ring, and landing heels first on the hard gym floor two feet below, bending the knees and then slowly returning to the upright position, with a little jump at the end for good measure. I do this five times, getting it right only once. I wonder if this is something that mere conditioning will iron out or if it will result in injury. I suspect the latter.

Jamie gives me a knee-friendly alternative. This involves sitting on a chair or, if in the gym, on the edge of the ring, standing up as fast as you can, while remaining in balance and then slowly returning to a seated position, adding a little jump in the middle if you can.

This seems doable, so I decide to start with this one. Boxing skills do not happen by accident, only by dint of practice and hard work. Events are pushed forward by a singular drum and bass track by Underworld called 'Dark & Long (Dark Train)', which proves to have the perfect tempo for practising boxing defences, and this track is for the time being ever on repeat as the boxing train rolls on and on, full steam ahead, with no time for anyone to get on or off.

The next few sessions at Kelly's gym are effectively boxing homework, as the youth club gym closes until January. In the final session in December only Peter and I are present, silently pummelling for all we are worth. We always seem to be the obsessive misfits who are the last to be kicked out the gym. I drive home, through very heavy rain and acres of brown floodwater, as one windscreen wiper suddenly snaps. I will get it fixed, ready for the next deluge.

Friday night is the blackest of nights as I miss the road turning into the gym and drive the unavoidable stretch of road past the abattoir, no doubt working at a killing pace because of the impending festive season. Its yawning maws are lit up by harsh fluorescent lights, as what goes in never comes out, and both animal and human souls are lost forever. A colleague invites me to a university Christmas social evening, where many others that I know will be present. The venue is on the same road as another abattoir close by, and I find that I have to decline for this reason alone.

I slouch round the heavy bag at Kelly's gym, trying to summon up some enthusiasm for slipping and rolling. My back right knee cranks further and further down, as I try not to lean backwards too much for the perfect swayback. I need to work more on my right arm strength, as my jab, once awkward, has somehow taken over as the power punch. The non-existence of a decent right hook is also a problem. Having spent over two years as an orthodox boxer, I also need to develop some southpaw tricks. Such is the encyclopaedia of things to be done and things to be put right. Someone has turned up the heating inside the gym, even though it is the mildest December ever known. The sweat slithers horribly onto the gym floor and from time to time I rush outside into the cool air.

Christmas is coming on like a sickness. It finally arrives and does not go away for far too long. All hopes of boxing are put on hold as my back finally gives in after days of twinging. Lifting too much stuff in the laboratory, plus the full range Russian twists I have been attempting have probably been the tipping point. I spend a few fitful codeine-filled nights lying completely flat on the hard floor in front of the fire.

There are violent storms, which send a barrage of hail down the chimney onto Tigger and me, and we both awake with a start. To our amazement, a small, bemused blackbird appears on the hearth, sucked down by the storm. In a deft movement, I bamboozle the bird, trapping it gently with a tea towel before

Tigger shows too much interest. It is at times like these that I really wish that *animals could speak*.

On Christmas Eve, in desperation, I ring my physiotherapist, Ted, in Kendal. As usual, he is calm and emails me a few exercises, and it is true that they do improve my situation, and I must just persist with them. He tells me that it is probably inflamed muscles pressing on the sciatic nerve. As I have no pins and needles in my left leg or loss of feeling, he is not unduly bothered, although I am.

Even though my leg feels a bit funny, I am allowed to go out walking, so I do. On Christmas Day morning I park at the Winskill cattle grid above Langcliffe near Settle, on the edge of Malham Moor, having driven a few miles along The Most Beautiful Road in the World. I limp across the cattle grid then walk on the slippery grass across several empty fields, grappling with a walking pole, making sure that I do not slip and cause further injury. Then to the left up over a stile, past the ancient stone water trough that is always there, onto the ancient stony track towards Jubilee Cave, and then out onto the expanse of Malham Moor, with splendid wide views of Fountains Fell and the area towards Malham Tarn.

It is wonderful to be outside again in the winter daylight. I immediately regret far too much time recently spent indoors, even for enjoyable and improving boxing pursuits. I hobble as far as a small, heavy abandoned truck used as a water bowser for animals in the hot summer. Now it is on its side on the cold, wet ground. I wonder how it came to be like that – surely no farm animal could have pushed it over.

On Boxing Day there is more of the same in the lashing rain, but alas no boxing. Terrible floods afflict north-west England again, and a few miles from my house I see that someone is paddling a white canoe across the washed out fields south of Horton-in-Ribblesdale. I enjoy another walk on the hills above Langcliffe, pressing on to the ancient Victoria Cave, a little way up a steep limestone scar, and scrabble around inside the cave, probably doing more than I should.

On my way down the hill I meet a man who like me is walking with some difficulty, clutching his side. He looks like he has been shot, but it turns out that he has recently broken ribs after a fall from his bike. Like two afflicted souls never giving up, we creep downhill even though the weather is filthy. Are we mad or just determined? I cannot decide. Dene, a local shopkeeper, runs towards us and stops for a chat. Dene is in his late fifties, a determined kickboxer and fell runner. We both envy him as he tells us of his planned eight mile round of the fells, and he zips on enthusiastically. I rue that only two weeks ago I was fighting in the boxing ring, but now appear to be moving around like an old crone.

For Christmas I am given a 2016 calendar showing Great Boxers of Our Time. Gennady Golovkin, appears on the January page. Although he is holding his hands aloft in a victory pose, gazing not at the crowd, he looks modest, even bewildered, as he clocks up thirty-four consecutive wins with no defeats. As homage to his Kazakh heritage he is wearing a blue velvet robe with gold embroidery.

I watch a video clip of his heavy bag workout. It has to be seen (and heard) to be believed. Golovkin has both power and skill. Opponents describe his punches as sledgehammer blows. In another video clip, he is shown finishing off various tall heavyweights, as middleweights in his own weight category are no longer deemed to be powerful enough to stand up to him. I read an appraisal of his skills in *Boxing Monthly*. His legendary punching power is attributed partly to genetics and the operation of natural selection on twenty generations of Kazakhs. I suspect that Golovkin has had some help from nature, but has also spent most of his short life in the gym, under the watchful eye of his skilled trainer Sanchez, who must take a good deal of credit.

Golovkin is the perfect marriage of nature and nurture, just as I am the perfect marriage of debility and neglect. I am now firmly in the negative zone, scrambling merely to get back to the zero mark and then off the starting blocks again. After watching some late night TV boxing, exhausted even by the vicarious thoughts of it all, I suck the air through my teeth. Tigger, who was asleep in his basket by the fire, pricks up his ears and looks up in annoyance as hail comes down the chimney for the second time.

30

COLD WAR

On New Year's Eve I go again to see my physiotherapist in Kendal. I fear the worst, as always, but the news is better than expected. After an examination, Ted confirms that my problem is a work-induced lifting injury probably coupled with a classic boxers' twisting injury, inflaming a set of pesky pyriformis muscles and other muscles that I have never even heard of at the base of my back – a literal and metaphorical 'pain in the a—e'.

I feel no compulsion to do anything that evening, so I do not, except watch the original 1970s version of *Tinker, Tailor, Soldier, Spy*. Back in the day, when at school, the episodes of original TV series were on a particular weekday night which always clashed with maths homework. It is a great pleasure to be watching it again without that particular spectre hovering.

I was never any good at maths, but had to endure it at A level and during my first year at university. It was always assumed by everyone that I would excel at maths, as my mother was a maths teacher and my cousin was an actuary. Nobody noticed that I was not like them. My passion was, in fact, natural history. As far as I was concerned this was an innocent branch of science untainted by the ephemerality of human affairs, whose simple laws stretched reassuringly across time and space.

Because education had lifted my parents out of lives of poverty in Liverpool and the East End of Glasgow, they wrongly felt that it was a panacea for everything. I think I disappointed my parents in every conceivable way, mainly by failing to automatically aspire to a future career they had mapped out for me as a professor of mathematics at Oxford University. In the end, I was pushed to go to there. During three miserable years, I was forced to live with chinless wonders from Eton and Harrow who had an outrageous sense of entitlement. I begged my parents' permission to leave. Due to vicarious pride, they refused. I never forgave them. In the end it made no difference.

In the *Tinker, Tailor* TV series, the brilliant Alec Guinness plays George Smiley, a fictitious aged British agent who is called out of retirement to flush out a Russian mole, 'Gerald', known throughout as 'The-Mole-Gerald'. The-Mole-Gerald has infiltrated the British Secret Service. Alec Guinness's raised eyebrow or tilt of his spectacles says far more than a thousand words. Over many episodes, the complex Cold War plot, full of twists and turns and unsayable nuances, is slowly revealed. It can be summarised as a critique of the old boy network and its stronghold on Britain, which allowed its traitors to operate in plain sight.

A wave of paranoia had crossed Britain in the late 1960s and early 1970s because of the threat that the Russians posed and the likelihood of nuclear war. This had been fuelled by the so-called treachery of the Cambridge spies Guy Burgess, Kim Philby, Donald Maclean and Anthony Blunt and also by the infiltration of the Atomic Energy Research Establishment at Harwell, Oxfordshire, by Klaus Fuchs, a Russian research scientist and Russian spy. Fuchs 'slept' for decades, becoming a trusted member of the local Harwell community, before starting his deception.

Tinker, Tailor takes me back seamlessly to those times, with the swirling 1970s interior decor, a complete lack of political correctness and taste, and everybody smoking. This is a sort of comfort, as life was simpler, and you knew who your enemies were. In the TV series there are long shots across grey, ploughed fields in Oxfordshire, and of earnest pipe smoking men meeting in Regent's Park, wearing Homburg hats and dropping things in dead letter boxes in London and Brno.

Bizarrely, I notice that Tigger is watching *Tinker, Tailor* with me, his ears and eyes trained intently on the ploughed fields and the plodding men in wellingtons and overcoats giving up their secrets for a full half hour. This is the first time I have noticed him doing this, and I have the horrible realisation that perhaps he is just plain bored and needs more entertainment.

On New Year's Day 2016, I watch a charming wildlife film about gorillas in the rainforests of the Congo. The gorillas are much more civilised than many people I know, looking out for their immediate family and community in a gentle, altruistic way. They are remarkably chilled and non-aggressive as the camera team continually invade their space and territory. After all, how would we feel if a load of strangers suddenly took up residence in our front room? Allegedly as part of an experiment, the wildlife camera team give the gorillas various objects to investigate, including a mirror attached to a camera. As one gorilla's face looms out of the television, Tigger rushes for cover under the sofa, which is a shame, as I think he had been enjoying the film immensely up to that point.

⊙

In the New Year, with my back just about holding up, sober and cold, we toil in the youth club gym, with the eight rounds on the heavy bags taking their toll. Dai looms right up to me as I vainly try to keep going on the heavy bag with a few weak twists and hooks, making double sure there is no slacking.

Matt and Dan, new recruits with the best New Year intentions, also join. One is a boxer, and both end up wasted. Russian twists, tuck jumps, running on the spot, sit-ups and then a round on the pads. Peter excuses himself from the other exercises and UNBELIEVABLY asks for MORE TIME on the heavy bag, while the rest of us gag, wheeze and double over with exhaustion.

Dai has been watching me trialling out my little slips and rolls like a hawk. He sniffs and says, 'We don't do that sh—t in the amateur gym.' 'Well, I do,' I say, glaring – feeling that it is my only chance of avoiding someone's future jab, as I am so slow off the mark. Dai snorts and looks at the floor, but I carry on, determined. On the pads I am very strong, relaxed and throw some much-better-than-usual jabs. Dai says accusingly: 'You've been practising.' I have to admit that I have.

Dai knows everything, and dissembling and even false modesty is pointless. As I huff and puff, Dai disses cross-trainers and other such new-fangled things. He snarls at fancy gyms, praising the two-mile-long Morecambe prom and its assortment of lamp posts as the perfect training ground. 'Walk, jog, run' between the perfectly spaced lamp posts. The sleet and Arctic westerlies will lash you in the face. Do a few press-ups with your feet on the park benches for good measure. Ignore remarks from bystanders and drunks and you are indeed well on the way.

On Wednesday it is more of the same, as more boxers appear. Javed is there with his sidekick, a small, macho man with an attitude. He upsets one of the youth workers on reception by taking a bottle of water out of the kids' tuck shop without asking. His unfit body is rife and stiff with predetermined machismo and he cannot skip for toffee in the opening session. This is a skill that has to be learned over time, but he is much too impatient. I have seen the small kids who routinely attend the youth boxing sessions showing much more determination. Totally knackered after a mere half hour, the nameless macho huffs a giant huff and exits the gym.

This is noteworthy, as it is only the second time I have seen *ANYONE* leave mid-session. Lord knows we have all been tempted, as Gerard and then Dai have pushed us up to various limits, but we have grit in our spittle and iron in our veins, and have somehow resisted. As Dai watches them leave, he narrows his eyes and growls: 'Well, f—k off out of my gym then!' and we all laugh, but Javed looks serious and stays on.

I drink gallons of water, and say to Dai with false confidence that I have been learning some defences. Ha ha ha. Everyone smirks including me: I'll be laughing on the other side of my face when these are put to the test, but what the hell – I can pretend for a while, at least to myself.

31

CYLINDER HEAD GASKET

The cylinder head gasket in my car engine has blown. Like every other human being on the planet, I have a heavy work schedule the following week, when my car will be hospitalised in the local garage in the Dales. As the long daily commute to work at the university is not humanly possible by public transport, I have booked a hotel room for the week in the conference accommodation section of the university until my car is fixed. I arrive on Sunday afternoon, where I am shown to a box-like room. It is clean, bland and comfortable and I am grateful for it. I sleep a deep afternoon sleep, and when I wake and open the blinds the sky is as grey as the ground and a few crystal flakes of snow are falling.

I then dash to the university sports centre, where four boxing bags are ranged along one side of a dance studio. There is nobody there, so I slug it out alone, contemplating my skipping action which is reflected in twenty giant mirrors – it is not a pretty sight. This is followed by a thousand 1-1-2-left hooks until I can no longer move arms or legs, and I double over, completely revived.

The following week passes in a blur of laboratory work, sandwiches and weak coffee. It is like being unexpectedly homeless, at work and on holiday all at once, and being paid and charged for the pleasure. A giant rucksack holds all my possessions and nothing is quite in the right place. Haydon works shifts and phones from home. He says with cold glee that I should prepare to be away from home for a month. I cannot see the joke. My sister is not contactable by phone, and I am out of sorts. Friends and family seem too remote.

⊙

On Monday night I seek the solace of other boxers. The university boxing club is very welcoming, as it has been in the past when I have been unable to attend the youth club sessions. Tommy is the affable Scouse coach. The treasurer is not there so they immediately waive the £4 fee. I have lost one of my boxing wraps, so Tommy lends me a beautiful championship pair.

Tommy knows Dai on the circuit, and ribs him by saying to me: 'So you've decided to join a *proper* boxing gym, now then, eh?' I raise my eyebrows by way of reply.

I am already a bit late, and the others are already hopping and leaping. The warm up is a tough forty minutes of side stepping, jumping about, then shuttle runs with press-ups, mountain climbing and sit-ups in teams of three. A rather geeky Chinese lad, who looks like a good boxer, is my designated partner. We slip and roll, reinforcing basic defences and each of us throws a series of light jabs. He suddenly looks unhappy and stops. 'Is everything OK?' I say, concerned. He hesitantly replies: 'No! You're SCARING me!' and we both laugh, as I feel that I could not scare the skin off a rice pudding.

Tommy tells me that I am dragging my feet and should be springing in and out of my opponent's punch zone, instead of effectively walking back and forth. Here the amateur and professional cultures clash, as Jamie has taught me to walk instead of jump. You never see Gennady Golovkin jumping, so I don't see why I should have to do it.

My front foot is flat and Tommy does not like this either, as he says that I should be up on the balls of both feet, but I don't think so. Tommy's default slip is different from mine, but I can't quite see how – he also uses a slick elbow-up manoeuvre to repel right hooks. I show him Jamie's upright-torso sway-back, which contrasts with his inferior leanback, where you end up in no position to punch, but he dismisses the swayback as '1950s-style boxing'.

After the end of the session, I walk across the university campus with Tommy and a few others as they make for the bus. The brutalist architecture is lit up with twinkling lights, but still looks brutal. Hushed figures stand near the bike sheds eating fried chicken, and Far Eastern students laugh in several languages. I ask Tommy if he is doing any sparring. Like an explosives expert holding up a hand with only two fingers, Tommy grimaces, revealing a fine set of missing-tombstone teeth, all gone at the front except for one. 'No, love. They can't make me a gum guard to fit,' he spits. 'Last time I sat in the dentist's waiting room it cost me £900.' I expect that Tommy's dentist actually screamed and ran away, overwhelmed by the scale of the structural engineering.

I walk back to my room down avenues of lit up matchbox rooms, aflame with zealous learners starting to burn the midnight oil. On a whim, I visit the university library, just to see what libraries look like these days. There are huge interactive screens, but also some books.

Most people enter a library with a specific quest in mind, but I go in to survey the length, breadth and depth of human knowledge just for the fun of it. I idly wander through the avenues of stacked books, marvelling at the diverse content. I see people crammed into tiny glass-fronted rooms called 'group-learning zones', whatever they are. I whoosh soundlessly along the aisles, eyeballing every facet of human knowledge, attracting looks of slight disdain. There is early modernism, modernism and post-modernism, and other types of modernism that I have never even heard of.

I take comfort in the fact that people have studied the lesser spotted something for their whole lives. The library is a sweltering engine of knowledge turning at full speed with the brakes off, fuelled dedication, where everything seems worthwhile and where the lights burn defiantly into the night.

On Thursday I join the college boxers again. I try out unfamiliar ten-punch combinations with Jules. She is of generous proportions, but nonetheless a very slick mover with a really excellent boxing brain, who defies immediate expectations. I try to slip (a jab) to the right, throw a right uppercut, throw a left hook, straight right, swayback, roll rightwards to avoid left hook, throw a left hook, straight right, left hook, roll to avoid a second left hook, throw a left hook, straight right, left hook, throw a left hook and finish off with straight right.

Second set: jab, right uppercut to body, right uppercut, left hook, straight right, left hook, roll to the right, then can't remember anything as brain fog reigns. These are great fun, and will speed up all my reactions and test my memory, but when am I ever going to throw them for real?

⊙

I am reunited with my car on Saturday and on Sunday I make it to Kelly's gym, struggling with new southpaw moves that Jamie has recommended. I see Frank for the first time in a month. He has trimmed up and is clearly working hard. I try and teach him to skip, and he tries to teach me an uppercut: I am not bending down far enough to the left, and he is jumping too high, but we are where we are.

I fetch up for a usual Monday session with Dai at the youth club. Dai is in a funny mood. I make an idiot of myself on the pads and in the first round, finding I am unable to throw the simplest shot. Second time around I am more relaxed, and at last a slap turns into a thud. Dai forces a smile. Eight rounds on the bags later, I unexpectedly have some fuel left in the tank. Dai gives over the last fifteen minutes to my choices, so we finish off with thirty full range twists, twenty burpees, twenty mountain-climbers, ten press-ups, and twenty squat thrusts. I do not know why I have chosen these killers at the end, and neither does anyone else. It is just sheer perversity, and now I will need a week's worth of tea and biscuits to recover (and I don't even eat biscuits).

Dai has been watching an American TV fitness programme called *Insanity*, where people are duped into parting with money to buy DVDs and are directed to try series of impossible exercises day after day. This is crazy sh—t of the first order, and I silently beg Dai not to get sucked in by it. Nonetheless, some of the crazy crab walks and hops are inflicted on us, and the following day, probably like the duped Americans, I find that I have difficulty walking.

Wednesday is more of the same only more so. Dai sets out laminated cards on the floor covered in green writing, detailing the exercises that we must do at the beginning and end of the session – a brutal set of circuits with eight rounds of bag punching in between. One person in the gym turns out to be colour blind which causes more than the usual confusion. I have been practising tuck jumps, and this pays off as I spring into the air like a jack-in-the-box like I have never done before. On the pads I throw some good thwacking jabs and feel very strong.

Intermittently, Dai describes all the curry houses in Morecambe that he has ever visited, but the reverberation of sound makes this impossible to follow. We nod in the right places, as the sweat drips from chins and eyebrows and we use any non-boxing brain cells that remain to decipher this one-way conversation.

Dutifully, I make it very late to Kelly's gym on a Saturday. There is only an hour left of workout time. The lad on reception says that I am one of the few that turns up at the weekend. This is meant well – to suggest dedication – but it inadvertently points up that I have indeed become rather a sad gym monkey. I think of possible dystopian alternatives which could fill a Saturday afternoon, such as carnivorous afternoon barbeques, watching *Phantom of the Opera* with compulsory audience participation or, worse still, the torturous Trafford Centre or IKEA, and the gym easily wins out.

On Monday, I fetch up at the youth club again, with its eternal draw. Javed appears, along with a newish lad Jon, and also Ben, a stalwart youth boxer who has recently graduated into the boxing seniors. As Dai is away, Javed offers to take the reins and offers me three two-minute rounds on the pads. This is a turn up for the books as he is a great pad-holder. He shouts genuine encouragement and I think is surprised at the nifty five-punch combinations that I can now throw, as I rarely get this type of practice outside the professional gym. All Jamie's training comes good, and I throw some really great jabs and straight rights. Javed assures me that he can feel the power and dynamism in the shots. The left hooks and body shots are still dodgy, and the right hooks even worse, but for the first time I throw a great left uppercut, getting right underneath the shot, my whole body pivoting underneath it, as brain and body working together, for once. Honour is satisfied, as I have been punching right to the end of the three three-minute rounds.

Javed says that he wants me to show more aggression, presumably expecting me to bare my teeth, but no amount of drama will make me a better boxer as I am technically giving it my all. I just want to throw a great jab/hook combination. I share with Javed some of the swayback manoeuvres that Jamie has recently taught me and we consider the difficulties of boxing somebody tall. Then, at my insistence, we haul out the Board of Death from the boxing store. We grind our way through, all trying to keep up with each other. Jon and Ben fall by the wayside, after valiant efforts. The Board dampens any bright illusion that you are actually fit. I slug through the first round, expecting a second, but we have all had enough. The Welsh expression 'Too much is plenty' comes to mind.

A few days later, I fetch up again at Kelly's gym. Frank is there, doggedly enthusiastic. I like Frank – although a relative novice he is really giving it his all and I can see that he loves boxing so there is common ground. After an hour or so of various routines, Dave, a rookie professional trainer, offers to hold up the pads, for Frank and then for me, for five one-minute rounds each. I shout encouragement to Frank. Dave holds the pads well, as Frank's six foot three inches worth of power comes crashing down. Initially, Frank is too tense and is only throwing the shots from his shoulders, and not moving around the boxing ring. I instantly make things worse by shouting: 'Frank – you are too tense!' Finally, he relaxes, starts to move, throws some great straight rights and left hooks which are angled downwards, but his jab is still only an embryo of itself. Frank has only been boxing for about six months, but under Jamie's skilled tutelage he has made excellent progress.

I step through the ropes for my turn feeling less than spry, but once my gloves are on and up, I feel good and ready. I am initially too tense, and the first round is full of stilted shots. Then I find my feet, as the boxing machinery clanks into action. I throw some great jabs, and I can see the surprise on Dave's face as the pressure of the jab on the pads shoves him steadily backwards towards the ropes. I make a few elementary mistakes, but overall there is some actual boxing going on, with slips, rolls and jabs effortlessly slewing out. I am not really tired at all after the five short rounds, and this too is a kind of vindication. Frank and Dave smile as they praise the power of my jabs, and a smile breaks across my face.

32

A REST IS AS GOOD AS A REST

I have been working too hard, and have broken out in a magnificent trio of cold sores, a virus and Athlete's foot. These are probably due to overtraining and overwork. For once, I am sensible and take a week's enforced rest from the gym. Numbers at the youth club gym have been dwindling recently and I particularly feel for Dai, who is now giving up his time voluntarily for hardly anyone.

I have had the day off work and the morning passes by. Snow falls outside and deadens any sound. Embarrassingly, I am still lounging on the sofa in dressing gown in the late morning when my neighbour rings the doorbell to leave his key, as he is going away for a few days. I shout through the letter box and sprint upstairs to get dressed and join the human race for the remainder of the day.

I go to the chemist's in my local town, mainly in search of foot cures. A man with windmill arms and designer glasses rushes into the shop, shouting and swearing in a loud, plummy accent. He says words that are never normally uttered in public, and everyone in the shop recoils in horror. The man is Toby, an upper-class alcoholic whose wife left him a year ago and whose brother has gone AWOL. Once handsome and successful, his life is now lived publicly in chaos and shame.

Like a bolting horse, he rushes headlong at the line of waiting customers, waving fists and shouting. In typical British fashion we say nothing and do nothing and the threat passes; someone who knows Toby fortuitously comes into the shop and calms him down.

When I leave I see Toby, with his companion, shakily clutching cigarettes and waiting in the rain on the town hall steps for help to arrive. I overhear him say in a rasping stage whisper, 'My life is just such a f—king mess.' He is so right. I toy with the idea of offering them a lift, but on this occasion I am the Bad Samaritan and pass by on the other side, sensing problems too deep to be rooted out in an instant. Besides, I am afraid that Toby will throw up in my car.

After a tough self-imposed workout at the Kelly's gym on Saturday, I head off to the local café, nearby. I sink into corner chair with a book. I am still reading Morrissey's *Autobiography*. The reviews of the book say things like 'bathetic, droll, deep', but for me funny covers everything important.

I read one hilarious section where, before they were both famous, Morrissey describes a visit to London to see his kooky, barely employable friend James Maker. Through a torpor of existential angst and cigarette smoke, James just about manages to answer the telephone for a firm of travel agents. James later reflects, 'It was good job – I had my own chair.' I splutter out my coffee at this epithet. At a loose end at the end of a dull day, Morrissey describes a visit with the same friend to a swimming pool in Peckham, where 'the smell of feet is awful, and I notice with horror that someone is still wearing their socks'. At the time they were both self-confessed no-hopers. Morrissey describes their situation with all the hilarious semi-hubris and fastidiousness of those who unconscionably sniff out those on a lower rung even than themselves. In the end, I find that the book is too funny to read in public and I have to snap it shut.

On Monday, we find out that Dai is still experimenting with the American *Insanity* fitness programme. There is no one sensible to spar with, and so it is the usual skipping and bag routine, with narrow-arm press-ups thrown in for good measure. Then Dai makes us bunny-hop the entire length of the gym and back, several times, carrying light dumbbells (presumably an *Insanity* exercise). The following day I feel as if I have been carrying a giant carrot in a *Bugs Bunny* movie, and can barely walk. I text the others and it turns out that none of us can walk, and the following week Dai confesses that he has not been able to walk either – a bad sign.

On Wednesday more punters appear, as Javed, Lorna, a new girl, and a man the shape of a beanpole, with incredibly long arms and legs splattered with tribal tattoos, join our ranks. Lorna blazes a trail as one of a very few female plumbers. In between the rounds we all listen intently as she explains to us how *not* to repair a toilet.

Javed tells me that he has had an 'enforced break' of ten years in his boxing career, presumably at Her Majesty's Pleasure, as Dai had commented. I blurt out, 'You don't want to do that again.' 'No,' he replies inscrutably. We argue about the Kray Twins and which bits of London they terrorised. Javed knows a suspicious amount about them. In the end we decide that they were born north of the river, moving to Wapping and the East End, hence the confusion.

As ever Peter is there at his appointed spot, giving the heavy bag a great, big pasting. Now aged fifty-seven, Peter complains to me, 'I SIMPLY CANNOT MOVE,' as he moves stealthily around the bag. We ceremoniously finish off with a round of The Board of Death. Peter shouts, 'I am TOO OLD to do this anymore, you know.' We know, but as usual Peter is first past the post, with a minimum of fuss, as Lorna, almost forty years younger, dry heaves up at the side of gym after only twenty minutes. Still we salute her determination. Once again, I am clambering up the fitness scale, but technique is lacking. I try a few tentative uppercuts on the pads courtesy of Dai, but I am just not getting the down-on-the-ground force up from the floor, again.

33

ME TEEF FELL OUT

Late on Wednesday night I watch a TV chat programme where the lead singer of the hedonistic Manchester band The Happy Mondays, Shaun Ryder, is an honoured guest. I watch because he will say the unsayable and be funny. Shaun is asked by a rather snooty Australian interviewer what he did on his travels: 'I went to Australia and me teef fell out.' Someone makes a weak Antipodean joke about being upside-down.

Unperturbed, Shaun drawls on: 'Actually, I got off me face wiv the Abos for six monfs.' Cut to a picture of Shaun with broken stumps of teeth and a badly shaved head, looking not very well. 'Vey never told me crystal meth were bad for me teef,' he growls, displaying a brand new set of replacement gnashers. Yet, in a substantive way, maybe the real down-under was revealed to Shaun.

Despite the horror of Shaun's sawn-off teeth and asylum-shaved head etched in my mind, I somehow manage to sleep a dreamless sleep on the sofa. I awaken at 7.55 a.m. sharp and get washed, dressed and out of the door in five minutes flat. Tigger looks on bemused as I scrape and bow to modern routines, then returns to his own primitive twelve-hour shift wrapped in The Comfiest Blanket in the World.

After a long session in the laboratory, mild OCD takes over and I find that I cannot leave until the lab looks perfect. It is late on a Friday evening and I have only myself to blame.

I dimble around one Saturday morning in February, going to the local doctors' surgery for a routine health check. As I am aged between forty-five and seventy-four, and this puts me automatically in the coffin-dodger zone. I only recall attending another similar check twenty-five years ago, and no one has been interested in the intervening quarter century.

Leila, a cheerful healthcare assistant who normally takes my blood for routine thyroid function tests, measures my weight and height, and announces with largesse that I have not shrunk. Compared with what or whom? Surely I am allowed to shrink a bit over a quarter of a century.

We talk about the medical dilemma of treating or not treating her beloved old dog who has a heart condition, about the excessive hormonal peskiness of middle age, and whether she should take up running again or the join the gym, based on our own cost-benefit analysis. Leila jumps on the scales herself and complains that she is too heavy. I think not, and say so. Leila has the slickness of one putting everyone at ease, but her funny, throwaway remarks cause me to laugh or comment, and my blood pressure shoots up as she tries to measure it again and again.

I unhelpfully recall the story of a man who famously died laughing in the 1970s watching an episode of the lunatic, slapstick TV series *The Goodies*. This series charted the madcap lives of three dysfunctional bachelors: a wimp, a mad scientist and a lovable goof in various escapades, aided and abetted by a gargantuan BBC special effects budget. One episode, 'Kitten Kong', stands out in the memory – where a giant kitten takes over London, wreaking havoc, and the three men have to rein it in. The kitten knocks down the Post Office Tower with a single paw. Surely this was the killer episode. We conclude that laughter is not always the best medicine.

'Shut up!' Leila shouts in exasperation, but she does actually remember 'Kitten Kong', and then knowingly cracks a Kitten Kong-related joke, forcing me to laugh or make yet another silly remark. I am then annoyingly compelled to have the last word. She gives up, and we go on instead to record my family's medical history. This takes ages as everyone is dead, and has died prematurely of something horrible. I say that, based on my ancestry, it is a wonder that I am alive at all, and Leila has to agree. My mother had a stroke three weeks before she died, and neither of us can decide if this is worth recording on the form.

Leila is a very slow two-finger typist, and she can't spell the names of any of the medical conditions. This exasperates both her and me. In the end she asks me to take over. Then, while I am still laughing, she takes blood, and the needle jitters painfully in my arm as we both giggle helplessly. She takes my blood pressure for a final time – it has lowered a bit, but the measured value is still much higher than it normally is, and I say this. 'Never mind,' she says. 'I can't change it on the system now – it is just too complicated.'

In the afternoon, I benefit from a productive session at Kelly's gym. Jamie happens to be there, and although I can still barely walk, he says confidently that bunny-hopping is the only real way to develop the required explosive power for many defensive boxing manoeuvres. We also discuss the ever-pressing issue of avoiding the quadruple jab. I have tried

Jamie's swayback defence manoeuvre in the ring when faced with Dai's quadruple jab and have come to grief many times. My defence is technically correct, but it is just not fast enough when pitted against the punishing speed of Dai. By the time I have swayed back, the quadruple jabs have been thrown, together with a sneaky hook, pivot and straight right.

When performing the swayback, Jamie encourages me to drop straight onto my back right leg rather than crank it down – this is much quicker and should remove me much more quickly from Dai's punch zone. Jamie says that I need to be much more creative, using a variety of shots and angles, rather the just the same old, same old. He suggests taunting my opponent with a dropped hand and employing more feinted shots, which seem to be my thing.

On Monday at the youth club, newbie Jon appears again, always with far too much energy, along with a newcomer, Jack, who is a military policeman. I instantly like Jack. He is not a poseur, but has clearly spent some time in the gym. I evaluate his boxing style from a safe distance as he bashes the pads with Dai for the first time. Jack is boxer through and through, and there is a telltale crack, crack, crack on the pads as Dai grins and nurses his shoulders.

Jack tells me that my posture is awful. I know he is right, as I feel my back arching forwards while doing squats and star jumps, but I protest that I am fighting nature, as my ancestors were all afflicted, pitiable hunchbacks, and in any case my physiotherapist has given me some corrective exercises. 'The trouble is,' says Jack sagely, 'that by the time you recognise that something is wrong, it is generally *too late* to do anything about it.' 'Yes,' I reluctantly agree, feeling myself to be a condemned mutant.

I follow Jack on the pads, and give Dai one of a few real surprises that I will ever give him by successfully slipping one of his very fast jabs. It is the first time that I have ever done this and therefore represents a significant leap forward. In fact, it takes us both by surprise, and Dai's fist falls in the air and he stumbles forwards. Then I score a rare and respectable point against Dai, as I catch his chin with an ace of a jab. However, I bask in glory for a millisecond too long, and Dai gleefully jabs me in the face four times. 'One point to you: four points to me, Marianne,' he pipes up.

Wednesday night is a harsh awakening. Dai is wearing his The Specials T-shirt – a coded warning that we are going to be trashed. The usual skipping and bag work is interspersed with tormenting bench exercises. Jon shows us a sideways lunge, and I skip backwards and forwards along the whole length of the gym, shamelessly showing off, as no one else can pull off this trick.

Dai has been doing a full range stretch that I have shown him, but he has omitted to rotate his feet, causing the ligaments in his knees to twist up like an elastic band. 'You must move your feet,' I shout through the cacophony of feet-thudding and panting. Then there is the nightmare bunny-hopping as the Wacky Races begin again.

I persuade Dai to hold up the pads for me. I lie and say that I will not hit the pads too hard. I practise some four-punch combinations. I get the shots wrong, then right, as Dai explains the mystery of the quadruple straight right, the feinted left-straight right, the straight right-left hook and finally the jab-left hook-straight right-left hook. Just as nobody expects the quadruple jab, nobody expects the quadruple right either, least of all me – and I am the one throwing it.

Val, one of the youth workers, has been watching us through the gym window. She later tells me that I am now throwing the shots really fast, and I am, but not fast enough. There is some speed there, but the hooks are still all wrong with nowhere near enough hip twist. My hooks are taking seconds instead of milliseconds to set up, and are clunky despite the punching power behind even the weaker ones.

Jon, Jack and I discuss the merits of ten, twenty and the possibly mythical fifty-punch combinations on the way out. They are a waste of time we decide, as too much brain power is expended on memorising and not executing the shots. Give 'em the old 1-2 we decide, as Dai beams approval. 'You don't need all that fancy sh–t,' he guffaws. But I do, Dai, I do need a few tricks up my sleeve, I silently say.

On Saturday, I practise hooks, hooks and more hooks at Kelly's gym as I defiantly stand at the bag for a full hour-and-a-half, oscillating between a southpaw and orthodox stance. The hooks are now less haymaker in style and more acceptably compact.

⊙

I watch the World MMA Championships in Dublin on TV, where most of the fighters seem to be Irish. These are basically boxing bouts with a few kicks and grapples thrown in. Those with the best boxing skills tend to triumph. Just getting into the cage requires nerves of steel, and these crazy bouts last generally only one round. There is no doubt that the Irish fighters are best, as their defensive manoeuvres are way superior. I have to admit that this is a bonkers game – there is a nauseating stain of blood permanently on the floor of the cage.

I feel guilty for watching it at all, but it is the impressive display of boxing skills that draws me in.

Extreme attitudes are also in evidence on the run up to the super-bantamweight world-title fight between Scott Quigg and Carl Frampton, which takes place 27 February 2016 in the Manchester arena. Quigg has a religious and unquenchable devotion to his boxing craft, which involves inhabiting a training camp at Amir Khan's gym in Bolton for three solid months, although this is a mere a mile and a half from his home. During this entire training period he claims that he has seen his family only once for an eight-hour stretch. He claims to have eaten Christmas dinner alone, which has consisted only of salmon, and then gone to the gym, missing out on all the usual festivities. I can't decide if this is pure grandstanding or not, but I guess that it is designed to intimidate his opponent.

Frampton claims to have a life, but then confesses that he would be willing to die in the ring, so he is not much better (or worse). I see in the media that the next morning that Frampton has triumphed over the religiosity of Quigg, having broken his jaw without Quigg even noticing, and I think that this is all a bit mad.

34

HOW THE PROS DO IT

I return to the Kelly's gym one Wednesday evening in March. The small gym is crammed full of professional boxers and I am anxious to see what their training session involves. I hide behind a large heavy bag, throwing my best continuous jabs, trying to fade into the background, self-consciously watching them doing their thing while pretending not to.

A pommel horse made roughly out of wood sits in the corner of the boxing ring. I wonder how the pros are going to use it. With its tapering back perhaps they are going to use it as a balancing bar.

Against all expectations, they vault over it sideways for three-minute stints, first leftwards and then rightwards, with both feet landing on alternate sides of the horse. This is followed by three minutes of sparring, and then continuous repeats of the vaulting and sparring for a whole thirty minutes. Even with the help of the sprung boxing ring floor, this gazelle-like jumping is a feat of eye-popping impressiveness.

Once the pros have finished, one of the trainers, Jocky, stands outside the boxing ring shouting indecipherable instructions in a thick Glaswegian accent to his rookie amateur boxer, whom he is training for a white-collar match. Next, in the ring with his client, Jocky shimmies sideways. I watch the poor, corpulent client, stomach bulging out of a shabby, green T-shirt, valiantly trying to keep up and keep going although he is very unfit. He tries first on the pads, and then four one-minute rounds of sparring. As he lurches out of the ring, his face blotched red and grey with effort, he looks like a man who has already suffered a cardiac arrest. He deserves instant admiration for giving it a go, and I can see that he is very, very determined.

When I ask Jocky how long he has been training him, I am astounded to hear that the client has been boxing for only six weeks, but will soon be fighting in the ring. I ask if he will be wearing headgear. Jocky says no. It is a luxury permitted only for female boxers. I show Jocky my headgear and we agree that it is State of the Art. Jocky tells me that Carl Froch, a famous pro, has the same headgear. Well, I think, this will be the only thing that I will ever have in common with Carl Froch, but just as Carl Froch's head is worth something to him, mine is just as valuable to me.

⊙

It is Monday night and there are new faces at the youth club. Tonight there are eight of us, including Peter. Unfortunately, Peter announces that we will no longer see him on a Wednesday thanks to his new zero hours contract. We all shake our heads and growl at the floor, cursing Peter's employer.

After exactly one hour of blood, sweat and tears, I try some left and right uppercuts in front of the mirrors, and Dai holds the pads up for me for a few minutes. He tells me that I am trying too hard and he is right. I am thinking instead of just moving, and dropping alternate knees just a bit too much, and make the shots clunky. It is partly Dai's fault as I am distracted by him singing 'There is a Light That Never Goes Out' by The Smiths while insisting that it is a song by The Jam. Indignantly I say that it is not, and this single thought abstracts any remaining brain power. Well, that's my excuse.

Wednesday has a good turnout too as Dai's small and faithful army appears. We punch six two-and-a-half rounds on the bags interspersed with dips, press-ups, step-ups at very high speed, and other ridiculous leaps and bounds; then the same again in one-minute rounds.

A new fashion victim with double-diamond earrings and a funny haircut appears. We are normally non-judgmental concerning matters of dress, but he is so vain and cocky that he annoys everyone by just being there. He crumbles after only fifteen minutes. This is not a crime in itself, but worst of all he is not really trying. I sail through the session.

Dai holds up the pads for me, but we have a contretemps as he tells me to leap backwards to get out of his punch zone by moving my front foot backwards first. I cannot do this, as I have been taught to step backwards using my back foot in the other gym. The simple matter of moving one's feet has become instantly complex again. We finish up with the Board of Death, and along with the others I grind through a single circuit. The younger boxers are reduced to their knees, and lie on the floor as us old fogies toil away until the bitter end.

◉

There is more and more of the same until it is early May 2016, and the clear prism of the night air is still lit by a yellow streak of the sun when we exit the gym. The year has turned and wheeled round again, in double-quick time.

Over the weekend I revisit an old friend not far from home. This is the snaky one-in-six road which runs out of the Dales village of Arncliffe towards Malham Tarn. Arncliffe is the land that time forgot, but in a good way. I have not brushed the dust off my bicycle for a month or two and this short outing will be a test, measured against things past. It is a dry, grey Sunday night, with the watery sun threatening to go down at any minute.

I toil up the road for forty minutes, the grey, linear limestone scenery grandly falling away into a deep defile where Yew Cogar Scar is just on my left. Only near the very top do I get off and push the bike, finally reaching the top cattle grid which marks the start of the wild, unenclosed land. I should be resting really as I will be sparring the following night, but what the hell. Instead of tiring, the stiff ride somehow resets the switch.

⊙

It is Monday, and after the usual skipping, Dai sets out the ring. I will be sparring with Aaron, who is nineteen. He is a nice, quiet lad, who is lean and does not look particularly strong. However, appearances are deceptive and I know that he is not a bad technical boxer having trained hard for the preceding four months.

This is the first time he is going in the ring, and I reassure him that there will be no hard punching (from me, anyway).

Dai snarls at me to stop chatting and to get in the corner. We box for three one-and-a-half-minute rounds until I fall victim to Aaron's continuous fast jabs. He is a good deal taller than me, and once again I have the frustrating feeling of being held at arm's length. He also moves well round the ring. I try to slip the jabs or effect a swayback, but I am just too slow.

I have some minor success with feinting shots, and then I implement a last resort strategy spoken of in the professional gym: just to walk forward straight into the barrage of shots, so that I can deliver my own or whatever. This is a heretical manoeuvre from an amateur boxing perspective, but it does occasionally work. It is best employed at the end of the round, as inevitably you will take a few shots. I do take a few shots, but then, keeping my hands up, deliver a couple of ace jabs. I see Aaron's head flip backwards as he looks momentarily confused – he has not been expecting me to move forward.

I box a further two rounds with Dai, trying the same tactic with limited success. I had noticed that Dai was not really paying attention to my rounds with Aaron. He does not expect me to come forward, so I do. Dai hunkers down on the ropes. I deliver a barrage of left and right hooks, with no opposition, and know that Dai is just biding his time, waiting for me to punch myself out.

He leaps out of the corner and delivers some very fast jabs and hooks. I feel these thud against my headgear, but I can do nothing as I am pinned into one hopeless position. I try to pivot out of the way, but Dai wheels round faster and faster. Then I make a fatal error: I adopt my new and shaky southpaw stance. This is all wrong and my body simply becomes an open book. Dai swoops down and comes in with a very hard uppercut which he stops just before my chin, and gives a stern verbal warning. This would be the finishing shot and I know it, but he has let me off. I am finished, and collapse over the ropes. Dai claps me on the back. At least he knows that I have tried.

Dai gets in the ring with Jon, then Jed. Jon is younger, more muscled up, macho and raring to go, but Jed is by far and away the superior opponent, always in control, measured and with a great movement around the ring. Jed makes little fuss of the considerable skills that he has, but he has the upper hand.

After two rounds of Dai pacing and snorting round the ring I notice he has a black eye. As usual Dai has been overenthusiastic and has paid the price. 'Well,' I say, unsympathetically, 'you've brought that on yourself.'

'That's boxing, Marianne,' Dai says, his boxing catchphrase, which can be applied to almost anything. This is always what he says if he or anyone else takes a shot, and I have to agree that it is, secretly awarding myself five stars for not getting punched in the face. This session will be Dai's last until next year's boxing season, as he has football refereeing commitments again over the summer. We exchange email addresses and say that we will meet at Kelly's gym sometime to marvel at the professional boxers. I know that if this comes to pass Dai will want to get in the ring with them, and for his own good somehow I will have to stop him.

35

ROLLING, ROLLING, ROLLING

At the next session in the Kelly's gym, Jamie and I discuss how ever and if ever I am going to avoid the barrage of jabs that I seem to attract each time I enter the ring, especially from Daï. This is not a new conversation.

Jamie puts me at my ease as we square up. As usual, he tells me to relax and not think. He encourages me to throw different types of jabs, so I feint a shot at first, and then he stops me before I throw a double jab. He encourages me to experiment with throwing different types of jabs and I do my best, trying not to telegraph the shots. Next Jamie tells me to completely drop my hands and simply slip or roll out of the way of his jabs which get increasingly fast. I slip to the right and left, duck, roll and swayback as best I can. Once things speed up, I am out of my league.

I say that I have had some success in just powering forward, and so Jamie tries to teach me to slip a jab by moving to my right, with his jab falling to my left, at what feels like my left shoulder. Next, I make a continuous movement involving a roll to the left, then, and only after the roll is almost finished, a step or spring forwards, so that my head ends up to the left of his left shoulder, but not too far forward. God willing, I will then be in the perfect position to deliver a left hook. Forthwith, I must produce a straight right, but snap it back really fast. This should provide me with the momentum for a fast pivoted left hook, with my right foot on the floor providing the fulcrum, but the left pivoting round, so that I end up facing rightwards.

I think of the children's board game Mousetrap, which was popular in the 1970s. Throughout the game, plastic pieces were incrementally added to a Heath-Robinson-like contraption. When the machine was complete, and the conditions were right, a ball bearing was released down a plastic runnel. This set in motion various other parts of the machine with the ultimate aim of an inverted basket falling and trapping an unsuspecting plastic mouse. In my case, various unconnected body parts creak into motion, trying to move in sequence and deliver the punch.

My feet are all over the place, and I am taking lots of dithering small steps instead of moving decisively. I practise the roll again and again, perhaps thirty times. As ever, there are basic mistakes also that need correction: I am keeping my back foot flat on the floor instead of with the heel raised, so I am not getting any torque in the right hand shot. I am shuffling forwards instead of springing, and I am also jumping backwards and completely losing my stance. I try so hard to get some swing in the pivot that I end up creating too much momentum, and I stumble backwards onto the ring floor, my head hitting the ropes. In a spectacular boxing own-goal, I have managed to knock myself down without the help of an opponent.

Finally, Jamie and I discuss strategies for improving core strength, and he suggests a bizarre exercise that involves hanging crucifixion-style for four short bursts of thirty seconds on a hanging bar.

As the summer stretches out like a wide path going anywhere, I decide that my main focus will be improving core strength, reaction time and learning the boxing-roll manoeuvre. In reality these are probably unassailable targets, but I have to believe that I can improve to begin to even try.

Frank, Jamie's protégé, is looking on, awaiting his session. He says that I have improved, and perhaps I have. I sneak a few sideways glances at Frank's efforts in the ring. Once he is relaxed, he moves really well, and for a big bloke this is a particular achievement. Frank has some new haymaker side swipes which look really good, and is rolling, rolling, rolling. Jamie and Frank take a thirty-second break, and I cannot help shouting across the ring: 'Someone has improved!' They both grin great big grins.

36

GRAVY TRAIN

May 2016 is marked by a seismic political change. The 'have-nots' of Blackburn and Blackpool outvote the 'haves' of the Home Counties, and The Establishment crumbles. The country votes to leave the European Union as the nationalists vow to 'take back control'. Over what and how? I appear to have as little control over my own life anyway as is humanly possible and I wonder how this could possibly change with the help of anyone's grandiose political statements.

Tigger watches the unfolding political shenanigans with me on late-night television. I think he understands more than me, as we survey the Old Etonians in grey suits and pink ties telling us how they could run our lives much better than the Eurocrats. The following morning bankers weep into their hedge funds as millions are wiped off shares and the pound plummets. Politicians of all hues resign, abandoning British people to their fate. To cap it all, England loses to Iceland in the European football cup. (Well done Iceland, by the way.) Hardworking Eastern European dentists and fruit pickers who have lived for years in the UK feel unloved and are spat at in the street. We choke on our croissants and jump off the Euro Gravy Train in favour of Bisto.

Boris Johnson has cleverly set the stage so that he can rescue Britain from all its ills and appear as the hero. He venerates Winston Churchill, whose attitudes and actions are not translatable into the modern age. I notice that Boris Johnson has even started to walk and talk like Churchill. Theresa May, the Home Secretary, has been too quiet, as she sets herself up as Prime Minister-in-Waiting hoping that the public will forget her repugnant racist remarks six months earlier, when her mask slipped and she spectacularly tripped over her Jimmy Choos.

I meet Frank at Kelly's gym, our paths not having crossed for a week or two. Frank has continued to work hard in the gym and now looks utterly transformed. He has definitely mastered the knack of the hook and shows me a fine variation where the right hand is ground downwards and twisted from above. Since Frank is very tall, he could use this to good effect in the ring, whereas I could not. It is a worthwhile and venomous shot, and much less boring than just slamming the hands straight in.

37

ALI AND FRAZIER

In June 2016 it is reported that Muhammad Ali has died. He gasps his last in an Arizona hospital, finally succumbing to breathing difficulties brought on by decades of Parkinson's disease.

As a young man Ali ran behind the school bus to gain boxing fitness. This was an early sign that he marked himself out from the crowd. He is a major loss in countless ways: as a consummate athlete, pacifist, decades-long black civil rights activist, wit and general stirrer-upper. The greatest accolade is bestowed upon him by his brother: 'He was a sweet, kind man.' Well, he was to some but not to others, and certainly not to Joe Frazier – except at the end.

Ali was a complex man who made both friends and enemies. Because of his failure to fight in Vietnam, Ali was pilloried by the US State Department and stripped of his boxing licence. During three years in the wilderness the hand of friendship was extended to him only by a few, including his major boxing rival, Joe Frazier.

Frazier lent him money and gave him lifts to and from New York out of the goodness of his heart. Ali survived by means of publicity stunts, films and pimping himself to the press. Once he got his licence back, he embarked on a shaming and vitriolic campaign intended to undermine Joe Frazier, in the run up to their famous boxing match which became known as the 'Thrilla in Manila'.

Ali goaded Frazier with the very worst of taunts – namely that he was an 'Uncle Tom', a white man's slave. Ali had joined a radical black civil rights organisation called the Nation of Islam, and through its influence he came to despise Frazier, whom he saw as the white man's archetypal victim. The cruel irony for them both was that Ali purported to speak for the black man, but saw Frazier as beneath him, referring to him as a 'gorilla'. Ali turned up on the road outside Frazier's hotel in Manila brandishing a fake weapon. No wonder Frazier was unhinged by it all, allegedly believing Ali to be mad.

I watch an extraordinary TV interview on YouTube where, years later, Ali, George Foreman and Joe Frazier all meet up, proclaiming brotherly love. Although they regularly beat the sh–t out of each other decades earlier, their palpable affection for each other somehow rings true. During the meeting, it's clear to see Ali has a very bad Parkinson's disease tremor, which was almost certainly in part due to Frazier's left hook.

Frazier had continued his devotion to boxing, living in a modest room at the back of his gym in downtown Philadelphia, quietly rescuing the poor off the streets, while Ali's star soared. It was as if Ali's original taunts eventually came true, with Frazier remaining the humble black man that he actually was, curiously unaffected and by his fleeting fame.

⊙

In mid-July, I sabotage any boxing hopes by managing to cut the finger on my left hand really badly at work, precipitating a visit to A & E. I fuss over my finger and the possible risk of infection, but it is still a nuisance a week or two later. There is no way I can get a boxing glove on my left hand, and I concede that it would be foolish to try, so I box right-handed for the next couple of weeks.

There is a works summer barbeque later in the month, which consists of a hog roast. I am at a loss to see how the execution, skewering and burning of another sentient being could possibly make for a summery atmosphere. Furthermore, as the staff of the environment faculty, I feel that we should be setting an example of vegetarianism or veganism, as setting aside the serious animal welfare concerns eating meat is one of the most environmentally damaging things that can be done.

During the event, someone has set up an open mike and amp to be used for the theme of 'international music'. This is a worthy idea, but a series of out of tune, folksy rants make it tiresome. In any case the whole idea (and reality) of the hog roast has put me in a bad mood. I long for auto-tune, and something a bit more toe tapping. Finally, I hide in my laboratory and everything feels safer. I get home and Haydon tells me that I represent food fascism and I am music snob. Well – good (on both counts), I think.

YEAR FOUR

38

DUBLIN DEVOTEE

During the late summer and early autumn of 2016, there appears to be an underlying decline in the function of my back which nobody seems able to halt. It is a roller-coaster ride, with various ups and downs, but my problem causes me to miss most of my boxing training over this period.

In real desperation I visit four or five different physiotherapists. My trusted physiotherapist in Kendal tries his best, but does not have a specific interest in boxing, so I visit others who claim to, but actually don't. They all have slightly different opinions and recommend slightly different courses of action. No one seems to get to the root of the problem, and I veer between pure paranoia and complete denial.

I have scans, take antibiotics in case there is some insidious underlying infection that has been overlooked, but the problem, left-sided sciatic pain in the region of the sacroiliac joint, is persistent. Although the pain and function vary, overall it gets worse. Everyone, except the physiotherapists, blame the boxing. The good news is that it is not a joint or disc problem, but still nobody knows how to put it right. I really miss my boxing friends and occasionally turn up to the youth club boxing gym when I am not really capable of doing anything; Dai and the others send me home.

I allow myself to be lulled into a false sense of security during periods of temporary respite, when there is some adventitious improvement. By early December 2016 I kid myself that I am almost back to boxing at full strength and find myself as sparring partner to Vic.

Vic is a newcomer to our gym and has bravely signed up for a white-collar boxing match at the Preston Guild Hall, scheduled towards the end of the month. Vic is an ex-youth boxer, now aged forty-eight. He has lost a bit of condition, but not an ounce of skill or much speed in the intervening decades. Dai does not have a license to allow him to train boxers to go into the ring competitively, so Vic has to do some of his training elsewhere, but it is Dai's job to train him like a racehorse. Vic's chosen boxing moniker is 'The Dublin Devotee', as a nod to his Irish heritage.

Unlike me, Vic is on a trajectory of improving fitness, and in our first encounter in the ring I find that he has already been training for a month. He is not particularly strong, but fast, and his ringcraft is really good. I find that I can punch through his double-gloved guard held up to his face if I just keep going with my jab. This is OK for the first two rounds, but then Vic has had enough. Once he starts to moving around the ring, I do so too, sluggishly at first. I do my old trick of moving forward and taking a few unnecessary punches. Dai shouts from the sidelines and, for once, I hear an emphatic 'Nooooo ...' through my headgear above the hubbub. I back off and stop trading punches.

Vic comes forward and I fall prey to his fast hooks left, right and left again. Then I raise my left arm high into the sweltering air for a millisecond. Just as I have predicted, his eyes dart upwards just long enough for me to launch a fantastic long-range jab. I swing my jab into action getting him square in the right eye. I do not really mean to hit him that hard, but it is a great shot. Dai shouts, 'That's boxing Marianne!' And I know that it really is. Despite my injured back, a rare and beautiful sweet shot has been conjured out of the ether.

Vic and I carry on in the same vein. Vic is much more skilled than me. Although we are evenly matched in three rounds, I would definitely succumb if it went to five, as I am relying far too heavily on my jab which I seem to have thrown continuously for three rounds. At the end of round three my left arm burns.

Throughout December, Dai puts Vic through his paces as best he can, and Vic's match in the Preston Guild Hall ends in a respectable draw. Vic is awarded a joint belt along with his opponent and parades his around the gym in a victory lap as we all heartily applaud.

Christmas is here too soon already, and I find myself on the boxers' night out in Lancaster, a few days before the big day. Our idea is to visit a few quiet bars in town and not do very much, but it is Dai's idea to dance, shout, play pool and generally muck about.

We fetch up at a quiet, civilised, rather bijou bar with potted palms and a man wearing a trilby hat playing innocuous Billy Joel songs on the piano. Dai insists on the pianist playing The Specials' best ska hits while he hops around the floor like a clucking hen. This is hilarious (up to a point) and the other customers look on with mild disdain. I make passable attempts on the pool table, as the drunks get louder and drunker. I take my leave at a reasonable hour, several bars and crowds later.

This is not my natural habitat, and I envy the ease with which the wall-to-wall glammed up crowds shuffle and jostle, calling to each other across the sticky carpet, balancing beer glasses and calling out the names of drinks I have never heard of. I guess I've just spent too long living out in the sticks.

39

DEAR DEPARTED

Just before Christmas I receive the worrying news that my aged Aunt Marion is increasing in frailty day by day. I speak to her daily on the phone. She still claims to have no sense of humour, as she chats on the phone, one blackly humorous anecdote following another. Her conversation is punctuated by dramatic pauses and phrases like 'I'm not having that', to allow the audience (i.e. me) to gasp. She remains firmly fixed on the present and the future, and as usual makes encouraging noises about my boxing misadventures. As ever, she also throws out the favoured waspish end-pieces as final barbs to her anecdotes: 'For the love of goodness', 'So that was that' and 'So that was it'.

Before New Year the prognosis is bleak, and I pray that she will rally as she has done so many times before, but she does not. She is at home, and although she has many friends, uncharacteristically she chooses to see very few people, only her son, Gordon, and his family. She has a very bad chest infection and is soon hospitalised. Dignified and ordered until the end, Aunt Marion, who is a tough and loving force, passes away on 3 January 2017.

Thankfully, her worst fear of residential 'care' is never real-ised. The shimmering, watery view from her Broughty Ferry flat overlooking the River Tay sustained her stoically beyond the expected span: the aerial views of the Tay Bridge, the sailing boats, people walking dogs along the shore, the sailing club boathouse, the trim, semi-tropical gardens, the railway, the joggers, the hope of a visit to Marks and Spencer's and the oil platforms towed mysteriously into port for repair. All were scrutinised and evaluated from a favoured window chair with burnt orange cushions, punctuated by Caesar salad and generous amounts of homemade watercress soup, almost to the very end.

Though she was failing, the knowledge of other lives still going along, close and far, kept her alive. Typically unselfish, she showed two last great acts of kindness: she asked that very few visit in those last few weeks except her son and his family, and she rather unexpectedly left her body to medical science.

The marvels of modern medicine had unquestionably extended her life by at least thirty years. Her actions ensured that she would be remembered exactly how she wanted to be remembered – stylish, dignified, fully in charge of everything and taking pleasure in a life that, near the end, sometimes appeared from the outside only to consist of a series of obstacles. She would have a lasting legacy. In typical style, we are instructed by her son, Gordon, to celebrate her life at an event in Dundee in the forthcoming spring. I decide that I am definitely up for that.

40

VIC'S REVENGE

With renewed confidence, Vic is at it again, preparing for a second white-collar match in the Preston Guild Hall in March, this time hoping for a win. Owing to my protracted back problem I have not witnessed much of his training, but when I fetch up at the youth club gym one February night, I see that he is much improved: fitter, faster and much more skilled.

He is now routinely boxing eight rounds in a single night, as Dai pushes him to the limit at every session. I notice that Dai's boxing technique has also improved, honed by the sparring. I box a single round with Vic on a busy Wednesday night. I put up a valiant fight but Vic's superior skill, fitness and speed instantly imposes itself. I think of the Battle of Crécy in 1346, when the Black Prince requested his father's help in battle, describing himself as 'sorely pressed' – an apt description of my situation. As I am thrown against the ropes and weaken in just one round, Vic throws out a great straight right to my left cheekbone. My whole head wallows backwards as his shot gets beyond my headgear and shoots right through my gloved hands. My head slews backwards then forwards, as I think, *This is not good.* I rally and finish the round, but Vic literally and metaphorically has the upper hand. He is well prepared and I give him credit.

Unfortunately, I have taken rather a big punch from my single round with Vic. There are the usual self-recriminations, worries about permanent damage and the inevitable judgement of others, usually from those who have never experienced the addictive nature of being in the boxing ring, even on the lowest possible rung. The truth is that I am not as fit as I was and probably should not have attempted any sparring.

I notice that over the next few days a very small blue bruise has appeared in the corner of my left eye. I think I have got away with it, but over the following two weeks there are insidious signs. The whole of the left side of my face swells up fast like an inflating tyre, and I have not one but two black eyes developing. It also feels as though an old, crude filling in one of my molar teeth on the left-hand side has worked loose due to Vic's punch, allowing an infection to take hold.

I see the emergency dentist, who takes some X-rays and tells me (in a way that only medics can) that she 'doesn't like the look of me'. She sends me to A & E for further evaluation for a fractured cheekbone or eye socket. It turns out that I am unbroken, but a dull Friday afternoon has been wasted away in casualty in the company of chatty alcoholics and those injured on construction sites or on the football field. I am put on antibiotics for five days and the face infection goes, but the tooth, loosened and infected, is a goner.

Vic tells me that he has the opportunity to dress up again for his white-collar bout in fancy boxing attire. As before, he has chosen a green designer robe with white trim, with 'Dublin Devotee' embroidered on the back.

Gutted that I cannot make it on the night, I am reliably informed that Dai is his self-appointed cornerman. Vic's fights a more formidable opponent than in his last bout, and I am delighted to hear that he wins outright, with the ref stopping the fight in the second round. Vic is deservedly victorious and has raised a large amount of money for charity. I am jealous not of his victory but of his philosophical calm, which I am fated never to have.

Remembering the recent fall against the ropes in the boxing ring with Vic and other past abuses, I awake one morning in late March feeling as if someone has shoved a red-hot needle into my back. Some temporary fixes are applied, but the truth is that this has been an affliction that has been gradually creeping up on me over the last year or two, which has never been satisfactorily resolved. Everyone assumes that this is a solely a boxing-related injury and immediately passes judgement: surely I have brought this on myself. I consider a lonely trip to A & E for pain relief but instead decide to tough it out with Paracodol. I feel that the demon has not been exorcised, and I need help.

41

SCOTS WHA HAE

In April 2017, with my back playing up, I drive to Dundee to attend a celebration of my late aunt's life. I arrive around 8.30 p.m. at the Woodlands Hotel on Panmure Terrace in Broughty Ferry on the Tay Estuary. It is comfortable and familiar. I drag myself into the bath, and then to bed.

I have a leisurely breakfast and walk towards the northern bank of the silvery River Tay, which is less than half a mile away. It is a beautiful spring day and I find myself in the Barnhill Rock Garden, a perfectly kept acre of flower beds, rare trees, mown lawns, ponds, pagodas and glasshouses, set back from Broughty Ferry promenade. The garden is punctuated with blobs of knobbly native volcanic rock. This gem, which I later discover is maintained entirely by volunteers, provides an hour of peace and tranquillity that I don't seem to have encountered for quite some time. (I can now say with pride that, in memory of my aunt, I am officially a Friend of the Barnhill Rock Garden.)

When I get back to the hotel, I shoehorn myself into respectable clothes and get a taxi to the Apex hotel near the revamped dockyards of central Dundee – an all glass-and-metal-mesh geometric shape which soars to the sky. The event is in the hotel's art gallery, a nod to Aunt Marion's career as an embroidery designer. On the taxi journey, I try and recall all that I know about my aunt and mother's early lives.

They were brought up in a tenement (location unrecorded) and then in a council house on Inverleith Street, Carntyne in the East End of Glasgow. Their father, Willie Gracie, was a railway worker, a platelayer then a crane driver on what is now known as the West Coast Main Line. Willie was a short, wiry, fine-looking man, with a shock of fair hair. He was plain talking, humorous, inadvertently tactless and very fond of gardening. Allegedly, one of his favourite tricks was to lay a slab of turf over the stove chimney of the platelayers' hut and smoke the unsuspecting men out.

Willie's wife, Isobel, was a competent housewife and loving mother, probably the main measure of a woman's worth in those days. From ancient photographs, Isobel looks to be rather a plain woman, with a tall, willowy figure. My mother recalled that she could not take part in the rough and tumble of family life, as her health was delicate and she was often ill in bed. Isobel died of a hereditary heart condition when my mother was aged twelve and her sister Marion was a few years younger. Thus, Willie became a single dad on the run up to the Second World War. Times were tough and Willie worked a six-and-a-half-day week to make ends meet. A lifelong smoker, he died of a brain haemorrhage before I was born, his hard life probably taking its toll.

As a young child, when I was under five, we made pilgrimages to my mother's family home in Glasgow. I remember the pebble-dashed building well. It was a flat rather than a house, as you had to go up a flight of internal stairs to get to the living area. Mrs Rae lived downstairs, a woman of good sense who seemed to me to be about a hundred, but was probably only in her fifties or sixties. Mrs Rae was an excellent baker and made a teeth-rotting Scottish confection called tablet. This was basically condensed milk and sugar boiled and set into a baker's tray. My mother spoke very fondly of Mrs Rae, whom I guess had been a mother figure to all the family after my grandfather was widowed. I got the impression that at certain times she had cooked food for the family, helping them along.

Willie was proud of his garden at the back of the building. He was originally from the small Scottish Borders town Newcastleton (known to locals as Copshaw Holm), in the Hawick and Kielder Forest district. Willie was used to country living and gardening was second nature. He grew vegetables, especially potatoes, which he admired from a long wooden railway bench set close the vegetable patch. Home-grown produce was an absolute necessity during the war, when there were shortages of food. Eventually, Willie asked for assistance from his late wife's younger sister, Pearl, to run the household, and Pearl moved in ostensibly as a housekeeper. She also cared for the two young sisters. It is a story with a happy ending, as Willie and Pearl fell in love and married. My mother described their wedding day as one of the happiest of her life.

Pearl was very house-proud, and after Willie had decorated their home she enjoyed showing it off to friends. Oblivious, Willie would feel obliged to point out all the imperfections. He had also taught their black cat, Trixie, to put her paw through a hole in a wooden stool, clawing the behind of visitors who dared to sit there. When my mothers' teenage friends appeared in fashionable new outfits, Willie would say cheerfully, 'Was that the only colour they had?'

Long after Willie had died, I remember sitting with my mother on the old wooden railway bench in the garden. The fallow vegetable patch and the remains of the Anderson air-raid shelter, which Willie had built himself at the bottom of the garden, were a testament to the sustained efforts he made to look after his family.

In the fullness of time, Pearl became my 'official' Scottish granny, even though she was really my great-aunt. Pearl was canny (in the Scottish terminology, 'fly') and could be quite strict, but she was also empathetic and had a huge sense of fun. Like Grandma Dunn on my father's side of the family, she had a subversive streak. She was very good at cards, fond of James Bond films and disaster movies, and could be a very good listener with a surprisingly broad outlook, considering her strict Presbyterian upbringing. My childhood memories of Pearl are of utter stability, sensible shoes and thick tweed or wool skirts. When I was a teenager, she acted as a wise confidante. Pearl was terribly fond of cats, and any available cat would make a beeline for her, sitting on her lap, glued to her Scottish wool skirt like Fuzzy Felt.

Willie had been born out of wedlock to an unknown father. Allegedly his mother, Isobel Marion Gracie, had been working as a housemaid when she became pregnant. She would never reveal his father's identity. Family folklore had it that Isobel was from Newcastleton, but had originally lived at Saughtree ('willow-tree'). Saughtree itself comprised no more than a few houses at a road and railway junction with a church nearby. I think that Willie and his mother both moved back to Newcastleton after he was born.

For a while the family lived at Riccarton Junction, an incredibly isolated village, 120 strong, which was only accessible by rail and had a Co-operative store, school and post office. Isobel later married Charlie Ferguson, a local church elder, and went on to have several more children. Some of Willie's half-brothers became railway workers on the Waverley Line between Hawick and Edinburgh and on the West Coast Main Line, as Willie also did.

According to my mother, Isobel was a handsome, rather formidable woman, ramrod straight with blonde hair, who looked so young that she was often mistaken for Willie's sister. Charlie was a decent man, who was also determined to provide for his family. He hunted hares and rabbits, fished at night and grew vegetables in a high-walled garden that he had constructed himself. A local barter economy ensured that produce was shared and no one went short.

During the Second World War, Glasgow was heavily bombed, and my mother and Marion were evacuated to live with their grandmother and grandfather, Granny and Granda Charlie, at Riccarton Junction and then in Newcastleton. They were city girls who found it hard to adjust to rural ways of life. They would be sent to walk miles to remote farms to collect milk churns, or would be expected to gut fish and make jugged hare soup for Granda and to help with tasks such as haymaking. My mother spoke fondly of Granda, of country fairs and celebrations including the annual Common Riding, where people would ride around ancient land boundaries on horseback as a way of protecting and celebrating land rights. She spoke of very remote farms that were totally unconnected to the outside world, and where rumour had it that brothers and sisters sometimes lived as man and wife.

My mother and her younger sister went to school in Newcastleton, where they were essentially taught how to be farmers' wives or domestic servants. Sixty years later my mother could remember the meaning of many obsolete North Country dialect words that she had learned at this time. These were ancient words of Viking origin used widely in northern England and southern Scotland that I had found listed in a book about the Yorkshire Dales published in 1789. For example, my mother said that her granny had worn a pirn-hat or pirnie-hat. *Pirn* was an old-Norse word meaning a round woollen cap, hat or striped nightcap that was used to contain bobbins for weaving.

Willie was determined that his two daughters would be properly educated and was aghast at the limitations of their rural education. He recalled them to Glasgow, despite the bombing risks. They were bright and went to the local grammar school, Whitehill School. My mother excelled at maths and science, especially chemistry, running off with various school prizes and becoming the dux (head girl) of the school. She eventually went to Glasgow University to read chemistry, unthinkable for someone of her background and gender. Aunt Marion excelled at art, studying at the Glasgow School of Art, and later became an art and design teacher and professional embroidery, jewellery and textiles designer at Dundee College. I have a treasured picture of her standing proud in her 1950s art studio wearing black.

Aunt Marion met and married Tom, a sailor. Our childhood name for him was 'Umple Tong', as we could never pronounce Uncle Tom. One of my earliest and very happy memories is attending their wedding in Glasgow. It was such a genuinely joyous occasion that I remember it well, even though I was only aged three. There were giant chandeliers hanging from the ceiling in the hotel reception room, made up of elaborate arrays of pear-shaped light bulbs. At my parents' house, there was a single, identical pear-shaped light bulb, which illuminated the tiny cubby hole under the stairs. At the wedding, I reputedly pointed to the chandelier and shouted, 'Dad – that's just like the light we have under our stairs!' Onlookers gasped as they wondered what kind of mansion we inhabited.

Tom was naturally quite shy and quiet and not the sort of man to push himself forward, but Aunt Marion could see his worth. He was an incredibly good-natured man with a dry, mordant wit. (Being funny seemed to run in all branches of the family, wherever one looked.) Marion and Tom lived first in a beautiful, large Victorian terraced house in Hyndford Street in Dundee, and then later in the flat near Broughty Ferry, overlooking the River Tay. The décor at Hyndford Street was very arty and adventurous, and as children my sister and I found this thrilling. There was one wall in the main sitting room that was entirely painted black, and some chrome chairs with only three legs. A large well-appointed cat, Nicholas, who lived to the age of twenty-one, also resided at Hyndford Street, mainly in a large basket on top of the fridge.

Aunt Marion's life was defined by exactly the correct amount of risk taking balanced against caution. Unfortunately, she had inherited her mother's heart condition and was told that it would never be sensible to have a child. She had already had open heart surgery in the mid-1960s when it was far less routine than it is now, and the family had held its collective breath on the day of the surgery. Now with a good income, Marion privately employed the best obstetrician in Dundee, and Tom and Marion went on to have a child, my cousin Gordon, who gave them tremendous joy.

⊙

At Aunt Marion's life celebration, Gordon has done a great job of putting together a collage of my aunt's life, using a variety of objects and documents. This assemblage showcases Marion's talent and waspish sense of humour and is an opportunity for hundreds of friends and family members who loved and admired her to come together. It is neither mawkish, disrespectful nor humourless. These occasions are always a strange mixture of jollity and sadness, where those present have not perhaps seen each other for decades, even lifetimes, and just want to catch up, but are also sad at the most recent loss. Like his father, Gordon is a funny man and an adept public speaker. His chatty style does not belie the obvious love and admiration that he had for his mother.

We remember that my aunt had terribly poor sight, and around the time of the Second World War decided that she would like to learn to ride a motorised scooter, in order to take my mother on a tour of the Scottish Highlands. She had no hope of being able to read the number plates at the required distance as part of the test, and so, on the evening before the test, she and my mother did a tour of the town square memorising all the number plates in the hope that the same vehicles would be there on the following day. The gods were kind, and as a result my semi-blind aunt passed the test and took to the road, and consequently she and my mother had one of best holidays of their lives. As far as we know, nobody died.

There is some debate as to whether the vehicle was a motorbike or scooter: Gordon says that it was definitely a motorbike; I say a scooter. From the back of a room, a woman of about ninety, raises her hand. It turns out that she rode on the actual conveyance and confirmed that it was indeed a scooter. It is the verification of these mythologised half-truths and hollowed-out tales that goes on in the room all afternoon and is strangely compelling.

In truth, I dread meeting those I have not seen for many decades, fearing that they will be heartbrokenly infirm, that I will not know what to say to them, or even worse I will not recognise them. My elegant and dignified 'Aunt' Lin, a long-time friend of Aunt Marion, comes into view hanging onto a walking frame. Truthfully, I cannot remember a great deal about her except that she was always incredibly stylish, and in fact she still is, even though she is now ninety.

I hastily remember that she is the only person I know who used to make the frequent and not inconsiderable round trip by train from Dundee to Jenners Department Store in Edinburgh, as she claimed that the perfume that was available in Dundee was never 'fresh' enough. I was secretly impressed with this, as it seemed an acceptably extreme form of behaviour. I seize the opportunity to quiz her about whether it was really true. She assures me that it certainly was, although she is obviously too frail to make that journey now.

We discuss the merits of various fragrances. I am no aficionado, but as I have become older, I have come to understand that perfumes are just another form of artistry and are not just to be sniffed at but fully inhaled. Lin extols the virtues of Coco Chanel, and as much as I hate myself for doing it, I champion Gucci, which I do actually like. I happen to have an atomiser of Gucci Sport in my handbag, and I spray it onto Lin's outstretched wrist which is way too thin. 'Too citrusy,' she says, and I find that I have to agree.

◉

By late afternoon I have had enough, and yet I cannot really say why, because overall the tone of the event has been ideal, perfect even. I think it is witnessing the unbridgeable gap between present, past and future, life and death, and possibly three or four generations that it is just too exhausting: the 1930s, the war, the 1960s and the 1990s, all in one afternoon. My sister and her husband offer me a lift to my hotel later on, but I get my prearranged taxi at around 5 p.m.

I get back to my hotel, where a wedding is already is in full swing. Men with bandy legs in kilts who have already had too much to drink are blocking the downstairs hallway, the sound of their tipsy laughter filtering upstairs. I repair to my curtained room and lie on the floor with a super-strong coffee for a good long while. If there were a readily available ice bath, I would gladly jump into it.

My back suddenly feels dangerously good, so foolishly I am tempted to test myself out in the empty hotel gym in the basement, my body like an old bicycle grinding on. For the first time in months, I throw some good jabs, hooks and straight rights, and I think of my aunt who was encouraging to me in every way.

42

KILL OR CURE

Eventually, in June, everything stops, as my back needs urgent attention or else. I pay privately to see a sports doctor at the Spire Hospital on Penny Lane in Liverpool. The doctor specialises in rotational and lifting injuries, especially those sustained in boxing and international rugby. I hobble in and, without appearing to look up, he says, 'You probably use your jab too much.' He instructs me to stand on my left leg, and I instantly fall over, which confirms his diagnosis. The consensus is that my injury is due to inflammation of the muscles in the region of the left sacroiliac joint at the bottom of my back.

He sends me to his colleague in Leeds, Dave Stringer, an international rugby physiotherapist who specialises in rotational injuries. I feel I am beyond hope, not only contemplating giving up sport of any kind, but also the norms of daily life.

However, Dave is a consummate professional with a methodical, scientific approach which inspires total confidence. Dave tells me that the basic boxing stance is one of the most 'unnatural' body positions imaginable, placing the body under various intolerable strains and torsions, which have to be balanced by other mitigating exercises (which I have not been doing). He confirms that it is a muscle and not a joint problem, and as such it is eminently fixable. Boxing is partly to blame, but the injury has also been exacerbated by too much lifting at work and also too much driving. It will take a few months to fix.

In my pained state, I do not really believe him, but after three months of tailored exercises, mainly Pilates and yoga, sports massage and a break from boxing, the pain gradually starts to subside.

I enjoy the Pilates and yoga and they induce their own sense of wellbeing, and Dave advises that they will maintain mobility well into middle and old age. He recommends a wider range of exercises to work different muscle groups and regain a balance that has probably been upset by throwing too many jabs. Dave explains all of this in a way that I understand, and I owe him a huge debt of gratitude.

Dave also recommends a programme of simple walking and cycling to aid my recovery. My boxing break has forced me to rekindle past good habits, as I remember what it is like to be in the outside world.

On a bright evening, I park the car near the Winskill cattle grid, above the hamlet of Langcliffe near Settle on the edge of Malham Moor. It is 6 p.m. and still the sun beats down. The sound of larks, lapwings and curlews is deafening. I was last here on Christmas Day, befuddled by back pain, but now feeling good, planning a four mile walk up hill and down dale through the finest sweep of limestone scenery. I know the placement of every single rock and crag on this beloved route and have viewed it in all weathers and circumstances over the last thirty-five years.

On this small square of landscape my life has been played out, in a way. I have walked, cycled, run and rock-climbed across its surface, descended potholes beneath it, been pinned down by blizzards, had to use an ice axe, lost my way in pea soup fogs, climbed over snow drifts, worn crampons, been baked by the sun, chased by weasels, cows and gamekeepers, found unusual wildlife (medicinal leeches), received very bad news and been lucky. Occasionally I have been exhausted and terrified, and I have unravelled a few geological mysteries, all in this tiny area. The landscape is impassive but the memories not.

I massively enjoy my walk. I chug along past Victoria Cave, Ben Scar, Attermire Scar, Warrendale Knotts, Blua Crags and Clay Pits Plantation, as the sunlight bounces off the limestone scars and eventually fades to a gloomy grey. Deep grey storm clouds gather over Fountains Fell to the north and rabbits scurry into their burrows. The first few spots of rain arrive as I return to the car.

43

SAVED BY SCOTLAND

By July 2017, Dave's prophecy has come true, and my back really has started to improve. Reassured, I plan a grand day out, visiting the Grey Mare's Tail waterfall in the Scottish Borders, close to the Moffat–Selkirk road. Moffat is a smaller Scottish version of my adopted Yorkshire hometown of Settle. Each acts as a hill sheep farming terminus. Settle has the Ye Olde Naked Man Café but Moffat has The Rumblin' Tum. Moffat also has a splendid sculpture of a fine ram in the centre of town, carved in rock and known as the Moffat Ram.

Moffat was visited as part of a family ritual about a thousand years ago, in the 1960s, on long journeys by car from Manchester up to the East End of Glasgow to visit my Scottish granny. Road travel north from Manchester was only possible via the grace and goodness of the A6 trunk road, as the M6 motorway had not yet been completed. The first stopping off point was Milnthorpe. This seemed to be light years away from Manchester, as my father would only ever drive at 30mph. Moffat, the second stopping off point, formed parts of the outer solar system. As a child I was mesmerised by the Moffat Ram, especially as it had no ears, and even now, if passing through Moffat, I always have to stop and doff my cap to the ram.

Scotland saved my life pretty early on. My mother went into labour very prematurely while on a holiday in Lochcarron in the Scottish Highlands in June 1963. She was driven by road ambulance to Glasgow Royal Infirmary, where I was born at only twenty-three weeks, to the surprise of both my parents. Fortunately, the infirmary had special expertise in caring for pre-term babies, and I spent my first three months in an incubator. My quality of survival was good, and so I rightly regard Scotland as my second home.

The Grey Mare's Tail is a spectacular waterfall in the rolling hills, just off the Moffat–Selkirk road about 10 miles from Moffat. It is classed as a tourist honeypot, but is well worth the visit. Even as a very small child I remembered the impressiveness of the landscape, a dark grey ravine topped by a 200-foot-high waterfall. A steep mountain path skirts the northerly side of the ravine and reaches the green, glassy calm of Loch Skeen above, framed by proper Scottish mountains for which there is no substitute.

The route from the car park involves a steep pull up a rocky path at the outset. This is no place to slip as a man to one side of me demonstrates. Temporarily distracted, he gazes at his smartphone, steps backwards and streaks down the hillside about ten feet, clawing at the air, then heather, just saving himself from a long fall. The footwear lottery is apparent, with flip-flops, Cuban-heeled boots (yes!), sneakers, pumps and actual high heels all worn as mountain attire. Fat Glaswegians, pink-faced in sweaty shirts, wobble up the mountainside, carrying ice creams. It is hard not to be a little judgmental, but the pull of the mountain is strong, and like a magnet it draws us back to our primitive selves.

To the west of Loch Skeen, the mountain of White Coomb looms up, with a line of ant-like people just visible in black silhouette on its crest, framed against an azure sky that is just too brilliant. I have had to take some antihistamine tablets as the Scottish plants have thrown out foreign pollen. I finish the walk and return to the car, and although it is only teatime, I fight sleep, eventually crashing out in a quiet layby. I come round, finally convinced that, whatever happens, Scotland is a lifelong addiction.

My physiotherapist, Dave Stringer, gradually encourages me to box again, even if it initially causes a bit of pain. He is very much of the 'use it or lose it' brigade and has always seen my muscle problem very much as a temporary setback. He sees the body as a malleable entity that can be modified to suit the user and reminds me how much good the boxing will do in other ways. By August, I am finally untwisted and totally pain free. Flamingo-like, I can finally stand on one leg again. I have missed most of the 2016/17 boxing season, but so what – I am ready to do it all again.

44

BLACKWELL'S WARNING

Over this long period away from the formalities of the boxing gym, I feel to some extent that I have lost my way. Not only have I severely missed my boxing companions and their easy camaraderie, despite dropping into the gym from time to time, but I have also craved the certainty, discipline and rigour of the boxing gym, which I never, ever found boring. I also think of the boxing-related injuries I have sustained, mainly the two black eyes and the lost tooth, not to mention the twisted back, and ask myself whether they were worth it? Yes, I definitely think that they were.

When I eventually return properly to the boxing gym in September 2017, I am welcomed back by the usual suspects, especially Dai, Mark, James and Peter, as if I have never been away. I learn that Peter too has had a period of absence, unable to attend due to a pesky new zero-hours contract.

A major topic of conversation in the gym has been the fate of professional boxer Nick Blackwell. In March 2016, a tele-vised professional middleweight fight between Chris Eubank Jr and Nick Blackwell ended in tragedy. During the last few rounds, Blackwell took an appalling beating and developed a huge, grotesque swelling over his left eyebrow, completely shutting the eye. The consensus was that the ref should have stopped the fight a few rounds earlier. At first no one formally objected so the fight was allowed to continue. Chris Eubank Sr was watching the fight and mentioned something about a stoppage to the ref, mindful of a similar situation in which he was involved, some years earlier, when his opponent Michael Watson was injured and brain damaged. Suddenly, Blackwell collapsed at the side of the ring, attended by an anaesthetist and was put on oxygen. He valiantly gave the thumbs up sign, before lapsing into unconsciousness as he was carried off on a stretcher. Aged only twenty-five, he suffered a serious bleed on the brain and was put in an induced coma.

Although he made a passable recovery, a few months later, against all medical advice, Blackwell sparred again in November 2016 at an unnamed boxing gym sustaining a second, extremely serious bleed on the brain. He fell into a second coma. His situation was monitored and analysed by the whole boxing community.

Nick Blackwell is in our minds as the press have picked up his story again. He has taken the whole of 2017 so far to recover from the second brain bleed, having had to learn to eat, walk and talk again. Of course, his boxing licence has been revoked.

We all feel the need to condemn the gym that allowed him to spar again, but the stark truth is that we can see the situation from both sides. Boxing at the amateur level has given all of us so much: levels of fitness that we never thought possible, self-belief, pride, discipline and induction into a global surrogate family, just for starters. We also think it is relatively safe.

⊙

I still secretly harbour a desire to fight in a white-collar match myself, although I have not had the courage to admit this seriously to anyone, yet, except in a joking way with Dai, I have only eighteen months left to decide, as then I will be over the age limit of 57. Dai has always joked that they could never find another boxer old enough to take me on. But *could they*? Daft as it sounds, if I did box in such a match I would really like to do it in some sort of style. The difficulty at my age is not committing to the training – it is merely getting enough rest between the training sessions along with the other ridiculous constraints of modern life.

Once you are committed to fighting in the ring, it is every man or woman for themselves, and the risk of injury goes up as survival instinct and inexperience kicks in. What if you are pitted against someone who isn't a boxer? A Radio3 or Classic FM listener with a massive ego would be *anyone's* nightmare. Someone who thinks they can box, but cannot. That really would be impossible. What if the headgear that you are made to wear is not as good as your own? All these uncertainties come to mind.

EPILOGUE

KEEPING ON KEEPING ON

For the record, we ignore Blackwell's warning and just keep on keeping on – for quite some time, in fact. When I next glance at my watch it is June 2019.

Against the odds, in his own redoubtable way, Nick Blackwell has been keeping on keeping on. Eventually, he managed to get out of his wheelchair and learned to walk with two sticks. The sticks became redundant as he began training himself to walk without them. In March 2019, he successfully ran the Weston-Super-Mare Half Marathon and he has set himself a series of ambitious goals stretching on into the future.

The youth club has taken pity on us and has allowed us to stay on a whole month after the usual May. Dai is on holiday for a week, so I take charge in the gym for the penultimate week of the boxing season.

Jonty, Paul and Mariella are toiling away. They are all under the misapprehension that I am a tough taskmaster. How I have managed to give this impression, I have no idea, because I feel older and tireder than ever before, mainly *because I am older and tireder than before*. Still, we skip till we drop and 'walk, jog, run' for ten lengths of the youth club yard in the sunshine. I haul out The Board of Death and crank through one round. Not for the first time, as I gag and wheeze, Jonty shouts cheerfully, 'Please don't die on me, Marianne.' I promise that I will not.

Jonty, Paul and Mariella all have the perfect qualifications to be boxers. Jonty has no feeling in one leg owing to a non-boxing accident, but you'd never know. He is a natural mover round the ring and has a great defensive boxing stance. I have spent six weeks trying to get past his defences, eventually managing only one great body shot and one good jab (only two, but they *are* good shots).

Paul is pushing fifty and claims to be very unfit, yet can box three two-minute rounds quite comfortably. He has a great chopping parry, which renders my jab totally useless (which to be honest, I am *none too happy* about, as nothing usually stops my jab). We all think he should go into the ring with Dai, even though he has been boxing for only two months, as he has great strength and lightning-speed reactions. When I ask him his secret, he says that he hauls bags of lentils around for three days a week for a vegan co-operative.

Mariella has never done any boxing (or so she says), but when I hold up the pads for her there is real power and skill behind the shots right from the off. More than that there is a steely determination that I instantly recognise and for which there is no substitute. Stealing Dai's boxing catchphrase, I say, 'That's boxing, Mariella,' and it truly is.

James is warming up on the new hook bag. Rather worryingly he has been concentrating on his boxing strategy as well increasing his phenomenal strength and speed. James is stronger and faster than we have ever known, as well as being the king of the shovel hook. His brother, Mark, has not appeared over the last few months as he has recently become a dad, so it looks like I'll be doing some defensive work with James – i.e. trying to defend myself in any way possible. After a year of intense practice, I can now actually throw a decent right shovel hook myself. Everyone is heartily sick of me saying that I can't throw one, but now I can, so I will stop complaining. But the left shovel hook is still weak, so I'm working on that now.

At the eleventh hour, Peter comes rushing in. He apologises *to me* for being a bit late (which seems quite ridiculous as I am definitely no substitute for Dai). He will not be budged from the new heavy bag for a full forty minutes, before pausing for a rest. 'I'm too tired for all this now,' he says. 'I'm pushing sixty, you know?' Yes, *we do know*. 'Have you been out running this week at all?' I ask. 'Oh no, not me, no. Oh, no. Not me. *Not at all*. I gave all that up *years* ago, you know. I'm *far too old* for that now. I'm retired. *Really* retired. Just a few walks round the park with the dog. That's *all* I'm up to nowadays.'

As we drag him off the heavy bag, Peter sails through two rounds of The Board of Death. No one else in the gym past or present can do that. As ever, we wonder what his secret is. (Perhaps he has been training as professional boxer somewhere else, but is too polite to tell anyone.)

For the final week of the boxing season, Dai appears. Before we have time to say anything in our defence, he greets us: 'You lazy f——kers. I bet you've done nothing while I've been away.'

ACKNOWLEDGEMENTS

Sincere thanks are due to Sara Hunt of Saraband for giving me the opportunity to tell my story and also to my editor, Charlotte Cole, for her professionalism and hard work, and Hamzah Hussain, for proofreading.

Thanks also to boxers Matt, Rob, Michael, Lucy, Vinny, Dylan, Joe, Arthur, Karen, Danny and Jordan – you know who you are.